THE SCHOOL SOLUTION

GETTING CANADA'S SCHOOLS TO WORK FOR YOUR CHILDREN

Paul Kropp & Lynda Hodson

Random House of Canada
Toronto

Published in 1995 by Random House of Canada Limited, Toronto.

Canadian Cataloguing in Publication Data

Kropp, Paul, 1948–

The school solution: getting Canada's schools to work for your children

Includes index
ISBN 0-394-22412-4

1. Education - Canada - Parent participation.
2. Home and school - Canada. I. Hodson, Lynda.
II. Title.

LC225.33.C3K76 1995   370.19'31'0971   C94-932316-0

Printed and bound in Canada

10 9 8 7 6 5 4 3 2

Table of Contents

CHAPTER 1

Introduction

School isn't just a big part of your child's life—it's the biggest and most important. Your child will spend at least 15,000 hours in class by the end of high school—more time learning in school than doing anything else except sleeping and watching television. If you include the time related to larger education, everything from homework to nightly reading to piano lessons, your child should spend far more time learning than doing anything else in life.

You want to be sure that such time is well spent. In the past, many parents simply trusted the schools to do their job and took a hands-off approach to their children's education. What everyone has realized over the past ten years is that "hands off" doesn't work, that getting the best education for your child requires a hands-on approach right from prekindergarten through high school. Even busy parents whose children are doing well in school should know something about homework and classwork, learning expectations and how to read report cards, and what can reasonably be expected of students at each grade level. Parents who have had problems with a teacher or a school—and there are many of you in this group—should know about power in school systems, teacher types and requirements,

What's Good about Canada's Schools

Quality of teachers: The average student entering an Ontario faculty of education comes in with an A average; the average student entering a Florida teachers' college has a C+ average.

Experience: The average Ontario teacher in 1991 had seventeen years in the classroom.

Library books: There are more books in the *school* libraries of Canada's major cities than in the *public* libraries down the street.

Equipment: Ten years ago there were one or two computers per *school*; this year there is an average of one computer per *classroom*, and some advantaged schools have a computer for every four students.

Retention: 84 percent of Canada's students finish high school, more than in any other country on earth.

effective use of parents' nights and just what options are available for your child's education. To put the matter bluntly: Canada's schools will serve your child better if you know how they work, what to expect of them, who controls them and the various strategies that can make change happen in the individual classroom. We'll give you as much of that information as we can over the following two hundred and fifty pages.

First the Good News

The good news about Canada's schools is that they do quite a good job for most of their students. Despite the howling of our newspapers and other media, Canada's schools probably do a better job today for a wider range of students than at any time in the past.

The principal reason for this is not at all mysterious—it simply has to do with money. Canada's provinces and local school boards or districts spend more per student on education than any other Western country, so the schools *should* be first-rate. As a group, our teachers are among the most highly paid in the world. That means the profession attracts top-quality prospective teachers and manages to hold on to them so that most are quite experienced in the classroom. Our school facilities are mostly top-notch, many of them quite modern or regularly modernized over the past few years. Our schools come equipped with computers, science labs, shops and technical facilities, gymnasia and swimming pools so good they are frequently used after-hours by the adult community.

Of course, money, qualifications and buildings are only some of the measures of education; achievement is another. Achievement in learning is difficult to compare from country to country because each society expects its students to learn a body of skills and information that can be very unique. Our children do not need to speak as many languages as students in Switzerland or Austria; nor do they need to know details of American or British or Chilean history; nor do they need the Latin and astronomy that were seen as essential skills in the seventeenth century. But our children do need to master reading and mathematics, Canadian geography and history and science, French and English and another language from the wider world; our children need to understand how our government works and how business operates; they need to be able to deal competently with computers and spreadsheets, hockey sticks and squash racquets. No one has devised a way to measure how successfully all these things are done, but what we can measure looks fairly good. Canadian schools provide adequate grounding in reading and math, at least according to international rankings. Our very best students stand up well in senior-level science and mathematics competitions. We win our fair share of Rhodes scholarships and other international fellowships. And we keep more of our kids in school than virtually any other country in the Western world.

Our schools manage to do all this and provide one other important ingredient—choice. In most communities, you can often choose what *kind* of school your child attends, just which *school* your child attends, what *courses* she takes, perhaps even what *teacher* she gets. The range of choice in our various school systems, especially in urban areas, is really quite impressive. There are public, separate and private schools; religious schools of various denominations; special schools for trades or gifted students or children with special needs. There are alternative schools often set up by parents like you, and home schooling if nothing else works for your child. Even the choosiest learner can usually find something suitable from this smorgasbord of offerings.

What Taxpayers Spend on Schools (1992–93)

Province	Number of schools	Education Budget (in millions)	Percent of provincial budget
Nfld.	507	$665	22%
P.E.I.	73	$126	20%
N.S.	525	$883	23%
N.B.	450	$802	20%
P.Q.	2,940	$7,824	19%
Ont.	5,800	$14,047	22%
Sask.	957	$1,493	17%
Man.	850	$1,175	17%
Alta.	1,830	$3,036	20%
B.C.	1,995	$4,080	19%
Yukon	29	$65	—
N.W.T.	80	$162	—

63 percent of this money went to elementary and secondary schools, 28 percent to colleges and universities, 9 percent to vocational and other training programs.

Curriculum Through History

The actual subjects or topics studied in school are called the curriculum, a word that sounds etched in stone. In fact, the set curriculum has changed radically over time.

- **c. 400–200 B.C.** The Greeks put a heavy emphasis on gymnastics, military training, logic and public speaking. Mastery of Greek oratory was expected: anyone who couldn't speak the language was thought to speak "baba," hence the word *barbarian*.

- **c. 600–1200 A.D.** Early schooling in Western Europe was church based and "scholastic," which meant an emphasis on divine topics over secular interests like math and science. The word *primer* comes from *primarium*: a child's collection of hymns, prayers, psalms, church rites and the Lord's Prayer.

- **c. 1400 A.D.** The beginning of the Renaissance was marked by a resurgence of Greek ideals, in a modified format. The *trivium*, from which we get the adjective *trivial*—as in Trivial Pursuit—consisted of three subjects begun early in school: grammar, rhetoric and logic. Children didn't begin the harder *quadrivium*—arithmetic, geometry, astronomy, music—until they reached university at age fourteen or so.

Then the Bad News

Unfortunately, Canada's schools do not always deliver their best for every child who enrols. Some children do get a better education than others, within the same system, even within the same school. As a parent, you must make careful choices about your child's education again and again throughout her school career, you must be vigilant each year as teachers come and go and you must use your position at home to bolster what happens at school, or your child's overall education will suffer.

All schools are not equal. Canada's schools do not receive equal funding from province to province, or even within the same city. The relatively richer provinces of Ontario and British Columbia spend, on average, about $6,700 per student on education. The poorer provinces of Newfoundland and New Brunswick spend about 25 percent less, so their class sizes are larger, their buildings less well equipped, their teachers paid somewhat less. While Canada does not have the extreme differences evident in the United States (where per pupil spending ranges from $2,400 to $8,300 in just one state, Illinois), we still have significant differences among provinces. Even local boards of education allocate money and facilities unevenly, frequently spending more on arts schools or schools for the gifted (whose parents closely watch over their child's education) than on schools in poor areas (where parents are often uninvolved).

Quality is slipping. Because our schools are educating more and more young people, in a society that values entertainment far more than education, the overall education of our graduates has declined somewhat. A grade twelve graduate in Ontario today has read less, spent less time in class and less time studying than a grade twelve graduate in 1955. Of course, far more students will make it to that graduation ceremony in 1995 than would ever have thought of it forty years ago, but many parents are upset that the decline has been so pervasive. The simple truth is that your child's 82 percent in physics this year probably represents the same achievement as the 72 percent you received, and may not be a sufficiently high-enough mark to get her into the university of her choice. Nor does that 82 percent in physics indicate that she is as well prepared as a high school student in Tokyo or at Bronx High School of Science in New York. Course choice, elimination of final exams and a generation of sympathetic teachers have led to mark inflation in high school and a real dismay about standards that needs to be addressed.

Choices are hidden. While Canada's various school systems offer a wide array of choices to parents and students, not all those choices are presented to the general public. You may well get a flyer from your local public and separate systems, but private schools rarely advertise door-to-door and alternative schools can't even afford to place ads in the *Globe and Mail*. Nor will those school board flyers readily tell you how to get your child considered for the gifted program, or into special education, or assisted by the resource teacher, or transferred to another school if the neighbourhood school is deficient. They will not tell you how to move your child from one class to another, or put pressure on a reluctant principal or lazy teacher. As a parent, you need a variety of tools and strategies to keep your child's education running smoothly. Few school boards will even tell you that there's a tool box.

Some teachers should be in another line of work. In preparing this book, we talked to hundreds of parents, students and teachers about their experiences with schools and their colleagues.

- **c. 1550.** Schools became more organized: King Edward VI issued the first English ABC, Valentin Ickelsamer of Augsburg, Germany, developed formal phonics. Even so, Thomas More complained that half the clergy in England were illiterate.

- **1700–1800.** The development of "charity schools" by religious organizations brought education to the masses in England. Democratic ideals led to general public education in France and elsewhere.

- **1870–1890.** Canada developed the public and separate school systems. Curriculum involved reading, writing and 'rithmetic in elementary school; commercial subjects, sciences and citizenship at secondary levels. Not much changed until…

- **1960s.** Beginning of "liberal reforms." Curriculum expanded, until some boards offered hundreds of courses from Latin to driver education. Proportion of time on English and math fell; later on so did student achievement in these areas.

- **c. 1985.** Educational backlash against reform leads to a "back to basics" movement, starting in Alberta and British Columbia.

Some Disquieting Stats

In the decade from 1981–82 to 1991–92, total spending on education increased by 117 percent. In the same period, the consumer price index increased by 78 percent.

The cost of education spending (1992):
- per capita: $1,943.
- per labour-force member: $3,813
- per student: $6,507

Expenditure per elementary and secondary student in 1989:
- Canada: $4,008–$5,894
- U.S.: $3,977
- Japan: $1,805

Among 24 countries in the Organization for Economic Cooperation and Development, Canada and Sweden were tied for a dubious distinction: world's most costly education system.

The general consensus on teacher quality was this: 20 percent of Canada's teachers are quite excellent; 30 percent are good, solid teachers; 40 percent do a good job for some students and an adequate job for others; and 10 percent should be in some other line of work. As a parent, you want to maximize the contact your child has with excellent teachers and keep your child away from teachers who ought never to have been hired. You want to match up your child with teachers who are compatible with how *your* child learns best, not on the basis of what's convenient for school staffing. Unfortunately, no school system in Canada will make this easy, and current funding problems will make it only more difficult in the future.

And all those other problems. There is certainly some substance in what journalists say about the schools. Racism is a problem. Too many kids drop out. Girls are *still* not encouraged in math and science. Higher-level literacy is declining. Marks are inflated. Elementary school behaviour is deteriorating and becoming more violent. Some urban secondary schools have become almost as dangerous as the streets outside them. Our kids are not being prepared for (pick one or more): the twenty-first century, the world economy, the computer age, entrepreneurialism, the next Olympics.

All these problems are becoming evident at exactly the wrong time. For many years, schools have closed their doors to parents, saying give us your children, trust us, and we'll look after education. But now we find that the schools have not consistently provided the excellence they promised. As parents we are disillusioned, and take out our frustration on provincial politicians, school trustees and the hapless teacher we may meet at a cocktail party ("Makes more money than me *and* gets the whole summer off," he grumbled). For this, schools have only themselves to blame. By creating the illusion that education is something that takes place within the four walls of a school, our education systems set themselves up for a major fall. We are seeing that now.

Our Philosophy—Parents as Partners

The phrase "parents as partners in education" goes back forty years or more. It's trotted out by principals and administrators, home-and-school executive members, even politicians when Education Week comes around. The problem is, nobody has ever taken it seriously. Many schools close their doors to parents for 198 of the 200 days in the school year. Many principals would rather talk to kids or board officials than have to deal with you and your concerns. Many teachers look upon their classrooms as their fiefdoms, and you, the parent, as someone who would only interfere with their daybook plans or the latest ministry directive. We wish it were otherwise, but this is the truth.

Nonetheless, parents *must* be partners to assure a real education for their children. Schools and teachers are not powerful enough to do the job alone. While they can handle *schooling*, the formal instruction and social engineering that will help your child fit into Canadian society, they deal with only a part of *education*, that process by which your child learns and grows to be a skilled, successful adult. *Education* is a parent responsibility.

This is not meant to lessen the responsibility of your child's school. Throughout this book, we will talk about what to expect and demand from your child's school. We believe that schools should be accountable—for their philosophies, their methods of instruction, their programs and their results. To say that parents are responsible for *education* only means that schools are especially

Norms Are Declining

Every few years since 1966, the authors of the Canadian Test of Basic Skills go out to set new "norms" for this standard test in reading and mathematics. To do so, groups of students are given both old tests and new versions of the same test. The results offer one measure of how our kids have changed on a standardized measuring stick.

Reading comprehension:
1966: 100 percent
1973: 90 percent
1980: 94 percent
1991: 91 percent

Mathematics:
1966: 100 percent
1973: 96 percent
1980: 98 percent
1991: 94 percent

What was so great about the kids in 1966? No one really knows, but it was also the high-water mark for the Scholastic Aptitude Test in the U.S.

Education Outside of School

Education is more than just schooling. Don't forget these other sources for your child's education:

- Sunday school, church camps, retreats
- Boy Scouts, Girl Scouts
- music lessons, community bands
- travel
- radio and TV courses
- museum and gallery Saturday classes
- farming clubs, 4-H clubs
- National Film Board videos and films
- athletics: organized community teams
- drama: community theatre
- the library: reading contests, books
- volunteering: seniors homes, Red Cross
- do-it-yourself—or with Mom and Dad
- dance, gymnastics, judo, karate
- summer camps
- a paper route or part-time job
- tutoring—or being tutored
- correspondence courses

responsible for the portion of education that is *schooling*.

Ironically, this was clearer generations ago, when schools were less grandiose in their claims and their offerings. No one in the 1920s expected schools to handle piano lessons, Icelandic heritage instruction, English for new Canadians, driver instruction, group-work skills, sex education and discussion of ethical issues. These parts of a child's education belonged elsewhere—at the piano teacher's, in the community hall, at union meetings, through the Boy Scouts and Junior Farmers clubs, at work in the fields, at church and at home. Parents expected to have many people in their community join in the education of their children.

Now we dump most of this on the schools. And the schools, foolishly, have said that they can do it all—all by themselves. Not only has this made for an impossible task for teachers, it has begun to cut into what ought properly to be done in school: instruction in reading, mathematics, history and the sciences. As any teacher will tell you, there just isn't enough *time* to do everything.

The first part of our fourfold philosophy in dealing with schools follows from all this.

1. **Remember that much of education takes place outside of school.**

   Jennifer Holder attends Kelvin High School in Winnipeg where her parents Chris Rhodes and Dave Holder expect her to get a solid education. They look to the staff at Kelvin to teach math and science, history and geography; they expect the school to develop Jen's love of reading and her curiosity in science; and they want that education in two languages because Jen has been in French immersion since kindergarten.

   But they don't expect Kelvin High School to do everything. Jen's education is larger than that—including Irish dancing lessons at the

Irish Club on Erin Street, diving instruction at Sargeant Park Pool, Polish lessons at her church and gymnastics on Saturdays out in St. Boniface. All this involves a fair amount of time and travel for both Jennifer and her parents, but it is what makes for a broader education that can ever be offered within the four walls of a school.

As a parent you may not have the time, money or energy to provide a smorgasbord of outside activities for your child. Nor should children be so loaded with classes, lessons and practices that they drag themselves through childhood without joy. But every parent should augment the formal schooling that goes on in the classroom with valuable experiences available only in the community.

Having provided all these caveats about the limitations of school as a place for education, we must still assert the obvious. More learning should take place for your child in school than anywhere else. School is vastly more central to your child's development than weekly hockey lessons, weekend canoe courses or educational television. And because formal education is so important, it can't be left to just any school. Your child's school should not be determined by convenience, or rumour, or family tradition. It is a matter of rational choice.

2. Choose and re-choose your child's school with care.

When Richard and Sandra Gulland moved to the small community of Killaloe, outside of Ottawa, the choice of schools was not large: one separate elementary school, one public elementary school. Neither had programs that particularly impressed the Gullands, who chose another option—a small, independent alternative school. They joined with a handful of other parents who enrolled their children in

How Canadians Feel about Their Schools

In 1984: 44 percent of Canadians thought that schools had improved; 36 percent felt they had gotten worse.

In 1989: 30 percent thought that schools had improved; 20 percent felt they had gotten worse.

Asked what letter grade they would give to their community school, Canadians marked like this:

A   6 percent
B   39 percent
C   34 percent
D   7 percent
F   4 percent

Anglophone Canadians were twice as likely to give their schools an A as Francophone Canadians.

Respondents in the Prairie provinces rated their schools most highly; residents of British Columbia were the most critical (half gave their schools a grade of C or lower).

Memories of Killaloe Alternative School

by Carrie Gulland

It was a long time ago. Back then there was only one room and one teacher (Kathy) and parent helpers. The room was divided in half by a monstrous curtain. On the one side of it were the older kids—the BIG kids. The rest of us little kids were on the other side. I remember before going back to school one year Mom telling me I was going to be on the other side of the curtain. I, of course, was thrilled and somehow managed to respond by saying, "You mean, I'm going to be with the BIG kids?" Obviously that's what she meant, but I couldn't believe that I was actually a BIG kid, a senior student.

I never used to dread going to school—at least not the Alternative School. Somehow, learning was made exciting and interesting. We learned how to appreciate not only things, but people too. I'm not saying that there weren't times when we got stumped, but that was easily solved by putting on our thinking caps and thinking it through with others. I think that was the key to enjoying the school—knowing that no matter what sort of wall we ran into, there was always a thinking cap beside you and a group of friends with theirs on as well.

the Killaloe Alternative School—a tiny school located first in various family homes, then in a rented schoolhouse, where the two "classrooms" were divided by a blanket hung over a rope. Fees were low and the teacher chronically underpaid, but family involvement was high and their daughter Carrie received a fine education from a remarkable teacher right through grade six.

Then it was necessary to rechoose: more of the tiny alternative school or the regular public school in Killaloe. The advantages of parent involvement, flexible curriculum and a truly committed teacher in a local environment made the alternative school an easy choice for the first few years. But public school offered the attractions of a broader world: working with different kinds of students, learning subjects that required particular teacher expertise and, later on, expensive laboratory equipment. By grade seven many of Carrie's friends were enrolled in the local public school, and the varied sports program offered there sealed the choice. The Gullands—Carrie now part of the decision—chose the public school, not because it was the best of all possible schools, but because it was the best choice given their family situation and the needs of Carrie's larger education.

Not every family lives in a location with a wide range of wonderful schools, or has the finances to afford private education, or can move the household just to find a better school for their children. Many parts of rural Canada offer only one public school: take it or leave it. As parents, our school choices are always hemmed in by the limits of the real world. Nonetheless, we have an obligation to survey the full range of schooling available, carefully investigate the final options and make the best choice we can on the basis of that investigation.

3. **Stay involved in your child's school.**

It would certainly be nice if parents could choose a school for their child and then trust the school and teachers to do their jobs with some measure of excellence. Alas, the real world doesn't work like that. In the real world, parents have to keep one eye on what's happening in school and another eye on what's happening to their child. This can be relatively easy in primary school, where parent involvement is encouraged and children are more the focus of family life. It becomes increasingly difficult through the senior elementary grades and into high school, when parents feel inexpert, or cut off from communication, or learn little of what's going on from their own teenage children.

The trick, of course, is to find ways to stay involved with the school. In this book we'll be talking about specific strategies at specific grade levels to help you stay involved and informed. Both are essential to protect your child from what can happen even in the best schools: poor teachers, unpleasant class groupings, changes in administration, cockamamie educational ideas.

There are times when it will be essential for you to take action on your child's behalf. If your child is in the hands of an incompetent or abusive teacher, you must do whatever you can to shield her and remove the teacher. No child can learn adequately from a teacher who, for whatever reason, can't teach. If your child is being physically threatened in school or the playground or on the school bus, you must take action to help her. No child can learn if she's frightened by the school experience. If your child's school is going downhill because of a poor principal, you should take steps with other parents to protect the school and the good teachers within it. This may involve

Seven Easy Ways to Stay Involved

- Read the school newsletter, monthly calendar, notes from the teacher.

- Go to parents' night, open house, the school musical.

- Join the home and school associations or parent advisory council.

- Chaperone a dance, supervise a school trip, help coach a team.

- Send notes to your child's teacher—or call her to keep in contact.

- Talk to your child about what she did in school.

- Eyeball your child's homework before it gets turned in.

Good Families Do...

Good families demonstrate the importance of school through what they say *and* what they do. They

- set aside quiet time for homework every night;

- eyeball projects at the planning stage—and again before they're turned in;

- read regularly with their children— and for themselves;

- never undercut a teacher verbally in front of their children (though they might have much to say to the teacher herself or the principal);

- support the importance of their child's learning and their child's involvement with all aspects of school life, from basketball to the French club.

removing or counselling the principal, documenting material for senior administration or lobbying school trustees. No child can learn in a school that is chaotic or without leadership.

It is difficult for us, who have spent a combined fifty years in teaching, to encourage parents to get out the hatchets and go after staff people at the slightest provocation. Teachers, too, have their ups and downs and personal crises. But such general sympathies can't stand in the way of protecting your own child. For every circumstance where we have seen a parent complain excessively about a teacher, we know of five others where incompetent teachers and administrators have carried on without a word of complaint—from anyone. Your child deserves better.

4. **Watch the subtle messages you give at home.** School will be as important for your child as you make it. In setting a value on education, what you *do* as a parent counts much more than what you say. We know families who tell their children that reading is important and that they should work hard at school. And we know that these same families don't have a book in the house, can't bother to take a trip to the library, spend their evenings plopped in front of the television set and really don't see any problem if their child goes to school late— or not at all. Their child is handicapped, not by what's *said* at home, but by the real message communicated by the actions of the parents.

If you hold up Uncle Fred as the family hero—who made a million with a grade six education and still says proudly, with your approving nods, "Who needs school to get somewhere in life?"—don't be surprised if your child declares at age sixteen that she wants to drop out. If you talk proudly about how you never had to do any homework because you were so smart, don't be surprised if your daughter declares that *she* doesn't have any homework, or doesn't have to bother to study for tomorrow's French test. You've already taught her a lesson that school can't undo.

School doesn't operate in a vacuum. It works best in an environment where everyone in your home supports what goes on in your child's classroom.

In This Book

In *The School Solution*, we've put together a compendium of approaches that should help parents deal with their children's schools. The next chapter talks about selecting the right school for your child: the options, what you should look for, what factors to weigh in the choice. Chapter 3 and Chapter 4 discuss how to work with teachers and administrators once your child is enrolled. Chapter 5 looks at some issues at home that will affect your child's experience at school.

The rest of this book seeks to make you an informed parent. We've grouped two or three grades together, then described the curriculum and the structure of the school day to the extent that these can be generalized across Canada, explained what your child should be learning and what the average child achieves. Along the way, we've got sidebars of advice, samples of student work, suggestions for outside-of-school activities, special terms used by teachers and a host of other items to help you understand what's happening in your child's grade. Chapter 15 provides honest answers to questions that frequently come from parents. Chapter 16 talks about some of the real issues in Canadian schools—not those making the headlines, but the ones that will really affect your child's education.

Characteristics of an Effective School

Research into what makes an effective school has identified six key factors for schools that deliver real gains for students and garner strong parent satisfaction ratings. In ordinary language, here's what the success factors are:

- The principal and teachers put a strong emphasis on high-quality teaching.

- There is a clear purpose for the school, which teachers, administrators and parents share.

- High expectations are set for all students to be successful.

- The environment is safe and students are calm and orderly.

- Adequate time is spent on academic tasks so all students can learn.

- Student progress is closely monitored and feedback is given to students and parents.

- Parents and school staff communicate and work together.

If knowledge gives power, and we believe it does, then all these chapters should make you more powerful in getting the best from your child's school. Perhaps more important, these chapters should help you support your child's schooling with effective parenting at home. These two are linked, like a loving couple holding hands. For your child's sake, don't let go.

CHAPTER 2

Finding the Best School for *Your* Child

When Blair Brandon was finishing grade six in Toronto's Beaches community, he and his parents had a wide assortment of choices for his next school: the Beaches junior high, alternative schools in Toronto and Scarborough, an academy in the public system complete with dress code, a full-time school for the gifted not too far from his home, the local Catholic school and an array of private schools. Blair and his parents did their homework—visited schools, checked out reputations and programs, talked to friends and students at the schools, listened to neighbours and colleagues give advice. They finally settled on University of Toronto Schools, the unusual public/private high school that counts among alumni both Nobel laureates and provincial politicians. Getting accepted was no simple matter. It involved a highly competitive written exam and a thirty-minute personal interview. But Blair made

What Does My Child Need from a School?

Discuss these with your child (if he's old enough) and rate their importance: 1-essential; 2-important; 3-doesn't matter; 4-No way!

Academics:
___ demanding academic standards
___ individualized program
___ formal homework assignments
___ enriched program in special areas (music, math, science, art, etc.)
___ special program for children with learning problems

Environment:
___ being with neighbourhood friends
___ a large school with many students
___ opportunity to meet new, different people
___ wide range of extracurricular activities; e.g., clubs, bands, sports
___ strict expectations for behaviour
___ opportunities to increase confidence and self-esteem
___ leadership opportunities
___ uniforms required

the cut, and his parents have found the tuition money to keep him enrolled.

Was it worth it? Did they make the right choice?

The answer, so far, has been yes—for Blair and for *his* family. The choice for you and your child might be very different, but that depends on your situation, your child and what you want from a school.

Making the effort to find the best school for your child is *always* worth it, even if you end up deciding that the local public school is best after all. You owe it to your own peace of mind to consider the alternatives, which we'll outline later on in this chapter. You owe it to your child to carefully select the schools he'll attend, at least through elementary school, and to select with him the secondary and postsecondary education he'll need.

All this means you'll end up choosing four or more different schools for your child at various times in his life. You obviously must choose a school when your child enters daycare, kindergarten, middle or junior high school and high school. You will also end up choosing a new school whenever your family moves to a new community—and the average Canadian family with children in school moves once every three years.

But there are other, less obvious, times when it pays to consider school options for your child. You might, for instance, want to think about a different *type* of school—say, French immersion, or private school, or alternative school—which might suit your family and your child better than your current choice. Or if your child is not thriving in his current educational setting and you see little chance that the situation will improve, then you owe it to your child to seek out alternatives. No child should be forced to vegetate in an unhappy classroom or ineffective school when there are often other options nearby.

Of course, you can always shrug off making choices and enrol your child at the school closest to your home, the same way you might pick the local garage to fix your car. If you're lucky, then your child will receive a reasonable education (and your car will hum along for many thousands of kilometres). If you'd prefer not to trust to luck (or you've seen the mess a local garage mechanic can make of your car), then the rest of this chapter is for you.

How to Start Choosing a School

You need information. The first place to begin assembling that information is at home, talking with your child, discussing matters with your partner, considering your own values and ideas about education.

Start with your child. Your child is already a person at age two or three, certainly by the time he's entering school. He will probably have opinions on the kind of school in which he would be happiest. These can range from the silly—"I just won't wear a uniform. You can't make me"—to the profound—"I went back to Crescent School because the standards were higher and I pushed myself more to learn in that environment." Obviously the weight you will give to such opinions depends upon the age and maturity of your child and the reliability of his information. Surveys indicate that the most important question for kids in choosing a school is this: *Do my friends go to it?* It's hard for young people to understand that friends change over time and that other factors might be more important over the long term. Nonetheless, your child might well have important things to say about his own education. A wise parent will listen.

You should also spend some time thinking about your child as a learner. Does he learn best

Instruction:

__ individualized program
__ teacher-directed, structured instruction
__ problem-solving opportunities
__ hands-on activities
__ relaxed, informal learning atmosphere
__ tutorials, special assistance
__ use of computer in program
__ rigorous physical activity

Parent Involvement and Communication:

__ frequent parent-teacher contact
__ parent help with homework assignments
__ parent participation on school trips and activities
__ prefer parents not involved

What Do I Want in a School for My Child?

Rate the features of a school that you value. 1-essential; 2-important; 3-doesn't matter; 4-No way!

Academics:

__ high academic performance and expectations

__ formal homework policy

__ high value on creativity, spontaneity

__ focus on building child's self-esteem

__ regular testing of student performance and end-of-term exams

__ ongoing teacher evaluation of work

Environment:

__ location near home

__ convenient bus service

__ strict behaviour code

__ informal student-teacher relationships

__ emphasis on individual student needs

__ wide range of extracurricular activities

__ competitive intermural sports

__ uniforms or dress code

__ high-quality facilities, labs, gym

__ extensive library resource centre

__ access to computers

in structured or unstructured situations? Is he a self-starter or a child who follows the crowd? Has he been successful or unsuccessful with certain types of schools or teachers in the past? What are his goals and interests? How important are sports, science labs, music programs? Answers to these questions will help you focus on your child's schooling needs.

Don't forget yourself. If you are going to be a real partner in your child's education, then you, too, have to be happy with the choice of a school. What are your family traditions? If everyone from your family has attended Upper Canada College, there's a good chance you won't be too happy if your son decides to head off to the West End Alternative School. How important is religion in your family? If you feel strongly that a particular religion should be an important part of schooling, you may have to seek out the small, church-based schools that will provide this. How important is it that your child "fits in" with the neighbourhood kids? If all the kids are going to Burrard Street School, while your son goes to the full-day gifted program at Granville, he's unlikely to get to know as many kids in your neighbourhood. This could be a good or bad thing, depending on how you feel about the local kids.

Getting beyond the usual moaning and groaning we find in newspapers and on radio call-in shows, what do you *really* think a good school should be like: structured, unstructured, organized, innovative, traditional, modern, "just the basics" or "educating the whole child"? It's difficult to get *exactly* the school you want for your child, but it pays to know what you'd like.

Then let your fingers do some walking. At this point it's time to start investigating the options in your community. Most areas have both a public and separate board of education that will have a school close to your home. Some areas will also have French-languague schools. All of these will be listed in the White Pages under "Boards of Education," so you really can let your fingers do the walking. A phone call to the general number, education centre or information officer will get you information on the closest local school and probably a pamphlet or two explaining the programs offered by that particular board of education. To find out what other kinds of schools are available to you locally, turn to the Yellow Pages under "Schools." This will give you a listing of private schools (under "Schools—Academic—Elementary and Secondary") and nursery schools (under "Schools—Academic—Nursery and Kindergarten").

For a greater range of schools, especially those outside your immediate area, you might want to check the advertisements in the special "Education" sections of your newspaper, which appear in August, September and January. The *Globe and Mail* also offers advertising for some schools in its Saturday edition. Small independent, alternative and nursery schools you'll have to find by word of mouth.

The Big Choices

Once you've talked to your child and your partner and completed some rudimentary research, you should carefully consider the major schooling options available for your child. This is probably the most difficult part of choosing your child's school, because these major options determine the character and sometimes the language of the school and school system where your child is enrolled.

Most communities in Canada have two school systems—the public and the separate—because of an agreement reached at the time of Confederation. In the days when most schools were operated by a particular church denomination,

Instruction:
__ structured, teacher-directed instruction
__ hands-on approach to learning
__ child-centred instruction
__ small class size
__ French-language instruction
__ special help for students in trouble
__ emphasis on problem solving and decision making
__ emphasis on skill development
__ emphasis on content or knowledge base

Parent Involvement and Communication:
__ frequent report cards and conferences
__ high parent involvement in making school policies
__ high parent involvement in making decisions for own child
__ open door for parent volunteers

Public Schools in a Nutshell

Some advantages:

- They're free.
- Your child will come into contact with a variety of neighbourhood children.
- The standard curriculum is well covered.
- Teachers are well paid and well qualified.
- They offer good special education programs, sometimes good gifted programs.
- They often have good physical facilities: gyms, labs, computers, etc.

Some disadvantages:

- Your child will come into contact with a variety of neighbourhood children.
- The curriculum rarely goes beyond the ordinary.
- The schools are locked into a large bureaucracy with limited flexibility.
- The schools are sometimes reluctant to give special attention to *your* child.

Quebec wanted to keep its school system Catholic; Ontario wanted to keep its school system either Protestant or nonsectarian. The 1867 compromise provided that each province would have both "public" and "separate" systems of education, though these terms have become confusing over time. Then add the recent surge in French-language education in English Canada, and you can have up to *four* boards of education in many Ontario communities. In Newfoundland there are different boards for various religious denominations, so some areas have Catholic, Integrated Protestant (including Anglican, United, Salvation Army and Presbyterian schools), Pentecostal and Seventh Day Adventist schools—all receiving public tax moneys.

Confusing, isn't it? Let's take this all a little slower and explain the options for your child within the various systems.

The public system. The public systems of education across Canada offer the largest number of neighbourhood schools, usually within walking distance from your house, and a great many well-equipped "consolidated" schools in rural counties, with bus transportation provided at no cost. There are no tuition fees. Books and supplies for your child are generally provided free, but there may be hidden costs for field trips, clothing for phys. ed., book clubs and special events. Most public boards offer a program that extends from junior kindergarten (age four) to grade eleven in Quebec, grade twelve everywhere else, and grade thirteen in Ontario (where students earn Ontario academic credits, so it's called "OAC year"). Some public boards now provide before-school, lunchtime and after-school child care to assist working parents.

The public schools have no particular religious base, though most begin the day with some kind of inspirational reading. Each school is run by a public board of education, which gets its money from both the province and the local property tax. Policies are set by the provincial Ministry or Department of Education on matters of curriculum, while fine points are handled by a local board of elected school trustees.

The advantages of schools in the public system have much to do with size and secure funding. These schools can afford to hire excellent teachers, usually have good facilities like libraries, gyms, computer and science labs and provide reasonable class sizes. Some schools can offer your child strong programs in music, art or drama and a range of extracurricular activities ranging from sports to astronomy. Public schools have access to system resources, including consultants, science kits, board libraries, psychological and special education services.

Large public systems in urban areas often have a range of specialized schools and programs as well. These can include special schools for the academically gifted, for elite athletes, for students specializing in arts or technology, schools with a particular philosophy or style and so-called academies, which are more traditional than many schools today.

Public schools must by law accept any student within their area who wishes to attend, though some special schools may set entrance requirements. The positive side of this is that your child is assured of some kind of education with children from his neighbourhood; the negative side is that the schools cannot insulate your child from the other children in your neighbourhood. This does not mean that good schools are necessarily found in wealthy areas (frequently we have seen quite the opposite), but that the local public school will always have a student body that reflects the local population. If the thought of your child attending class with the neighbourhood kids sends a shiver down your spine, better

Ranking Schools—on the Cheap

There are many parents who want their provinces to do the job of rating schools, as if this will make it easy to choose the best school for their child. Alas, it's not so easy.

- Quebec is the only province where average provincial examination marks and graduation rates of high-school students are made available on a school-by-school basis (the Montreal *Gazette* publishes a full-page list). Does this mean your child will get a better education at a school where the average mark is 67 or 72, or 100 percent of the students who sat for the exams passed them—or does it just tell you something about the neighbourhood and teachers teaching for the exam?

- In Ontario, standardized reading and writing tests have begun to be written by students at grades 3, 6, 9 and 12. Overall rankings of the various boards of education have a limited use. Some boards are making school results available, but these say much more about neighbourhoods than the schools themselves, and really give no information to compare teachers or programs.

We're afraid you just can't reduce education to a set of numbers—not for your child or a whole group of children.

Catholic Schools in a Nutshell

Some advantages:
- They're virtually free.
- Catholic religious education is mandatory as part of the program.
- They are often conservative in terms of values and discipline.
- The teachers are well paid and well qualified.
- They sometimes have good physical facilities: gyms, computers, labs.
- The usually have a better "tone" than public schools.

Some disadvantages:
- Even if you're not a practising Catholic, Catholic religious education is part of the program.
- They are sometimes too conservative in terms of values and discipline.
- The physical facilities (gyms, libraries, science labs) may not measure up to those of local public schools.

shop elsewhere for a school or choose one of the specialized schools and deal with the transportation problems that follow from your choice.

Many of the disadvantages of the public schools have to do with size. The boards tend to be large, bureaucratic and slow to respond to change. Principals and teachers are restricted by everything from provincially set curriculum, to official textbook lists, to negotiated contract requirements. The character of the schools themselves depends greatly on the principal, who can move within the system on very short notice. Because the public schools must educate *everyone*, a disproportionate share of teacher attention can in some classrooms be spent on students with behaviour problems or special needs, while ordinary children twiddle their proverbial and actual thumbs.

In our experience, Canada's public schools do a good job for most of the students who attend them. Like a North American car with a proven V8 under the hood, the public schools offer power, some luxury and dependable value— unless you end up with a lemon.

The Catholic or separate system. All the provinces in Canada have a system of religious schools given some support by public tax dollars. The largest such system is that connected to the Roman Catholic Church. In French Quebec, the schools and course offerings of the Catholic system are larger than those in the competing English Protestant system. In Ontario, Alberta, Newfoundland and Saskatchewan, the Catholic separate systems are about as large as the public systems and receive strong tax support from ratepayers, who are asked to designate whether or not they support the Catholic schools. In British Columbia and Manitoba, the Catholic schools receive very little government money, but do get support from their local diocese. In these provinces tuition fees of $700 to $1,000 a year are likely, though they are sometimes waived for families who cannot afford them. The three Maritime provinces, the Yukon and Northwest Territories do not have Catholic schools.

In the provinces where Catholic schools receive tax support, their schools share many of the advantages of the public schools: well-paid teachers, well-equipped schools, good support from consultants and board facilities. A casual observer walking into the average separate elementary school would have a hard time observing many differences between the environment for learning there and that at a public school down the street.

But there *are* some significant differences, and these can be perceived as advantages or disadvantages, depending on your own family values. Catholic schools maintain that they have a spiritual component missing from the public system. At one time, when priests and nuns did much of the teaching, this component was obvious. These days, well over 90 percent of the teachers in Catholic schools are lay people; some of them may even be Jewish or Muslim or Hindu. The administrative structure of the school, however, is Catholic and this affects everything from textbook selection to how misbehaving students are dealt with. All the students at a Catholic school will be expected to join in church services on certain religious holidays. This may be fine for many families, but it could prove awkward if you or your spouse would prefer not to have your child take part.

Twenty years ago, when the Catholic schools were significantly underfunded in relationship to public schools, they could rightly be criticized for dumping their problem students on the public system or failing to provide quick remedial help

Getting into a Catholic School

If you want to enrol your child in a Catholic school and you're Catholic, there's no problem at all. You probably already support the separate school system through your municipal taxes (it's a check-off when you buy a house or register to vote) and you probably go to the local Catholic church.

But suppose you're not a practising Catholic and you think the local Catholic school is superior to the local public one. What then? To enrol in an Ontario Catholic elementary school, you must:

- provide a baptismal certificate for your child,
- or provide a letter from a parish priest,
- or prove via baptismal certificate that one parent is a Catholic *and* agree that your child will take part in all religious services,
- *and* you must designate your school taxes to the separate system.

In Ontario, under the legislation in 1984 that gave full funding to Catholic high schools, however, any child of secondary age can register at a Catholic high school regardless of religious background.

for students with reading and learning problems. These days the two big systems are about equal in funding and student service. The real differences lie in values, atmosphere and the tone of a particular school. Visits to your two local schools will likely make clear which system offers the better choice for your child.

Other denominational schools. Our comments on the Catholic schools apply fairly well to other denominational systems in provinces like Newfoundland, where these are supported by tax dollars. In the rest of Canada, however, groups of parents of a particular religious affiliation have sometimes gathered together to form independent schools tied to their church. These schools range from a dozen children in a church basement in Sundance, Alberta, to the sprawling Guido de Brès High School, which buses students in from all over Ontario's Golden Horseshoe.

What these schools have in common is a strong religious base and a sense that religious values should be part of the day-to-day school experience for your child. Because denominational schools generally do not get tax revenues, they must charge tuition fees, which range from $1,000 to $4,000 a year, with some break given to families who enrol more than one child. These schools are subject to provincial regulations for private schools and thus have to follow the provincial curriculum guidelines, but are quite free in other respects. Teachers may or may not be certified; students may or may not be accepted or removed without cause; rules on dress and behaviour that would cause an uproar in public education are accepted as the norm. Often these schools have very strong parental involvement that overcomes spotty teaching and deficits in buildings, libraries and laboratories. Would such a school suit you and your child? We've found that variations within this group are so substan-

Growth of Private Schools

Year	Public enrol	Private enrol.
1971–72	5,628,218	139,929
1974–75	5,416,366	175,298
1977–78	5,178,753	189,389
1980–81	4,855,766	209,399
1983–84	4,700,448	229,860
1986–87	4,661,332	228,179
1992–93	4,934,000	247,200

tial that you really must investigate carefully, even if all the other members of your church send their children to the church school.

Private independent schools. The fastest-growing group of schools in the country, at least during the heady 1980s, was the private schools. A number of factors led to this growth—a rise in family income for the upper middle class, growing disenchantment with public schools and partial public funding for private schools in British Columbia. Often the staunchest defenders of private schools—and campaigners to get public funding for them—are teachers from the public school system who have chosen to enrol their kids in private schools, and pay from $3,000 to $13,000 a year for the privilege.

Privilege is a key word in thinking about some private schools. While there are many small independent schools operating in church basements on shoestring budgets, the real private school alternative has always been for the privileged at places like Ridley College in St. Catharines, St. George's in Vancouver and Lower Canada College in Montreal. These and many other elite private schools offer a traditional and very expensive education for those who can afford it or whose intellectual and other merits will win a scholarship and admission. Your child will find that classes are small, programs are demanding and sports participation is usually mandatory. The actual quality of education is quite high, as you would expect from schools that can screen their applicants and "send down" any student who violates the honour code. But the real long-term payoff of these schools may well be in association rather than education. As Peter Newman pointed out in *The Canadian Establishment*, the network of friendships and acquaintanceships formed at such schools remains powerful—and sometimes profitable—throughout life.

Private Schools in a Nutshell

Some advantages:

- Your child joins with a select group of other children, probably from a higher socioeconomic class.
- Learning frequently goes beyond basic province-wide curriculum.
- Elite private schools have often excellent sports facilities and libraries.
- Teachers are freer to use special methods and develop higher expectations of students.
- Some offer boarding at extra cost.
- There is more flexibility in dealing with family travel, special demands.

Some disadvantages:

- They're expensive: up to $20,000 a year.
- Your child will be isolated from neighbourhood friends.
- Your child may have to travel long distances or become a boarding student to attend.
- Teachers vary more widely in credentials than in public systems; some lack teaching credentials altogether.
- Physical amenities are uneven: dormitories, computer labs, even chalk may be second-rate.

Elite Private School: A Case Study

Adam was a very bright child who had been identified as having superior intelligence, but also a mild learning disability. Adam's social skills were somewhat weak and he had yet to establish good friendships with the other kids. Mom and Dad wanted him to make friends, especially those who were "socially acceptable," so they enrolled him in an elite private school.

Unfortunately, Adam's academic skills were weak, despite his intelligence and a large vocabulary from spending so much time in the company of adults. He cared little for the athletic team sports required by the private school. He often found himself in disputes where he was the butt of other students' jokes.

With much parent-school discussion, it was decided to move Adam back to the public school system, but into a new school. Although he would be required to share classes and time with a wide social and academic range of eleven-year-olds, he would receive some special help for his academic and social needs. This helped to compensate for an increase in class size from eighteen to twenty-eight.

After a year of hard work by the public-school staff, including frequent setbacks, Adam made major gains in both attitude and achievement—and was able to work well in the full program the following year.

There are some down sides to all this, however. Students at the elite private schools are sheltered within a certain social class, and this sometimes shows in their values and occasionally snooty attitudes. As a parent you must find funds not just for tuition, but for uniforms, residence fees, transportation to and from the school, books and supplies, so total expenses can run $2,000 over tuition and sometimes much more. And despite tuition fees of up to $20,000, the physical amenities at the elite private schools may not measure up to those at a good public school, especially in expensive science laboratories, libraries and computer facilities.

Other private independent schools can be quite different from the elite schools, sharing only a relatively high tuition and a lack of tax dollars. There are schools that go after a specific population of students—intellectually or artistically gifted, physically or mentally challenged, visa or English as a second language students. There are schools that have a specific educational focus, like Montessori schools, which emphasize the importance of play as a kind of learning, or Waldorf schools, which emphasize music and art. These schools are frequently smaller than the elite schools, combining different grade levels into single classes.

All private schools receive a cursory "inspection" from their provincial government to make sure they follow general educational guidelines, but are quite free to establish their own policies on a wide range of items, including hiring and firing of staff. Supporters would maintain that this gives private schools the option to get rid of incompetent teachers (who are rarely unionized) and to encourage gifted teachers who may not happen to have provincial accreditation. Detractors say that lack of job security drives good teachers to the better paid public system and puts private school students at the mercy of untrained amateurs. In our opinion, both views are highly exaggerated and the actual quality of teaching in good private schools is virtually identical to that in good public schools.

Is a private school the best choice for your child? Obviously there are many factors that will go into the decision: your child's needs, your family's goals and your budget. Both of us have spent some time in private and quasi-private schools, and find their day-to-day functioning much closer to that of your neighbourhood school than to the gorgeous New England academies you see in Hollywood films. Are they really worth the money? Some would argue that good public schools, like a well-equipped Ford, offer better performance than some very prestigious private schools. Nonetheless, there is *something* about driving a BMW that supersedes simple logic.

Alternative schools. In the 1960s, a number of experimental schools sprang up as an alternative to public, separate and expensive private education. The alternative schools were often based vaguely on the ideas of A. S. Neill's Summerhill School in England, where a child would learn at his own pace, often in untraditional ways. These schools made extensive use of parent volunteers and kept tuition low by scrimping on staff salaries and facilities. By and large an alternative school would survive for a few years in rented homes and church basements until it ran out of money, students or stamina to keep going.

Nonetheless, the *idea* of alternative schools refuses to die. In Ontario, for instance, an enrolment of five students with a teacher and a nominal principal is sufficient for application to the Ministry of Education to operate as a school. This has made it possible for a number of very small schools to survive—and sometimes offer an excellent education—on a shoestring. Other alternative schools have kept going by becoming part

Alternative Schools in a Nutshell

Some advantages:
- They cost less than larger private schools.
- Some are part of the public school system.
- They are often close to home.
- They are responsive to parent concerns and issues.
- They have a wide curriculum: from the basics to astronomy and ballet.
- Classes are often small.
- The atmosphere is informal.
- They sometimes make wide use of community facilities.

Some disadvantages:
- They have often poor physical facilities.
- Unqualified teachers differ widely in quality and experience.
- Shoestring finances make continuity a problem.
- Their atmosphere is too informal to suit some parents.
- They can rarely offer expensive science labs, shops or libraries.

Getting Info: Your City Magazine, Your Local Newspaper

Some magazines and newspapers have begun to rank schools the way they might rank pizza parlours. *Maclean's* started the trend with its ranking of Canadian universities; now *Toronto Life* has begun a yearly ranking of Toronto high schools. We imagine the trend will quickly spread.

How good is this information? It's great—as far as it goes. If you want to know student population, staff size and physical aspects like wheelchair access, such surveys give you plenty of data very quickly. But the schools themselves tend to be described in guidance-counsellor hype rather than in useful terms. And ranking schools is a very difficult business. You can't say that school A is better than school B because it has more computers or a higher rate of university acceptance. We still have no measures for the tone of a school, or the commitment of the staff, or the experience of the average student. Nor can any data predict how your child will get on in a particular school or with a certain set of teachers.

So clip out the section from your city magazine or local newspaper (often there's a whole section in the last week in August) that has such information, but don't make it central to your decision.

of a public board of education "umbrella" that offers a number of different types of schools in an urban area.

By nature, alternative schools differ greatly from one another. Some in the public systems concentrate on difficult students; others attract artsy or druggy types; others attract high-achieving, independent learners. Your child will find that most alternative schools provide innovative and flexible programming that may only loosely resemble the provincially set curriculum. Classes are small and personalized, the atmosphere is informal and much use is made of the community and visiting experts. In some secondary alternative schools, learning is negotiated between staff and students on a contract basis. You and your child will often be involved in the leadership and operational decisions of the school, including hiring and firing staff, dealing with behaviour problems and sometimes even cleaning the floors.

The tremendous advantage of alternative schools is their flexibility and responsiveness to what your child needs. At the elementary level, they can provide a level of attention that isn't possible in the traditional school. At the secondary level, they can cater to students who find the regular high school too rigid or too restrictive to suit their intellectual interests. The disadvantages have to do with size, instability and the vagaries of personality. Alternative schools are frequently shaky operations, getting by year to year, dependent on the goodwill of a handful of staff and parents. If your son finds he doesn't like his teacher at the alternative school, there may not be any other teacher for him to go to. Even if everything is going well, the plug to the school can be pulled by a group of angry trustees, arguing parents and staff, even a nasty landlord. One of your authors has had significant involvement with alternative schools and French automobiles over the past twenty years. To sum up in a kind way, both are wonderful when they work.

Home schooling. Despite what you may have seen in the popular video produced by Phil Donahue in 1993 (where wonderfully successful home schoolers send four of their sons happily off to Harvard) the truth is that home schooling is difficult, time-consuming, lonely and virtually impossible to do on your own. In Canada, it is the schooling of last resort. If all your other options seem hopeless, if you have the time to spend four hours a day teaching your own child, if you can somehow make up for your child's isolation from his peers, then perhaps home schooling is for you.

As a home schooler, you are both parent and teacher, following the provincial curriculum in a program that must be monitored by someone in your local public school system (but don't expect much real help from there: after all, you're the competition). Actual instruction can be done informally, at your own house, following your own theories on education. It can be supported by correspondence courses available from your provincial Ministry or Department of Education and by any friends or relatives you can dragoon into helping.

For some families, home schooling provides an opportunity to go far beyond the public school curriculum by incorporating travel, personal expertise and intensive one-on-one teaching as part of an education you really believe in. For other families, home schooling becomes a tiresome exercise for children isolated from their peers, forced to deal with Mom and Dad twenty-four hours a day, who grow to resent their family's standards and expectations. It is difficult to give home schooling a try and then abandon it if it doesn't work out. Home schooling is a commit-

Home Schooling in a Nutshell

Some advantages:

- The program can be highly individualized.
- Education will reflect family values.
- A wide range of interests and subjects can be addressed.
- It is very efficient: three or four hours a day will match six hours in a large class.
- You are not restricted to "official" textbooks.
- School hours can suit family convenience, to some extent.

Some disadvantages:

- The parent must be teacher, principal, disciplinarian, tutor as well as Mom or Dad.
- Few parents have sufficient expertise to tackle all senior-high subjects.
- Alterations in a regular schedule will interfere with your child's learning.
- Few parents have training in teacher techniques.
- The educational bureaucracy is often not supportive.
- You must select and purchase all textbooks and equipment.
- Children are isolated from their peers.

French Immersion in a Nutshell

Some advantages:

- Your child will learn to speak and read French quite fluently.
- Students often come from a higher socioeconomic class.
- Class size is sometimes smaller than in regular classes.
- Often trips to Quebec, even Europe, are part of the program.
- Future career possibilities are extended because your child will be bilingual.

Some disadvantages:

- English reading and writing skills are typically one to two grades below those of nonimmersion students.
- Your child may not be in the same class as neighbourhood children.
- The recent explosion in French immersion means that some teachers are not as well qualified or prepared; some will have difficulty speaking to you in English.
- Unless you can handle French, it will be difficult for you to assist in reading, writing or homework.

ment and a philosophy, but one shared by only a handful of families, most of them in rural Alberta and British Columbia.

The French immersion question. Arching over all the categories we've just gone through is one more choice: the French immersion option. Because Canada is a bilingual country, and because facility in French and English has become essential for Anglos in Quebec and anyone working for the federal government, many English-speaking parents have taken to enrolling their children in a French-speaking school. The most popular form of this is called French immersion, which suggests that a student dipped into a French environment will metaphorically soak up the language. Such programs grew by 200 percent in enrolment in the 1980s, while other forms of schooling increased only marginally. It is possible that this growth was related to parental commitment to a bilingual Canada and a sense that two languages would be a good investment for children, but we suspect that FI simply became *chic* in the 1980s and provided a way for advantaged parents to send their children to an elite, quasi-private-school experience at taxpayer expense.

If your child enrols in an early immersion program, he will start in kindergarten or grade one with a program where reading, writing, math and virtually everything else will be presented in French. After one or two years English will be introduced as a core subject, and the time spent on it increases in the higher grades, but your child's basic language of instruction (and response) is always French. Other French immersion programs can begin in grade three or four (intermediate immersion) or grade six or seven (late immersion). All receive some federal financial support.

As might be expected, if your child is enrolled in early French immersion, he really will grow up to speak French with some fluency. Unfortunately, his progress in reading and writing English almost always falls behind, usually by a grade level, sometimes by almost two. Nor will his facility in reading and writing French ever reach quite the same level as that of Francophone students in French schools. These truths often lead to panic in grade four or five, when you might wonder if French immersion has held back your child's reading and writing forever, especially when comparisons are made to the illustrious nonimmersed kid next door. If you can get past this point, you'll find that your child's facility in reading and writing English improves until a normal level is reached in high school—with the bonus that your child is also fluent in Canada's other official language. For children who get hung up at the crisis point, damage to self-esteem may make it best to withdraw from French immersion and return to the regular school program.

Moving toward the Final Decision

As you move closer toward a decision, it's time to widen your sources of information. The first source may well be next door, mowing the lawn.

Check with neighbours and friends. The reliability of what you hear is highly variable, ranging from nasty teacher gossip you might pick up from the lady across your back fence to a careful evaluation of a school music program by your son's piano teacher. Sadly, the opinions of people who do not have children in the school are practically worthless. American educators have found that the fastest way to raise public approval for local schools has nothing to do with class size or quality education; the only thing required is fresh paint on the doors to the school to clean up graffiti.

Nonetheless, the *real* experience of parents in your neighbourhood is important. You'll have to

French Immersion: A Case Study

Jason entered French immersion in grade one after a successful kindergarten year. His parents wanted him to have the opportunity to learn French and Jason's kindergarten teacher supported the decision. After two years in the French immersion program, Jason's mother began to notice some moodiness in her son and a reluctance to go to school. Jason had made few, if any, friends in his class and was having trouble reading both English and French.

Jason's mother was assured her son would soon adjust. He did not. By December of this third year, Jason's parents decided to remove him from the program and return Jason to the regular program in the neighbourhood school.

Even before starting at his new school, Jason was given a collection of easy readers to begin with. His mother received a few tips on reading with her son. On Jason's first day, he marched into the office with his bag of borrowed books, thanked the principal and proudly announced that he and his mom had read them all.

In a year, with some help from a reading-buddy program, Jason was making good progress in the regular grade three program. What's more, he was enjoying school and had made a set of friends. Sometimes a change of school and program is essential to keep a child learning.

discount the natural tendency of people to prefer choices they've already made, but having done so, you'll get some idea of the strengths and weaknesses of your local school. Several opinions are always more valuable than a single view; the opinions of parents with ordinary children are probably more important than those of parents who are upset over the handling of their "special" child. Ultimately, the opinions you receive will be only as reliable as their sources, and not nearly as important as your own investigation.

Check out the school yourself. Once you have narrowed the choice down to two or three schools, it's time to do some looking around on your own. You can't judge a school for your child on the basis of paint on the doors, ivy on the walls or the cars in the teacher parking lot; you have to go inside and start talking to people. In most cases, the person to talk to is the principal, though large high schools sometimes assign these duties to a member of the guidance staff.

Make an appointment. The principal should find time to see you within a week—or find someone else to talk to you if she is unavailable. If you say to the secretary when you phone, "We're thinking of enrolling our son at your school next year," this should get you at least fifteen minutes with the principal and someone to take you on a tour of the school and its facilities. Any school that can't manage this much probably won't do much for your child either.

When you arrive for your appointment, the principal will probably talk to you about the school and its facilities for ten minutes or so. She's probably done this several hundred times, so the information will be accurate enough. You'll learn about hours, attendance procedures, gym clothes, lunchtime supervision, bus schedules. You might get some sense about the principal's personal philosophy or special programs at the school. What her talk won't give you is a real sense of how good the school might be. For that, you'll have to listen carefully to her answers to your questions. Try these seven for starters:

1. **How are students evaluated? How will I know if my son is meeting the standards for his grade level?**
   The response will give you a sense of how the school approaches curriculum and the whole question of standards. An answer about individualized programs and individualized progress likely means that your child won't be measured against a norm or given many standardized tests. This might be fine for you and your child, but for many parents it's not good enough. In response to parent demand, many schools and boards across Canada have begun producing clearer statements about expectations, called student *outcomes*. These permit a personalized approach to student learning, but still give parents a sense of how their child is doing compared with other children in the grade.

2. **Do teachers encourage parents to be involved with homework?**
   The answer to this question will tell you whether or not there is homework at your child's grade level. It will give you a sense of how demanding the school is of its students. It will also say something about how welcome your involvement is likely to be at the school.

3. **What kinds of extracurricular activities are available for my child?**
   A school that provides a smorgasbord of activities—sports, lunchtime house leagues, clubs, drama, music, art, chess, debating—will be better for your child than a school with just classes and a football team. Some schools offer trips at Christmas or March break; some make

Choosing a School for Your Child:

Seven Steps in Brief

1. Talk with and think about your child and what he needs and wants.

2. Think about your own values and what you expect of the school.

3. Phone your local schools for information.

4. Consider the major options available to you for your child.

5. Check with other parents, neighbours, friends for their opinions.

6. Visit the final choices; look around; talk to the principal; evaluate what you've learned.

7. Talk the choices through with your partner—and with your child—then decide.

extensive use of neighbouring community facilities; some use local trips to augment geography and history programs; some have special camping or leadership opportunities for students. Your question allows the principal to lay out the menu. Let's hope the selection is wide.

4. **What are your expectations on behaviour?**
You might already have learned some of this in the principal's opening talk, but there's always room for more information How are parents involved or informed when students get in trouble? Do teachers handle their own discipline through detentions or other tactics, or is the administration involved? Some schools have a written behaviour code: ask to get a copy. And try to get a feel from the answers just where on the discipline spectrum this school lies. Do three lates merit counselling or a detention or the strap? Which would you want for your child?

5. **How large will my son's class probably be?**
Class size varies from year to year, according to enrolment and teacher contracts and a host of other factors having to do with groupings and split classes. But a principal should be able to give you a reasonable guess at any particular grade level. According to research, class sizes closer to twenty-four work better for students than those above thirty. The reasons for this are simple: more individualized attention, more flexibility in lesson strategies, easier control of the classroom environment. Statistically, the next bump up in education effectiveness doesn't occur until class size drops to twelve students—something you won't find in many schools.

6. **What type of help is available if my child is having difficulty with school work?**
Listen for such terms as *resource teacher*, *reading booster*, *peer counselling* and *special*

Balancing What you Hear

Marge was completing the purchase of a house in a new subdivision outside Calgary. In her dealings with the real-estate agent, she asked about the public school in the area. The agent enthusiastically endorsed the school, saying that her nephew had gone there and that they had the best sports teams in the district.

Marge made the same inquiry of her new neighbours after moving in, only to be told that their son had had a terrible experience at the neighbourhood school, that the staff were incompetent and the principal quite arrogant. The neighbours had moved their own child to a new school, which still wasn't living up to their expectations.

Marge's own investigation took in both the neighbourhood school and the one where the neighbours had finally sent their son. She looked at facilities, the principals, the report cards and the provisions for parent involvement. Marge ended up choosing the neighbourhood school, which suited her son well, and has yet to regret the choice. As for her neighbours, they're still unhappy and thinking about a third school.

assistance. Any of these indicates that there is special personnel available to help children with learning problems. A principal who responds that her teachers provide all the extra help any child may need is dodging the question or hiding an inadequate program.

7. How can I be involved with the school?
This question tells the principal not only that you want to know what's going on, but that you're ready to share in the partnership of educating your child. Many schools have a home and school organization, or parent advisory group, or ask parents to help out with trips, school teams, reading and library programs. If these aren't mentioned in the principal's response, don't panic. For many administrators this is uncharted territory and there is some fear about where parent involvement is heading. Nonetheless, a school that actively encourages parent involvement is much more likely to be a good place to learn than one that keeps its doors locked all day.

Look around on your tour. After you've finished talking to the principal, someone will take you to have a look around the school, the playground and—with luck—into a classroom. Sometimes schools ask senior students to conduct such tours—and this is always a good indicator of a good school—but the information you get from your guide isn't nearly as important as what you see and feel.

Observe the school's general appearance and the care shown for the building and equipment. A well-kept school indicates more than effective custodial staff; it shows that staff and students have pride in their school. Schools littered with garbage and plagued with graffiti by their own students may be places where staff have thrown in the towel in their attempts to inspire and motivate. On the other hand, displays of student work

Checklist for a Good School

All these items can be seen in a good school at any grade level:

❏ The school seems clean and well cared for.

❏ There are displays of student work and activities in the halls and classrooms.

❏ The principal is welcoming, friendly, businesslike.

❏ There is a busy, well-stocked, staffed library.

❏ The students seem happy and enthusiastic.

❏ The computer laboratory is functioning and in use by kids and staff.

❏ There is a schedule for extracurricular activity.

❏ There is a house system, or at least house league sports.

❏ You can see parents and other volunteers helping children.

❏ Classroom doors are open, and what's happening inside looks productive.

- ❏ Children are reading for enjoyment—not just in the library.

- ❏ There is a strong music program with a band or orchestra.

- ❏ There is a school musical or art show or a number of special-event evenings.

- ❏ Teachers are not stuck behind their desks, but up teaching or working with students.

- ❏ There are classroom displays of current topics, samples of "final draft" student work.

- ❏ Students seem busy and engaged in their work.

- ❏ If you visit at lunchtime or recess, the cafeteria and playground seem reasonably under control.

- ❏ The school has a tradition of excellence.

- ❏ Teachers greet each other in the hall as if they were friends, not just nod to each other as colleagues.

Scoring: award 5 points for each check. An excellent school will score 80-90; a good school 70-75; an adequate school 60-65.

and photos of student activities and achievements show a school where teachers take pride in the kids. Surely this is what you want for your child.

If you can time your visit to coincide with an outdoor recess period, step outside and watch how the children play and socialize. How much supervision is available in the schoolyard? How many organized games or activities are going on? Remembering that any school can have a disruptive day, what is the general *feel* of the recess period? It often says much about how students get along with one another.

As you wander around, try to get a sense of the rapport among the staff, and among staff and students. There should be a *feel* to the school or climate that indicates people like to be there. We've been to schools where the hallways are silent and there's nothing to see but a teacher disciplining a student and a custodian wringing out a mop. And we've been to schools where kids come and go to the library, other students do projects on the hall floor, the teachers seem to know every child and always have smiles and jokes for one another. What kind of environment do you want for your child?

If you get a chance to observe a classroom, don't generalize too much from what you're seeing. A particular classroom more likely reflects that teacher and her students than the teacher your child is going to get; nor is it possible to generalize about everything that goes on during a day or week from ten minutes at the back of the class. You'll get a more reliable sense of what's going on by listening to student-teacher talk and looking at examples of student work.

Decision time. If there was ever a time for all of you to be involved in a family conference, this is it. You, your partner, your child, sometimes your ex-partner—everybody should have a say. How you value particular aspects of program and philosophy is up to you, but give all the options some careful thought before you act.

Then act. The actual procedures for getting into a particular school vary, but time makes a difference. There may be entrance exams to write or scholarships to apply for. Some high schools like to have course options selected in the January before your child enters in September. Your neighbourhood elementary school would prefer to know about your son's September entrance by May to arrange classes and seek appropriate staffing. While it's still possible to wander in off the street in September with your child, such surprises don't do either the school or your child much good.

A Homework Policy or Guide

Ask to see a copy. A good one will include:
- a philosophy of learning that shows the role of homework;
- responsibilities of students, teachers and parents;
- suggested times to be spent on homework for various grade levels;
- recommended schedules for study or homework;
- recommended settings and procedures for study;
- ways in which parents can help;
- procedures for checking assignments;
- consequences for unfinished homework (homework club, study hall).

We feel that homework should be expected at every grade level, starting as early as kindergarten. If your child consistently has "nothing to do," better have a serious talk with the teacher and the principal.

CHAPTER 3

Working with Teachers

Teachers—the blessing and the curse of our educational system. Technocrats and bureaucrats would like to get rid of them altogether: human beings are too fallible, too variable, too likely to mess up "delivery of the program." Parents whose children are suffering under the yoke of a bad teacher would do everything short of voodoo—maybe even including voodoo—to rid the school of someone who can cause so much damage. Even our newspapers, which once applauded teachers for the nobility of their calling, have now taken to blaming them for everything from declining test scores to violence in the school parking lot.

It's a shame. There are many, many good teachers out there and quite a few excellent ones, all working little miracles despite declining budgets, fragmenting families, TV-inspired violence, mouthy students and a host of societal contradictions that can pull a good teacher apart. Just when more kids need a hug than ever before—and are less likely to get one at home—our teachers can be charged for putting an arm around a student of the opposite sex. Just when our kids most need stability and order someplace in their lives, teachers find it increasingly difficult to enforce order in the classroom. Just when teachers are making a real effort to reach each child as an individual, society blames them for the collective problems of an entire generation. So let us begin with a plea for understanding for the species *didacticus*; it's a tough job, but somebody's got to do it.

Knowing the Species: Who Becomes a Teacher

At one time teachers were mostly underpaid and mostly female, a gender that had few other professional possibilities. This collective unfairness resulted in a very cheap and somewhat underprepared group of teachers who kowtowed nicely to mostly male educational authorities and did what they could for oversized classes of young people.

This system of entrapped, cheap labour began falling apart when enrolments increased in the 1960s and more professional jobs opened up for women in the 1970s. More men were drawn into the system, and teachers of both sexes became more aggressive about contracts, salaries and teaching load. The old order exploded. Some of the initial results of this explosion were good: smaller classes, more teacher preparation time, more teacher empowerment. But the long-term fallout has been less than splendid: teacher burnout, strikes that idle students, soaring school budgets.

What do we have today? The average elementary school teacher, Ms. Watson, is probably a woman, probably married to a middle-class husband who also works, and probably has a couple of kids of her own at home. Ms. Watson came into teaching because she loves kids, did reasonably well in school, completed a three-year B.A

The Teacher Index

Percentage of teachers who teach: 84
Percentage of teachers who are principals or vice-principals: 7
Percentage of teachers with "nonteaching" duties like guidance or library: 7

Median age of an Ontario teacher in 1978: 34.6 years
Median age of an Ontario teacher in 1991: 41.6 years

Chance that your child's primary (K-3) teacher is a man: 1 in 17
Chance that your child's high school teacher is a man: 1:1

Chance that your child will be in a split-grade or mixed-grade classroom: 1 in 5

Chance that your child's teacher will have less than 5 years' experience: 1 in 7
Chance that your child's teacher will have more than 20 years' experience: 1 in 3

and a one- or two-year teacher training program. She was born into a lower-middle-class family and regards teaching as a step up on the social ladder, but she's uncomfortable dealing with professional-level parents and she doesn't want to cause problems for the school principal, whom she regards as her boss.

After thirteen years of teaching, Ms. Watson is still happy with her work in school, focussing on her students, guiding class discussion, setting up group work, creating games and simulations, even dispensing bandages when required. She worries about her students as individuals, as kids, and wants to be sure they get the basics. She sees the rest of the curriculum as relatively less important, but does the best she can to follow the dictates of the board or division and the Ministry or Department of Education. While she feels important to her students and reasonably well respected in the community, Ms. Watson also feels quite powerless to move the educational establishment: the principal, the board or district, the Ministry or Department of Education. Nonetheless, she'll do the best she can in her classroom, with whatever situation comes her way.

The average secondary school teacher is a somewhat different creature. To begin, he is more likely a man, more likely interested in his subject area than in the joys of working with young people and more likely dissatisfied with his job. Our average high school teacher, Mr. Farrow, is probably married, probably within ten years of retirement and probably looking forward to that. After eighteen years in the profession, he's worried about burnout, loss of job prestige and increasingly difficult students.

In class, Mr. Farrow lectures, gives tests, assigns homework and occasionally entertains class discussion. At the top of his salary scale, Mr. Farrow makes a good dollar—more than $60,000 a year in most provinces—but the money is heav-

Joys and Sorrows of Teaching

Percentage of teachers who are "proud to be a teacher": 89

Percentage who "look forward to coming to work each day": 77

Percentage who would choose to go into teaching if they could begin a career again: 61

Percentage who feel they are respected in their communities: 49

Percentage of teachers who sometimes worry about being injured by students in the school: 17

Percentage of teachers who sometimes "find it difficult to maintain discipline": 30

Percentage of Newfoundland teachers who say that "fear of legal action" affects how they deal with students: 19

Percentage of Quebec teachers who say that "fear legal action" affects how they deal with students: 5

Percentage of art, library and guidance teachers who are "very satisfied" with their jobs: 23

Percentage of French, math, technical and computer teachers who are "very satisfied" with their jobs: 12

What Do Teachers Earn?

Teacher salaries vary from province to province and rise sharply as teachers gain in classroom experience. Here are the 1994 teaching salaries across Canada for a teacher with a four-year university degree and the highest level (often twelve years or more) of experience.

Province	Specific Location	Salary
B. C.	(Vancouver)	$56,883
Alberta	(Edmonton)	52,273
Saskatchewan	(provincial)	49,184
Manitoba	(Winnipeg)	53,015
Ontario	(Carleton Board)	64,779
Quebec	(provincial)	47,971
New Brunswick	(provincial, 1993)	46,742
Nova Scotia	(provincial)	53,489
P.E.I.	(provincial)	45,235
Newfoundland	(provincial)	40,786
N.W.T.	(territorial)	69,249
Yukon	(territorial)	67,691

ily taxed, his union dues are high and there are few job perks besides the short school year. He resents the way neighbours envy his salary and time off, feeling that they don't understand how hard he works. Some of his colleagues at school are suffering from stress or burnout, especially those who haven't adapted to a new generation of students who frequently challenge their teachers and often regard their jobs at McDonald's as more important than an upcoming math test. Mr. Farrow spent four years studying his subject at university and another year at a faculty of education getting his teaching certificate. He loves his subject and wants to impart that love and excitement to his students; sadly, the teenage students increasingly look to each other for love and to the media for excitement. This truth leads to grumbling in the staff room, but Mr. Farrow refuses to give up. Every year he can reach a handful of kids and that, maybe, makes it all worthwhile.

As a parent, you'll have to work with both these "average" teachers, and dozens more of their real-life counterparts, so it helps to understand where they come from and what's going on in their minds when that blank look comes over their faces.

The Right Teacher for *Your* Child

We have said earlier that in our best estimation, about 20 percent of Canada's teachers are excellent, 30 percent are good, 40 percent do a reasonable job for some students and 10 percent should be in another line of work. (Most of the teachers across Canada whom we asked confidentially would agree with these percentages, but feel we're being too kind with that bottom 10 percent figure.) We must also tell you that your child has a fifty-fifty chance of getting "the right teacher" for her needs in any given year. You'll note the figures don't gibe. Here's why: the right teacher for your child depends on the mesh of personalities, teaching style and learning style almost as much as it does upon teacher excellence. For example, Mr. Starr is an excellent teacher with a flamboyant technique, who puts a heavy emphasis on class participation and rarely encourages formal note taking. But, excellent or not, Mr. Starr may not suit your shy Deirdre, who learns best in a structured setting, hates group work and is deathly afraid of getting up in front of her classmates.

Theoretically, teachers should have enough variety in their teaching style to accommodate all students. Theoretically, Deirdre should benefit from the demands and excitement in Mr. Starr's classroom. But the truth is more complex than the theory. Deirdre might well learn more from Mrs. Drudge down the hall, even if we rated that teacher's dull board work, silent classroom and rigid discipline in the mediocre category. It's a matter of meshing teaching and learning styles.

So let's consider a number of different teaching styles and the types of students who profit from each.

The traditionalist: Miss Tudd. The traditionalist teacher keeps her pupils' desks in rows, with her own desk front and centre at the head of the class. On the blackboard will be a list of assignments and procedures, perhaps a penmanship chart at the early grade levels. Miss Tudd's daybook is carefully structured and she follows the text rigorously in each subject area. You can expect her to assign homework nightly, collect it the next day and mark it conscientiously. There will be little fooling around in the class—"Raise your hand before speaking, Johnny"—but that doesn't mean there won't be joy in learning and effective teaching.

The children who thrive with Miss Tudd are those who like order, who can deal with arbitrary structures, who can focus and stay on task. Girls

Teachers as People

Why teachers decided to teach—and stay teaching. The first percentage relates to those teachers who considered the reason "very important" for starting in the profession, the second percentage to those teachers who considered the reason "very important" for staying in it.

"To work with young people":
   55 percent—56 percent

"Job security": 27 percent—41 percent

"To render an important service":
   36 percent—35 percent

"Length of work year":
   21 percent—35 percent

"Interest in subject":
   35 percent—33 percent

"Salary": 11 percent—26 percent

"Pension": 7 percent—25 percent

Chance that your child's teacher has a spouse who is also a teacher: 1 in 4

Chance that your child's teacher has a parent who was in a profession: 1 in 10

Chance that your child's teacher has a parent who is a farmer: 1 in 5

Chance that your child's teacher has a parent who does unskilled labour: 1 in 5

Teachers Moving up the Ladder

Teachers who wish to spread their influence further afield (and earn a little more money) can become a vice-principal, principal or consultant. The pay in these positions is about $6,000 a year more (after taxes) than a teacher at the top of his or her salary category, some compensation for the fact that the jobs require eleven months of work rather than ten.

Upwardly mobile teachers generally start by applying for positions of responsibility in their own school, then demonstrating their skills through committee work, seminars or workshop presentations for other teachers in the system. Getting promoted involves jumping through a number of hoops that involve written submissions by the teacher, evaluations of the applicant at work and "the interview" (often a gruelling, three-hour "simulation" of some school administrative crisis).

Collective agreements with teacher unions cover promotions up to the superintendent level, so vice-principals who wish to move up (and there are very few "career V.P.s " around) must go through the same process again to become principals. The format is almost the same for those hardy few who aspire to a supervisory-officer job, but the board can set and change the rules for those competitions without dealing with the unions.

are more likely to do well with the traditionalist teacher than boys, quiet students more than outgoing ones. As adults, the teachers we often remember most fondly are the traditionalists: they were stern, but when they smiled at us in approval it meant something. We tend to forget the stifling atmosphere in their classrooms, the lack of creativity and the mind-numbing drudgery of their daily worksheets.

The coach: Mr. Gung-ho. Remember basketball practice? The coach tends to teach a move, run a drill, then help individuals to master the fine points. So too, Mr. Gung-ho will do a lesson, lead the large group in discussion, give out some instructions and then move in on individuals and groups to ensure that they are on task and understand what the lesson was about. The technique works well with a high-energy teacher who can respond quickly to the needs of many different children. It also requires pretty clear routines for behaviour in the classroom, so Mr. Gung-ho will be less freewheeling than other teachers. He'll be perfect for a child who needs structure and direction, for kids who like lots of activity and group work. For the shy child who wants to work alone, or the creative genius, Mr. Gung-ho is the wrong man at the blackboard.

The hands-on teacher: Ms. Tactile. Ms. Tactile's classroom is full of *stuff*: blocks, lab equipment, toys, games, books. The student desks may be in groups or rows, but the action is in activity centres throughout the room. The day will be organized not around lessons so much as around activities: the reading selection will be introduced with a prop or a game; the math lesson will use blocks, metre sticks and bingo chips. Ms. Tactile may not teach all the theory, but she'll get the kids involved with the work.

The children who learn best with the hands-on teacher, logically, are the hands-on kids. If your son loves taking apart clocks or your daughter loves building with Lego, then your child will thrive with this teacher. If your child isn't that curious, or needs more careful explanation, or doesn't like getting his cutting knife right inside the metaphorical frog, then this teacher may not be the best. Or maybe, just maybe, Ms. Tactile will help your reticent child develop her creativity and problem solving.

The child-centred teacher: Mr. Love. Some teachers put their classroom emphasis not on lessons or skills or curriculum, but on the needs of the child. This requires individualizing a program for twenty-five kids and enough energy to run all those groups and individual activities at the same time. With a teacher's aid to help, it's sometimes possible for Mr. Love to do all this and still maintain his sanity.

The classroom of the child-centred teacher is set up with pupils' desks grouped in four or with kids sitting together at tables; the teacher's own desk can be anywhere *except* the front of the room. There are few notes on the blackboard about assignments and due dates because the kids are doing so many different things. Homework will be erratic, sometimes nonexistent, sometimes an enormous project requiring a whole weekend. Somehow Mr. Love will tailor-make each assignment to get the most from each student, or at least he'll try.

Bright students often thrive with a teacher like Mr. Love, as well as students who are self-disciplined enough to put together their own learning and structure. If your child needs order and rules and a structure imposed from above, then he's going to have a hard time in Mr. Love's class.

The instructor: Mr. Wright. When we think of teaching, we picture a teacher in front of a classroom, chalk in hand, and thirty kids paying rapt attention to the lesson. This kind of Norman

Dysteachia: What to Look For

Not every child who has a problem in school is a problem child; sometimes he just has a poor teacher. Educator Arn Bowers's term for this is *dysteachia*. Here are some signs.

- the homework is busywork, copied from a teacher's resource book, or nonexistent;
- marking is done late (a reasonable turnaround time is two days) or not at all;
- record keeping is spotty or "lost";
- the class is frequently out of control or many kids end up being sent to the office;
- even "good" students are yelled at or given repeated detentions;
- the teacher is frequently "sick" and takes days off, leaving the kids with supply teachers;
- there is lots of attention to form ("name, date, title") but no attention to learning.

Rules and Regulations of Victoria Central School (c. 1880)

Duties of Pupils

1st. After having entered their respective Class Rooms, not to leave them without permission.

2nd. To present themselves at School at all times neat and clean in their person and dress.

3rd. To take necessary Books home to enable them to prepare their lessons for the upcoming day.

4th. Always to pay proper attention and respect to the instructions and admonitions of their Teachers.

Duties of Teachers

1st. To be in their respective Class Rooms at 1/2 before 9 A.M., and at 25 minutes past 1 P.M., for the reception of pupils.

2nd. To open and close the School with prayer, not occupying more than 5 minutes on each occasion.

Rockwell vision of education is a thing of the past in most classrooms—if it ever did exist anywhere—but there remain many teachers, especially in high school, who simply like to teach. The advantage of "direct instruction," as it's sometimes called, is the speed with which it can get across information and sometimes build skills, hence its value for children who are distracted or who have fallen behind. The disadvantage of Mr. Wright's style has to do with all that information on the blackboard and not in the heads of the students—and the fact that bright children who want to race ahead hate getting stuck behind slow-moving vehicles such as a teacher and their peers. Not every child feels that guessing what's in Mr. Wright's mind is the best kind of class discussion.

The manager: Ms. Digit. As schools adopt more and more business models and the teaching contingent ages, you're more and more likely to find a manager teaching your child. All teaching involves some management: record keeping, organizing groups, coordinating due dates and field trips and project work time. But Ms. Digit takes all this a step further, often seeing the organization of class activity (frequently on a computer) as more important than actually teaching. For children who enjoy working on tasks and doing self-directed learning, Ms. Digit provides many avenues to make these things happen. For the disadvantaged child, or the child who has fallen behind, or the child who really wants to talk about things with the teacher, Ms. Digit lacks the personal touch.

The performer: Mr. Starr. Some teachers really like to do "a show" in class, with themselves as the star. If your child's teacher is a performer, you'll find a centre-front desk, with pupil desks pushed up close. Homework will tie into the day's lesson, which can be an extravaganza that will rivet the attention of a child. A gifted teacher of this type—like Robin Williams's John Keating in *Dead Poet's Society*—will make a lasting imprint on your child, even if he doesn't actually teach all that much.

If your child enjoys sitting back and watching —and doesn't want to steal too much of the limelight himself—then the performer can be a wonderful experience. For a child who needs special attention, or wants to get involved, or would rather *do* than *admire*, Mr. Starr can be less than the best.

The martinet: Colonel Martin. No teacher could be worse: tired, burned out, boring, with nothing left for children than the authority of his position. Look for a classroom of rigidly neat desks, a fearful silence in the air, students working "independently" on seat work that seems to go on forever, shaky hands if students dare raise them to ask a question. Some parents think Colonel Martin is just the kind of teacher their child needs to bring an errant boy in line. But all Colonel Martin really does is bottle up youthful energy, stifle enthusiasm and creativity and teach kids that learning is synonymous with terror. Get your child out of his classroom—fast.

You Often *Can* Choose Your Child's Teacher

Despite everything you hear officially, parents really can have a powerful say—almost a choice— in who teaches their child. Here's the situation. At any grade level, in almost every school, there will be two or more teachers assigned. Your first job, as a parent, is to pick the best teacher for your child from those available. You do this in similar ways to choosing a school.

- *Look around.* If you're in the school for any reason, look in the classrooms. What's going on? What kind of teaching style is in evidence?

3rd. To teach the branches required in their respective Divisions, according to the standard of preparation adopted by the Board of Trustees.

4th. To keep in the books provided for that purpose a record of attendance, recitations and deportment of each pupil, and to furnish each parent or guardian with a correct transcript thereof on the 1st Monday of each month.

5th. In no case to grant leave of absence to any pupil except in the case of sickness without a note from his or her parent or guardian.

6th. And generally to conform to all the duties of Teachers as laid down in the Common School Acts for Upper Canada.

7th. In all cases when any doubt may arise as to the most effectual method of carrying out the spirit of these regulations, application shall be made to the Principal.

How Teachers Really Mark

Boards or districts and curriculum consultants will give you complex statements of how teachers evaluate students. But if you ask the teachers themselves, this is what they say they look for:

(Percentage of teachers who said this item was "very important" when asked by the Canadian Teachers' Federation)

Effort: 80 percent
Tests/exams: 25 percent (rises to 55 percent by grade twelve)
Homework/notebooks/ class assignments: 30 percent
Projects: 20 percent
Attendance: 30 percent
Behaviour: 55 percent (drops from 80 percent in kindergarten to 30 percent in grade twelve)

Are the kids happy, learning, on task, or are they bored, sitting stone silent, with one or two kids obviously removed for punishment? The arrangement of the physical classroom will also tell you a great deal about the kind of teacher who inhabits the place. If you're a volunteer, watch prospective teachers in the staff room. The way teachers relate to their colleagues often speaks volumes about the way they treat kids.

- *Ask around.* Teachers get reputations, often richly deserved. Try to find out from neighbours and friends what the reputations are for the teachers available for your child. The words of other parents—especially those whose kids have studied with a particular teacher—definitely have value. You have to remember that their child may not be like yours, or respond to the same kind of teacher, but we have found that parent word of mouth is remarkably accurate in describing teacher quality and teacher style.

- *Talk to the teachers.* In a good school, teachers themselves often know which of their colleagues would be best with a given child. If your child's grade three teacher was first-rate, she'll likely know which of the grade four teachers will be best for your child. Teachers are forbidden by their professional code from bad-mouthing one another, so you can't begin your talk by saying, "I've heard that Mrs. X is a witch. Is that true?" But you can say something like "I want to be sure that Deirdre gets the best teacher for her needs next year. Do you think Mrs. X or Ms. Y would be better for her?" You'll usually get a straight answer.

- *Consider the choices.* The teacher with the best reputation may not always be the best teacher for your child next year. You have to consider the mesh between your child's learning style and the teaching styles of the teachers assigned to a given grade level. You may also want to look at the class assignments: a split-grade class is rarely as good a learning environment as a single-grade-level class, regardless of how good the teacher may be. And then there are the other alternatives: gifted class, French immersion or nonimmersion, the music program with Ms. Y or the shop class with Mr. Z. All these factors have to be weighed carefully before you meet with the principal.

- *Speak to the principal.* Once you've selected Mrs. X, Ms. Y or Mr. Z, it's time to speak to the principal. The best time for a discussion like this is in May, before next year's class lists are engraved in stone. Some principals will go out and ask for your input before arranging classes for the following year, but such farsighted principals are rare. For the rest, you'll have to make an appointment to suggest which teacher would be best for your child. Every principal we've talked to will *try* to place your child with the teacher you request.

Unless the principal has specifically asked for your suggestion, it's best to approach this matter with some discretion. Don't walk up to the principal in the front hall and announce, "I want my child with Mr. Z next year." Better to go into the principal's office, close the door and chat about your child, the year just past and your concern that she have a good teacher next year. It's often best to talk in generalities, about Deirdre getting along best with "a motherly type" or "needing structure in the classroom." Then pop the key phrase: "I was hoping that you might be able to see that Deirdre gets in Mr. Z's class next year." Don't expect a simple response. No principal can *promise* that a child

The Myth of "Retribution"

Many parents think that teachers are vengeful creatures. We've heard the idea hundreds of times: "If I make a stink about something, I know that the teacher will take it out on my kid."

Wrong.

Teachers are not nearly as vengeful as they are timid. In our combined fifty years in the classroom, we've run across only a handful of teachers so spiteful that they'd respond to parental criticism with unpleasant treatment of a child. But we've known thousands of teachers who will suddenly give a child kid-glove treatment when they know a parent is concerned and watching carefully.

Kid-glove treatment is not always the best approach to education or teacher-student relationships, but it certainly beats abuse, fear and distrust.

If you must take action to change what's happening in your child's class or school, chances are that the teacher won't like you much, but it's not going to end up damaging your child.

That Time of Year...

How you deal with your child's teacher may well depend on the time of year. Of course, if the teacher turns out to be good, you can relax about all this, but if the situation is otherwise...

- August/September. Be nice. Wear a sweater. Introduce yourself. A little ingratiation goes a long way.

- October. Watch. You'll have a hunch by now that things are going well or going poorly. If well, volunteer your services and keep the good stuff happening. If poorly, start your file folder (see the sidebar, p. 51). Get your suit dry-cleaned.

- November. Act. Use the information in your file folder. Speak to the teacher about changes. Allow two weeks, then speak to the principal.

- December. Get aggressive. Just what does the teacher or principal promise to do? Get a superintendent or trustee on your side. If you want your child moved in January, you have to be aggressive before Christmas.

will be with a given teacher, but she does have considerable power in making that happen.

You should also listen to what the principal has to say about the choice you've made. She may have more information about your child and her own teachers than you think. She'll certainly know if Mr. Z is scheduled for transfer, or whether his teaching performance is under review, or if your impressions are close to correct, though she can't reveal any of that to you.

Remember: you cannot demand; you can only ask. Do not request a particular teacher in writing, or in a roomful of people, or with another parent present. You are engaged in a delicate verbal negotiation. Most principals will do whatever they can to accommodate you, but if you try to bully or bluster or do any of this too publicly, you'll get nowhere.

Dealing with Teachers Throughout the Year

You're going to be invited to meet your child's teacher at least twice during the year. Go. Whether that teacher is excellent or incompetent, you'll be literally powerless unless you've made the effort to attend orientation night, or parents' night, or the parent-interview afternoon. Many, if not most, parents find these events uncomfortable. School may not have been a place where you excelled or of which you have fond memories. Teachers themselves are frequently defensive on these occasions, trying too hard to put their best foot forward. And these events are always held on the teacher's turf and according to the teacher's timetable, putting you at an immediate disadvantage in power and comfort. Nonetheless, you really have to grit your teeth and go.

Why? Because you are the best advocate your child is going to have for his first dozen years in school. Because teachers tend to treat more carefully those children whose parents are involved. Because any complaints to higher authorities are worth nothing unless you've talked to the teacher first.

So go. The first meeting will usually be early in the school year, August or September, often a presentation by the teacher to a captive group of parents wedged into tiny student desks. After the twenty-minute lecture, there's time for questions and then everybody is supposed to go for coffee with the principal. Don't leave yet. Introduce yourself to the teacher as Deirdre's parent. Smile. Mention something positive about the class that you've noticed or that you've heard from your child. Then go for coffee. In most schools, teachers rarely have enough information at these first encounters to say anything substantial about your child anyway.

The second meeting, in October or November, is a serious interview with the teacher about your child. By now the first report card will have appeared and probably given you a great deal of information that you don't need ("Deirdre displays evidence of strong interpersonal skills") and not much that you really want to know (Is Deirdre reading at the norm for her grade level?). So bring the report card and use that for the discussion. How is Deirdre doing—really? What are her strengths and weaknesses? How can you help at home? If you suspect that the teacher is really going to be a problem, you'd better start a file folder to keep notes on what she's doing or not doing. This can be vital if you have difficulties later on.

Any teacher will be most comfortable giving you the good news about your child, slightly less comfortable telling you the unpleasant truths and very uncomfortable if you begin asking her about teaching techniques or suggesting that her classroom is less than ideal as a learning environment. Your approach at this meeting should be to look

An Essential Parent Tool: The File Folder

If your child has ended up with a truly incompetent or mediocre teacher, or in a dreadful school, then you have to take action to change the situation. Your first tool is a file folder. Here's what to keep in it:

- notes sent by the teacher or school;
- copies of notes you send to the teacher or school;
- notes on conversations with the teacher or school;
- notes on particular events at school that you've heard about from your child;
- your observations on your child's behaviour or learning;
- quotation said by your child or other children about the teacher or school;
- copies of marked tests, homework, handouts;
- report cards.

Remember to date all the material. You will never have to use all this as you might in a legal case, but it is vital to be able to refer to specific incidents or specific meetings on a given date. This gives you credibility.

For Parent Interviews

Start with the easy material:
- The report card—what does it really say?
- How is your child doing compared with the other kids or her potential?
- How is your child behaving?
- How can you help at home?

Then move to the middle-level material:
- Is Deirdre happy or unhappy with school, and why?
- Are there problems with other kids or distractions in school?

Only at the end should you broach criticism:
- Is the reading/text material too easy/too hard?
- Shouldn't the homework be more regular?
- What is the marking scheme?
- You've heard that some students think the marking/teacher behaviour is unfair...

Keep smiling. Never raise your voice. Don't take notes on the spot, but later on jot down what you remember.

at what's happening as a common concern: for you, for Deirdre and for the teacher. You all have a stake in working out a relationship that will lead to an effective year. Remember that Deirdre is all important to you, but only one of twenty-five children (or 150 in high school) for the teacher. Remember that teaching is the teacher's business, that she's had a year of training and probably several years of experience in doing that—a lot more than you. Remember that most teachers are doing the best they can in a given situation, including trying to do a good job by your child.

But don't get overly sympathetic. Yes, it's difficult to teach a class of thirty-two kids, three of whom have special needs, but it's not impossible. Yes, homework can be just busywork, but it does much to involve families and let Deirdre know that learning is important. Yes, current theory says that each child learns at her own rate, but couldn't Deirdre get some extra help because she seems to be a grade level behind in math? Nothing will change unless you ask for change to happen.

If your child seems happy in school, if the lessons you hear about seem fine, if the work that comes home looks good, if your child seems challenged but still enthusiastic about school—then congratulate the teacher. Teaching is an exhausting job to do well. Teachers who do that—and those who put in extra effort at teams and clubs and school activities—should be applauded for their work. Sometimes a little praise from a parent, especially in writing, keeps a good teacher perking along.

But if things aren't going well for Deirdre, you mustn't be afraid to ask for changes in the classroom, or in teacher behaviour, or in the way your child is treated. We have rarely seen teachers "take it out on the child," as parents always fear. More often, we see children being very carefully treated after the parents' concerns are made clear—sometimes with benefits for the whole class. By speaking up on Deirdre's behalf, you are not just making trouble, you're trying to help the teacher do her job that much better. By working to change what goes on in class, you may well be helping the teacher improve—a real boon for hundreds of future students.

Some Special Resources

If you're having problems with your child's teacher, the first place to work those out is with the teacher herself. Failing that, you might want to move up to the next levels: department head or chairperson (in high schools), vice-principal, principal, superintendent, chief superintendent or director, trustees. We'll discuss those options in the next chapter.

But smart parents should be aware that there are other teachers who can influence the education of your child right within the school. You don't have to complain or go to senior administration to contact the school librarian. In some schools, the teacher-librarian is a real curriculum leader, with the capacity to make suggestions to classroom teachers that can improve at least the content of what they're teaching. In many schools, the teacher-librarian runs some part of the program herself—a research project, or regular library reading time, or one-on-one counselling. If you can get the teacher-librarian on the side of your child, you have made a powerful ally without having to lodge any complaints at all.

The other important ally for some children is the special resource teacher. With the rise of special education programs, almost all schools now have at least one resource teacher. These individuals serve as both advocate and tutor for children identified as having special needs. As advocate, they run interference with teachers and administration, try to make sure the child is matched

On Teaching...

In teaching it is the method and not the content that is the message...the drawing out, not the pumping in.

—Ashley Montagu

The Really Incompetent Teacher

Principals frequently complain that they can't get rid of incompetent teachers once they're past the two-year probationary period. But that's not true. Here's the procedure in Ontario; it's lengthy but not impossible.

1. The principal or vice-principal does a classroom observation.
2. The teacher is given a written report, an offer of assistance and a specified period of time to improve.
3. The principal or vice-principal does subsequent observations, completing written reports (the teacher can ask for an outside supervisory officer to do so as well). Two unsatisfactory reports within twenty-four months put the teacher "on review."
4. The teacher receives written notice from the superintendent that he or she is "on review." This must include requirements for improvement, the frequency of subsequent observations and the length of the review process. A teacher may be asked to submit an "action plan" outlining his or her own ideas for improving.
5. The "on review" period can continue for up to twenty-four months. Then the teacher is either free from the process or his or her contract is terminated.

with instructors suited for her, push to have the program modified so the child can fully profit from school. As a tutor, special resource teachers provide time for one-to-one assistance, a room to write tests and essays in a less pressured environment and a counsellor to deal with the slings and arrows of childhood fortune. In a sense, these teachers work as ombudsmen in the system, trying to optimize the education for the child. They also have access to outside agencies that can assist your whole family.

But here's the rub: only 10 to 20 percent of the kids have access to resource teachers: kids who are identified (or "designated") for special education. That group includes slow learners, the gifted, the physically handicapped and kids with specific learning problems. The vast middle range of students may never even get to *meet* the special resource teacher in the school. Too bad for them. If your child is having difficulty in school or finds herself bored or uninterested, it might well be wise to go through the procedures to have Deirdre designated for special education. In the old days there was a stigma to this—"only dummies end up in the rubber room, you know"—but with so many different kinds of kids requiring special attention, that stigma has virtually disappeared. Your child might well be better off designated special needs—with a resource teacher as advocate—than stuck in class with a teacher who doesn't pay her much individual attention and doesn't see why you're so concerned about her. We have more information on all this in chapters 13 and 14.

Don't Despair

By and large, Canadian teachers are among the best prepared and best educated in the entire world. Unlike American teachers, who expect to be paid for coaching a team or looking after a club, Canadian teachers regard themselves as professionals who provide these extra services as part of their commitment to education. Again unlike their American counterparts, Canadian teachers are almost always drawn from the top of their university classes. Our teachers don't have to be forced or paid by state authorities to take upgrading courses—most do it on their own. In any given summer, about a quarter of Canada's teachers will be enrolled in a summer course to learn how to teach that much better. The vast majority of our teachers work hard at their jobs, putting in seven or eight hours at the school and another couple of hours at home getting ready for the next day. Teaching is tough work—imagine keeping the attention of twenty-five squirrelly nine-year-olds who would rather be playing Nintendo while you're trying to do a lesson on long division. Teachers who do teach well deserve every penny we pay them, and probably a nice collection of soaps and jellies at Christmas. If your child has an excellent teacher, then there is no spatula thick enough to spread out the praise such a person deserves. If your child's teacher doesn't measure up, at least you know how to begin to take action. The next chapter will tell you more.

CHAPTER 4

Working with Principals and Higher-ups

When you were a kid, the principal was that very large man in "the office," the man you saw when you were in trouble, the man who administered "the strap" and otherwise brought terror into your fearful heart. Even your classroom teacher trembled before the authority of this individual—and your parents treated him with a respect that verged on awe.

As an adult, you find that much seems to have changed. The principal is now far more likely to be a woman; she passes out awards and smiles more than metes out discipline and punishment; and the strap is either banned or so dusty that it hasn't been used in years. You see the principal in the halls of the school, chatting with teachers, begging to find someone to do dance supervision, politely asking the custodian if the front stairs could be swabbed down one more time—and you wonder if you've just gotten older or if principals really are a different species now.

How Do Principals Spend Their Day?

According to a Canadian Teachers' Federation survey in 1991, here's how principals spend their time in an average seven-hour school day:

- administrative tasks: one hour thirty minutes;
- meeting/talking to teachers and staff: one hour twenty minutes;
- meeting/talking to students: one hour ten minutes;
- disciplining students: three-quarters of an hour;
- evaluating teachers: half-hour;
- meeting with parents: twenty minutes;
- dealing with building problems: fifteen minutes;
- planning curriculum: ten minutes;
- everything else: an hour.

The answer is both. Principals never were quite as fearsome as you thought, but they were men in a world where most teachers were women, they were bigger than you (many were former athletic coaches) and they did have far more power over schools and teachers than they do now. The principal today is closer to a middle manager, spurring on a group of mostly competent professional teachers, hemmed in on one side by superintendents, trustees and Ministry or Department of Education regulations, hemmed in on the other side by teacher unions and CUPE shop stewards, trying the best she can to help her teachers teach, her kids learn and her kids' parents have faith in her school.

If all this makes it seem that the principal isn't important, then we've given the wrong impression. *Nota bene*: A principal does more to influence your child's education than any teacher in the school. A good principal sets the tone so education can happen for your child. A good principal both inspires teachers and directly encourages them to do their best. A good principal gets the teachers he or she wants, and gets rid of the bad ones quickly. In our experience, a good principal can turn a mediocre school into a good one in a year or two; a bad principal can reduce an excellent school to mediocrity within five years. Even if your child is currently having a fine time with fine teachers, keep an eye on who's in the front office. That person makes a big difference.

Who Becomes a Principal

You know the old aphorism "Those who can, do; those who can't, teach; those who can't teach, go into administration." The idea is cute, but really quite incorrect. The average principal really *was* a good teacher. Indeed, many of the hoops a teacher must jump through to become a principal relate entirely to excellence in the classroom. This is ironic, because what you and your child really need in a principal is not just a good teacher, but a good manager who can pluck the strings of administration the way Joshua Bell can play the violin.

Those who become principals and vice-principals tend to be a little more ambitious than their colleagues, a little more concerned about curriculum issues and kids and a lot more willing to go through the long process of becoming a principal. In most provinces, school principals are expected to have a university degree, hold teacher's qualifications, have five or more years of teaching experience, display evidence of excellence in the classroom and extracurricular involvement, take leadership courses and the summer principal's course and sometimes to already have a master's degree in education. The reward for this is a longer working day, evenings supervising dances and sports events, days of board meetings and parent discussions, a shortened summer vacation and higher stress levels—all for an extra $6,000 a year after taxes. Is it any wonder that many fine teachers have no intention of ever leaving their classrooms for the front office?

By the time a principal climbs up from the ranks and ends up in that front office, he or she will have a very definite style. How you deal with a principal depends much on the way that person manages the school.

The firm hand. There are still some principals who think they're the boss, the way principals really were back in the days when teachers could be summarily fired for failing to stoke the coal stove properly. This principal likes to run a "tight ship," doesn't like problems that "rock the boat" and will act quickly and decisively on small items. On larger items—dealing with a lousy teacher, redesigning the report card—this principal is dumbfounded by a system that doesn't surrender

Two Different Worlds

Teachers and principals sometimes see issues in education quite differently. Notice the differences in response to these CTF survey questions:

- "In mandating new policy, the government understands the role of teachers as key agents of change."
  Principals who agreed: 26 percent
  Teachers who agreed: 12 percent

- "Our principal encourages teachers' participation in professional development activities."
  Principals who agreed: 97 percent
  Teachers who agreed: 78 percent

- "My principal provides helpful feedback regarding my teaching performance."
  Principals who agreed: 65 percent
  Teachers who agreed: 25 percent

The Four Big Lies

- **"The teacher unions are so powerful that my hands are tied."** Wrong. Teacher unions are often pressing for the same changes you are. Most school board contracts have a "management rights" clause that reserves a great deal of power for principals and administrators.

- **"I don't have much power over what Ms. X does in her classroom."** A principal can't be in Ms. X's classroom every minute, but he can observe her regularly; he can look in her daily plan book; and he can ask colleagues to work with her.

- **"The board or district has a policy against that."** This is sometimes true, but many board or district policy books are hundreds of pages long and frequently ignored. A strong principal has much more freedom than senior administrators would like to admit.

- **"I can't do anything to get rid of a poor teacher."** Not true. Principals can document, set expectations, provide counselling and call for help from senior administration. Given six months to two years, they can have any incompetent teacher fired. For serious matters, a principal can remove a teacher from the classroom *immediately*.

enough power and whose administrative tricks he or she will never master. For big problems, you'll have to go up the administrative ladder to the superintendent.

The big old jock. At one time, many principals were selected from the ranks of school football coaches, under a philosophy that went something like this: "We can't tell if anybody will be able to run a school, but that guy sure did win the city championship." Those days are largely past, thanks especially to employment equity, but such principals hang on. Despite the appearance of effectiveness, you'll likely find the old jock will agree with everything you say and then do nothing about it. Only persistence on your part will see changes made.

The rising star. This principal is so slick you'd think you were talking to a stockbroker or a telephone sales representative. He or she is angling to move higher up, to look good in the eyes of senior administrators and the trustees. If you can put forward something that will help this climb, the rising star will love you. If you bring forward a problem that will tarnish his highly buffed image, this principal will either move quickly to solve the problem or else try to bury the whole issue using damage-control techniques. As a parent, don't push too hard or too fast, and whatever you do, try to keep an upbeat spin on things.

The technocrat. You can spot the technocrat because he's busy on the computer when you walk into the office and seems reluctant to shake hands for fear that a power failure will obliterate the file on his machine. The technocrat wants quick, efficient ways to deal with a problem: send an administrative memo, change a timetable, bring in the special ed. teacher. Don't look for sophisticated people skills, but rest assured that something will get done.

The kid-centred principal. One of your authors will confess to falling into this group. She went into administration because she loves kids and stays in it because she thinks a good principal can make a big difference. She knows that schools are about people: that teachers and students both need nurturing and encouragement, that sometimes even parents don't have their kids' best interests at heart. Don't approach this principal by saying "I want..."; begin by saying "My child needs..." The flip side of this style, unfortunately, is that kid-centred management seems pretty loose by business standards. Don't be surprised if every clock in the school is set to a different time and the administrative handbook is buried someplace in that pile over in the corner of the office.

The bumbler. There are some principals who have discovered the delicate art of appearing to be incompetent, while actually running an effective school. The bumbler manages to avoid heavy pressure from parents and senior administrators because he just seems to be a "Joe Nice-guy," but he can be remarkably effective working behind the scenes to get the kind of school and teachers he wants.

The incompetent. Not many of this variety have survived affirmative action and the new demands of senior management, but we've run across more than a few in the past. There was the principal, a year from retirement, who virtually hid behind his desk for ten months before finally waving goodbye. There was the principal, excellent with politicians, board officials and powerful parents, who let his school go to rack and ruin while he glad-handed the powers above. There was the principal who could have been a case study for the Peter Principle and rose by seniority far above his level of competence. Within a year, three quarters of his staff had applied for transfer.

A Few Truths

- **The better the principal, the faster he or she will be transferred to a new school.** There's a great deal of turnover in administration and good principals enjoy a new challenge. To rise to a superintendent's position, a principal is expected to have led three or more different schools. Hence the good guys move.

- **Principals are like icebergs—much lies invisible beneath the administrative waters.** An effective principal doesn't have to splash around to make things happen; frequently he or she knows just whom to call to make change happppen.

- **The principal will *seem* to support the teacher and the status quo, even while he or she takes notes for the confidential file.** Don't assume that nothing is happening just because you can't see it happening—the smartest principals work invisibly.

- **Good principals attract good teachers; bad principals drive them away.** Hervé Langlois of Saskatoon asked 200 teachers why they had changed jobs. Reason number 1: the principal. He concludes: "Lack of consideration shown by principals destroyed the transferees' sense of being valued members of a team."

Do such miserable principals still exist? Sadly so. If your child's school is burdened with such an administrator, ally yourselves with worthy teachers and take your dealings directly to the area superintendent.

Getting to Know the Principal

Rule one: if you get to meet the principal *after* your child has a problem, you're meeting the principal far too late. The best time to meet your child's principal is before signing up at the school. In Chapter 2, we talk about the importance of visiting the school and speaking to the principal *before* enrolling your child. If you've done this, then you've already made your initial contact with the administration. If you haven't— or if a new principal has been appointed—then you'll have to make an effort to meet her.

Why? Because teachers change year by year, but a principal often lasts for four or five years. Because teachers are the people your child adores or complains about, but the principal sets the tone for the school and establishes the programs that make learning rich for every student. Because you'll need to have the principal on your side if you ever have to deal with a problem teacher.

Often you can briefly meet the school principal either at the initial orientation parents' night in the fall or later at the official meet-the-teacher evening. At either event you'll find the principal standing somewhere near the office, waiting for parents to come up and introduce themselves. Go ahead: "Hi, I'm Marion Jones, Amanda's mother. She's in Mrs. Parkes's grade two class." The principal will respond with something like "Nice to meet you," and then it will be your turn to say something. Our advice is to say something nice: "So far, Amanda is really enjoying the class." Or "This is just a wonderful building. We feel so lucky that Amanda is here." These introductory

---

Rule of Thumb
Meet First, Complain Later

As a parent, you can either make an effort to meet the principal at the beginning of the year—at a parents' night or in his or her office—or you can wait until your child has a problem.

If you meet the principal early on, then he or she will already know you when you come in to discuss a problem and the principal will have some sense that you're a reasonable person rather than a chronic complainer.

If you meet the principal *after* a problem has developed, then you're starting off a relationship as a whiner and complainer. You may still get results, but only grudgingly. At worst, you may just be ignored as some kind of loony.

comments will be long forgotten if you have to come back with a problem in November, but the initial impression you make—that of an involved, caring, upbeat parent—will last.

Never, ever try to discuss a substantial problem with the principal on these evenings. The principal has two hundred parents to greet and only a minute or two for each one. There's only enough time for your compliments; there's not nearly enough time for your gripe.

Taking Problems to the Principal

If you do find that a problem is developing for your child, then the first step is always to discuss the problem with your child's teacher. There's no sense going over the teacher's head right away—that just wastes the principal's time and raises the teacher's hackles. If Amanda is having problems with Joey, or you think the teacher is favouring the boys, or you feel the classroom atmosphere is stifling, or you think the homework is spotty and unproductive—talk to the teacher. Give the teacher a chance to fix things up.

But if that gets you nowhere, then a principal is the next person to see. In some larger elementary schools and most high schools, there will be both a principal and one or more vice-principals (sometimes called deans). Technically, the principal is the one who deals with school-wide programs, educational policy, curriculum and classroom practice. The vice-principal deals with nuts-and-bolts matters: timetables, class changes, school trips and discipline. In a school with both administrators, the vice-principal spends 200 to 300 percent more time on discipline problems than does the principal, though we are beginning to see more of a team approach to school management, especially in elementary schools, than we have in the past.

Lord Give Me the Strength and the Wisdom...

In our experience, parents who feel that their children are having a problem in school are almost invariably right. The difficulty, as in medicine, is in figuring out where the problem lies and how to solve it.

- **40 percent** of problems can be easily resolved by discussion with the classroom teacher: discipline techniques, homework, special needs, etc.;

- **30 percent** of problems are probably unresolvable—or will take a very long time to resolve: a personality conflict between a good teacher and a good student; a serious disagreement over instructional methods or textbooks in use; changes in the curriculum (set by the province); items requiring substantial tax dollars;

- **20 percent** of problems are resolvable with the help of the principal or guidance counsellor and some cooperation from the teacher;

- **10 percent** of problems are really at home and should be resolved there, or with the help of a psychologist or family counsellor.

In addition, many problems have a component which will need new policies set at the board or district, Ministry or Department of Education level.

When you've figured out the exact nature of your concern, you might be able to decide whether you want to see the principal or vice-principal. If you're in doubt, shoot for the top.

A serious meeting with the principal requires serious preparation:

- Make an appointment. You can't just come by and expect a busy administrator to drop everything to deal with you.

- Bring your file folder. You may want to refer to specific dates when you spoke to Mrs. Parkes, or show the principal some of the work that concerns you. Walking into a tough conference with a principal and having to ask for notepaper is as embarrassing as having to borrow a tie to get into a restaurant.

- Know what you want. You can always come in and toss the problem on the principal's lap and wait to see what happens, but you're more likely to be satisfied if you have some idea for a specific change that would make an improvement.

Allow serious time—between fifteen minutes and half an hour—but be prepared to stay for an hour. Present the problem, make your case and offer a suggestion or two. Let's say that you don't like the reading program being used by the teacher. You'll want to point out the failings in the text, the limitations on what the teacher is doing in class and the fact that Amanda doesn't seem to be reading as well as you'd hoped. The principal will invariably be thoughtful and concerned—it's a practised attitude—but this tells you little. Don't expect instant action. Nor should you expect the principal to agree with you entirely. The only really definite response you should anticipate is a promise that he will reply to your concern in a week or two (in fact, it's wise to ask for a specific date: "When do you think you can get back to

Conversation Stoppers

If you want to be given short shrift as a concerned parent, just try any of these conversation stoppers on the principal:

"I think Ms. Parkes should be fired." Firing a teacher takes months or years and never happens just because a parent complains. Better to be specific about what Ms. Parkes is doing wrong.

"The textbook is lousy. Get a new one." School textbook and book budgets are chronically low (about $30 per child per year). Ordering is done only once or twice a year, and even then a particular grade or subject has to wait its turn. Patience!

"I want Amanda moved." Sometimes moving your child is a good solution, but first the principal will want to talk to the teachers involved, to Amanda and maybe to higher-ups. Don't expect instant action.

"I need bus transportation for my child!" Maybe you do, but a new bus route costs more than $30,000. There had better be a few other students out there who need the route too.

"The whole problem is little Johnny." The whole problem is never just one other child, even if Amanda says so. Ease up on your judgement calls.

me?"). Results will be slow. At this stage, action is not enhanced by putting your concerns in writing. A letter to the principal tends to tie his or her hands in dealing with a situation and is more likely to give you a formal or defensive response than to make change happen in the classroom.

After you leave, the principal will have to talk to the teacher about what you've said and get her perspective on the situation. He might also seek an opinion from your child, or other teachers, or senior administrators at the board or district. A good principal will then get back to you, arranging another appointment to discuss the issue and what he and the teacher are prepared to do.

If the principal fails to get back to you, then you already have indications of a more serious problem in the school. Allow a week, then call to inquire about how the principal is doing in following up on your concern. A reminder call is good enough to start with. After two weeks, *you* should arrange an appointment to speak with the principal again.

The second appointment will likely include your child's teacher. By this time, the principal should have some plan to deal with your concern. Let's say that he's found a different textbook for Amanda to use and the teacher has agreed to offer a different style of homework. You may or may not be satisfied with the plan—and you should say so straight out—but you'll have to allow some time to see (or not see) results before you press further. At that point, you might want to write a letter to outline and formalize your concern; or you might want to continue working at the problem within the school; or you might want to bounce the whole matter up the administrative ladder.

If You Still Can't Get Satisfaction

If you suspect that your principal is not really working at your concern, or you're still not satisfied with the response that you get, then you'll

The Power Chart

School power starts at the top (provincial level) and trickles down. As a parent, you have to start at the bottom and pester your way up.

- Your provincial ministry or department of education
- Your local elected board of education trustees
- Superintendents of your school board or division
- Subject supervisors/consultants— especially in English, reading and libraries
- The principal of your child's school
- The teacher of your child's class
- You
- Your child

Beware the Hose...

A principal who doesn't want to deal with your concern will sometimes give you a hose job. It's the fireman's trick: throw a little water on the fire and see if it goes out. Unfortunately, the hose is also a way of avoiding real problems.

You know you're getting a hose job when:

- your second meeting isn't just with the principal and teacher, but you find the office crowded with consultants, advisors, superintendents and psychologists;
- the principal keeps saying he can't do anything, or it's out of his hands;
- you feel you need a dictionary to understand what the principal is talking about;
- you've listened for half an hour and the principal and teacher still haven't said they'll do anything.

have to move up a level. In a private or small denominational school, you'll have to go to the board. In most public and separate boards or districts, the next level up is a superintendent.

Superintendents are the senior officials in a school board or district hierarchy. Usually they're school principals who have taken additional courses (supervisory officer's qualifications, or S.O.s, as they're called in the trade) and have done a good enough job with local school politics that they've been promoted to oversee a number of schools in a local area. Other superintendents look after a particular aspect of school management such as curriculum, physical plant or special education. You can find out which superintendent looks after your local school or area of concern simply by calling the board or district office and asking. Many boards or districts publish a flowchart showing all their superintendents as well as the school trustees—a handy item to have if you're taking your concern to the top.

By the time you've raised your problem with the superintendent for your area, he or she will probably already have heard about it from the school principal. If not, present the situation as you see it, refer to specifics from your file folder and then *follow up by letter*. We've italicized the last item, because at this level written communication is essential if you're to be taken seriously.

The average superintendent simply wants you to go away so he or she can carry on with other business. There's nothing necessarily awful for you in this predisposition—you, too, have better things to do than harass those in the school hierarchy. While superintendents have little power over the average classroom teacher, they can make powerful phone calls to principals that tend to get things moving. That is exactly the kind of phone call you want. If it works, you'll see changes happening both in the classroom and in your local school.

If it doesn't, then you're going to need political help. In Canada, our public and separate schools are "run" by a group of elected individuals called school trustees. Public-school trustees, like aldermen, represent a particular area or ward in your jurisdiction and must be re-elected every two or three years. Separate school trustees are often elected from a long list of possible candidates and are supposed to represent the entire district. In both elections, only about one voter in five bothers to mark this section of the ballot, so school trustees are often very responsive to even small groups of voters with a particular issue in mind. For an individual parent, a school trustee may act as an ombudsman who will help you deal with the school, the board or district bureaucracy or even the Ministry of Education. At the very least, your local trustee knows exactly how the system works.

It's important to remember in all this that there is little real power in our educational systems. Various higher-ups can make the working lives of the level below more difficult—frustrate special requests, cut budgets, limit career aspirations—but they can rarely order something to happen. Our schools don't run in a military fashion, or even in the style of a large corporation. Concerns tend to be handled by discussion and consultation, with results that are painfully slow both for parents and for those of us who have to work with senior administration. Trying to wrestle changes out of principals, superintendents and trustees can be like wrestling with a marshmallow—good exercise, but hard to declare a winner when the match is over.

A Few Other Vehicles to Make Change Happen for Your Child

While there is always the formal route for dealing with concerns—the one we've just outlined—there are a number of informal ways to make

School Committees that May Include Parents

- homework policy development and review
- reporting to parents (report cards)
- race relations
- communications
- school partnerships with business
- fundraising (formerly the chief role of parent groups)
- parent council (in Ontario)
- parent education planning
- community school planning
- safe school policy
- discipline/behaviour code policy and procedure
- athletics and arts promotion
- curriculum advisory
- assessment and evaluation communication
- library advisory
- volunteer coordination
- reading booster
- special events—such as meet-the-teacher night, barbecue, career awareness day or arts month

Home and School Associations

For help to set up a home and school group, contact one of these organizations:

- British Columbia Confederation of Parent Advisory Councils
  #1540-1185 W. Georgia Street
  Vancouver, B. C. V6E 4E6
  (604) 687-4433; Fax (604) 687-4488

- Alberta Federation of Home and School Associations
  #312-11010-142 Street
  Edmonton, Alberta T5N 2R1
  (403) 454-9867; Fax (403) 455-6481

- Saskatchewan Federation of Home and School Associations
  221 Cumberland Avenue North
  Saskatoon, Saskatchewan S7N 1M3
  (306) 933-5723

- Home and School and Parent-Teacher Federation of Manitoba
  Box 158, 905 Corydon Avenue
  Winnipeg, Manitoba R3M 3S7
  (204) 489-7741

- Ontario Federation of Home and School Associations
  252 Bloor Street West, Suite 12-200
  Toronto, Ontario M5S 1V5
  (416) 924-7491; Fax (416) 924-5354

changes happen in school to benefit your child. Consider these:

- *Home and school association.* The home and school association (or parent-teacher association in some areas) is a group of parents who organize together to support their children's education. Often there is a meeting called early on in the school year, with a presentation on an education issue and then an election of officers. Like many organizations, an HSA usually has a president, secretary, treasurer and however many other officials it needs to function. This executive, and the organization as a whole, can have real influence on the overall tenor of the school. At best, the HSA becomes a powerful advisory committee for the teachers and principal, having a say on everything from behaviour codes to report cards. At worst, an HSA can just become a fundraising committee doing bake sales to buy books for the school library.

  Assuming that your HSA is effective, becoming a member of its executive is a good way to share informally in some of the decision making at the school. You'll have proven your seriousness as a parent by taking on a position of responsibility; you'll be physically in the school every few weeks to deal with HSA duties; and your opinions will have greater weight because you'll be known to have a commitment to the school.

- *Volunteering.* We've spoken before about the value of volunteering as a way to get information about teachers and the school. Now let's add the importance of volunteering to get you known, informally, as a mature, respectable parent *before* you have to go to the principal to deal with problems with a particular teacher. Good schools seek out volunteers for a variety of tasks—from working with slow readers, to helping the librarian, to supervising kids on trips, to working on board or district committees, all of which gain you credibility should you ever have to deal with a problem.

- *Special ed. and guidance teachers.* Nothing will help your child's cause within a school as much as a strong teacher working *inside* the system. Often special education teachers can take on this role for students who have been identified as either gifted or having difficulty in learning; sometimes they can do this for other students as well. Their job is to intervene to create the best possible educational environment in the school for the students they look after; they might also be able to do this for your child.

  The guidance department in a high school can sometimes be effective in helping out students who are in trouble. These teachers provide personal counselling and goal-setting advice, as well as make high school program changes on their own authority. They also have a strong voice with the principal and can access board or district services such as psychologists and consultants. If your child is smart enough to get a strong guidance counsellor on her side, her school career can be much smoother sailing than otherwise.

Where the Power Is

Even if your child attends a private school, you can't underestimate the long-term impact of what happens in your provincial legislature and at your provincial Ministry or Department of Education. If the new Minister of Education decides that there will be a province-wide language-arts test involving all grade nine students, which will take up two weeks of classroom time and cost millions of dollars in taxpayers' money (recently the case

- Quebec Federation of Home and School Associations
  3285 Cavendish Boulevard, Suite 562
  Montreal, Quebec H4B 2L9
  (514) 481-5619

- New Brunswick Federation
  c/o 8 Teesdale Street,
  Moncton, New Brunswick E1A 5K5
  (506) 855-9556

- Nova Scotia Federation of Home and School Associations
  209-515 Prince Street
  Truro, Nova Scotia B2N 1E8
  (902) 895-4618

- Prince Edward Island Federation of Home & School Associations
  P.O. Box 1012
  Charlottetown, P.E.I. C1A 7M4
  (902) 892-0664

- Newfoundland & Labrador Federation of Home & School & Parent-Teacher Associations
  P.O. Box 23140
  5 Merrymeeting Road
  St. John's, Newfoundland A1A 4J9
  (709) 739-4830

in Ontario), it will happen within a year. If the premier decides to roll back the salaries of everyone on the public payroll (recently the case in many provinces), then that will happen almost instantly. Both of these will have a major impact on schools, education and teacher morale—despite the best efforts of your local teachers and principal.

Much of the real power over education policy and education financing is at the provincial level. It is not subject to parental power as much as voter power. If the current political bandwagon is to slash and burn government services, it might be wise to remember that schools are one of these. Big classes are lousy. Schools without books can't work. Teachers who are angry or on strike don't help your child. Try to remember this the next time you vote, and mark your X accordingly.

Generally speaking, we don't think parents should have to harass teachers, principals or other officials to get the best education for their children. Good schools and school systems are responsive to parents, sensitive to special needs and intelligent in the choices that are made. If yours is not, reread Chapter 2 on making choices and vote with your feet. If you have a problem with a particular teacher in what seems otherwise to be a good school, then be prepared to take action. But if you are more generally disgruntled, if you find that *no* teacher measures up to your expectations, then it could be the problem is with you. Don't launch into a crusade against your local school unless you've carefully examined your own motives. But having done so, don't be afraid to fight for the best education for your child. The kid is worth it.

Four Fingers Point Back

Remember the old adage about pointing the finger at someone else—that four fingers will always be pointing back. Sometimes the problem that you *see* at school didn't start there, but merely shows up there. Be prepared to have the teacher and principal make suggestions about changes you can institute at home. These suggestions will only come forward after considerable thought—sometimes with fear and trembling—and they deserve hearing. Remember:

- a child who acts up in school is often having a problem at home too;
- a child whose parents are suffering through a messy separation and divorce will do less well in school and sometimes act out with other students;
- a child who won't read or quits reading may just be modelling the attitude of one of his parents;
- a child who is violent in school is learning that violence somewhere else.

CHAPTER 5

Home and School and You and Your Child

Let's be frank: no family is perfect. Well, maybe yours is exemplary, but we know that our families aren't perfect, nor were the ones we grew up in, nor are any families we know. The only perfect families used to be on shows like *Leave It to Beaver* and *The Brady Bunch*, where understanding parents neatly solved every problem within the twenty-two-minute script allotted for each program. If only real life were like this, being a parent would be so much easier.

It is not our business in a book about schools to say a great deal about fixing imperfect families. But parents must be aware that education takes place in a context defined by the home—and that much of what you hear about your child at school may well be caused by what you aren't aware of at home. In this chapter we'd like to talk about the factors in your home that might be affecting the education of your child, some of the predictable patterns in families and the resources that are available to help families function better in these post-*Beaver* times.

Toward the Year 2000: Tough Times for Families

The modern family doesn't have it easy. One family in two will go through a separation and divorce at some time while the children are growing up. One family in four suffers from fairly serious poverty, so that even essentials like books and shoes must be budgeted for. One young family in three will suffer a period of unemployment this year.

Obviously all this can have an impact on children in school. A child whose parents are in the midst of separation and divorce will likely see his marks fall by 10 percent or more for a period that lasts from six months to a year. That child is also likely to begin acting out—seeking attention by fighting, crying or mouthing off to the teacher. If the school principal and teacher are aware that a family breakup is in process, they're likely to be more understanding in dealing with all this, but that won't stop it from happening. Be prepared.

Child poverty takes its own toll on young people. We're not talking about children who have to save their allowance to buy a new Nintendo game; we're talking about kids whose parents are having trouble finding the cash to buy shoes. As unemployment grows among young families, the effects of child poverty can be seen in more and more children: envy, loss of self-esteem, petty theft. In the 1930s, when almost everyone suffered economically, the effects on children were not as serious. Today we are becoming a society of haves—whose lifestyles are celebrated on television and in the movies—and have-nots, who are made to feel increasingly disconnected and devalued. The capacity of schools to bridge the gap and draw children together is simply not as

No More *Leave It to Beaver* Families

Canadian families have changed since the days of *Leave It to Beaver*. Here's the latest from Statistics Canada:

- Most moms work: 64 percent of mothers with children under sixteen hold a job (62 percent with children ages three to five).

- You're not better off: real income of Canadian families has not grown since the early 1980s, even with more mothers working.

- Some parents never do get married: 10 percent of all families are headed by common-law couples. Single-parent families now make up 13 percent of the population.

- Some kids have it tough: 18 percent of children under eighteen live in a low-income family.

- More than half the children in school will have been through a family separation and divorce. In Canada as a whole, we've had more than 75,000 divorces every year since 1986.

- The average family spends 23 percent of its income on taxes, 12.6 percent on food, 16.3 percent on shelter, 12 percent on transportation, 7 percent each on furnishings and recreation and 2.6 percent on cigarettes and alcohol.

great as it once was, nor have families found real advocates among our political leaders in Canada.

Almost every family, rich or poor, one parent or two, will go through several periods of stress while the children are growing up. The causes are many—job pressures, career change, goal changes, moving from place to place, house renovations, elderly relatives, health problems—but the effects are not limited to adults in the family. Children are frequently the ones who show the distress of the entire family, especially if all the adults keep their responses under wraps. If your child is having certain kinds of problems in school, he may just be displaying the anxiety and upset of the entire household.

If teachers were better connected to the families of students they teach, they'd be in a better position to help you and your child during these difficult times. Because teachers are too often not connected (in fact, they're rarely encouraged to be), a great deal of attention is sometimes placed on classroom seating or textbook selection, when the real problem is that Dad is out of work. You can't always wait until Dad gets a job again to begin dealing with problems showing up at school, but it's always helpful to understand where the real problem may be.

Some Predictable Patterns

There is enough research on families now that certain patterns can be predicted. This doesn't mean that such patterns are always true for your child, but they do make sense of what we see in our children as they grow up.

- *The first child.* Birth-order research tells us that the first child is always the most anxious to please the parents. This child is the one who usually excels in school, learns to read most quickly and gets more than her share of

Stages in Accepting a Problem

Denial. Your family suspects that your son Jerry has a problem; you sometimes wonder why your child behaves a certain way—but nobody wants to say anything—"Jerry will grow out of it... there's nothing to worry about."

Growing suspicion. A teacher, a close friend or a relative suggests that Jerry might really have a problem that needs attention—and you begin to admit the possibility to yourself.

Shock of recognition. The problem is confirmed, either by crisis or diagnosis. Jerry has a real problem that he won't just grow out of.

Anger and guilt. Secretly you feel angry at Jerry for letting you down, for failing to be a perfect child. And you feel guilty yourself—those are your genes, or it was something you did that made him this way.

Taking action—or copping out. Some parents finally stop blaming themselves and take steps to deal with the problem, accepting the limits of improvement that can be expected, but still doing what they can. Some parents cop out and dump Jerry on the schools, who do what they can in six hours a day, 185 days a year, but rarely work miracles. Only families can do that.

Getting Another Opinion

If you suspect that your child has some kind of problem, you'll want to double-check your suspicion with someone else. Try these sources:

- **Relatives.** They've watched your child since birth and sometimes have experience with their own families.

- **Friends.** They tend not to speak out unless asked, but your close friends have opinions about your parenting and your child's development. If you ask, they'll tell you...gently.

- **Neighbours.** With many families so spread out, neighbours sometimes serve the same functions as relatives. A teacher, social worker or health-care professional might be especially useful.

- **At the church.** If you attend with some regularity, clergy and lay people at the church are a good source for opinions about how your child is developing. Priests and clergymen also have a good knowledge of community resources to help with difficult situations.

- **In your community.** You might have friends among parents in minor league hockey or baseball who can offer a casual check on how other families deal with problems.

the parents' attention. The first child is also more likely to display family distress, because she is most closely bound to the hopes and dreams of her parents and grandparents.

- ***The middle children.*** *Independence* seems to be the key word for middle children. They are freed from the heavy expectations and careful parenting of the first child, but often have to compete for attention against that child. Middle children will often choose to excel in their own way, but not in how parents expect. If the first child has made reading her area of excellence, don't be surprised when her brother is slow to read and would rather spend his time on math or sports. Sibling rivalry is probably far more important in setting up life patterns than we currently acknowledge.

- ***The baby of the family.*** Your last child is always the baby, somewhat spoiled, somewhat indulged by parents who have decided there won't be any more. The baby benefits from a family that is assured in its parenting and frequently has more income than when the first child was born. The baby also enjoys the advantages of older siblings, who have paved the way in the neighbourhood and at school. The result is a certain assurance in his identity that can make the youngest child seemed spoiled or bratty. The baby can do well or poorly at school—and often not care as much about it as older children. All this can be quite harrowing to parents, but the last child frequently does very well in adult life because of that same assurance that drives you crazy.

- ***The only child.*** Sometimes the only child behaves more like a miniature adult than a child. He spends so much time in the company of adults that his vocabulary and mannerisms take on those of a thirty-year-old's. This premature maturity is coupled with a heavy dose of family expectation, so the only child simply *must* excel—and frequently does, but often at the price of personal happiness. Much has been written about the loneliness of only children, less about their achievements. For them, parents should be aware that school becomes a social, as well as a learning, centre.

- *The problem child.* Sometimes a particular child will take on the role of the problem child within a family. Especially when this child does not have the ability or charm of his other siblings, the problem child will get his share of family attention by causing problems. The solution, as any behavioural psychologist would tell you, is to praise the achievements of the problem child, while making punishment for problems quick and boring. Even better, try to pass around the "problem" tag: each child should have an equal chance to end up in the proverbial doghouse.

Good teachers have seen enough families and have enough training to recognize some of these patterns. If they have courage enough to speak about such matters, it would do well for us to listen.

School Can Reveal What You Can't Always See...

Sometimes school will reveal problems that don't become obvious anywhere else. Hearing and vision difficulties are an obvious example. Your son George may have gotten on well enough for his four years before school despite a partial hearing impairment, but that problem will make it difficult for him to do well in school. Similarly, farsightedness or astigmatism are not terrible or even obvious in infants and young children, but either condition makes reading incredibly difficult.

Family Doctors: What They Can Do for You and Your Child

A family doctor is important for much more than just treating disease. A doctor can also do preliminary diagnosis of conditions that affect learning in school:

- hearing problems;
- vision difficulties (though a thorough exam requires an ophthalmologist);
- hyperactivity or attention deficit disorder (though beware an instant prescription for Ritalin).

In addition, a good doctor can offer advice on parenting and some brief counselling on personal and family problems. Doctors also can refer you to specialists for further diagnosis and community facilities for treatment and support.

If you have recently moved and don't have a family doctor, check the phone book under "Physicians and Surgeons" or phone your provincial medical association and ask for the physician referral service.

Family Counsellors: What They Can Do for You and Your Child

If you suspect that your family isn't functioning as it should, you'll need some help to get it working properly. That's the role of a family counsellor. By sitting down once or twice a week with the whole family, a counsellor tries to help everyone understand what's going on and develop new ways of behaving.

To access a family counsellor, you can:

- get a referral from your family doctor;

- if you're working, call your employee assistance plan at work and explain the problem as you see it;

- if you're on social assistance, tell your caseworker that your family would like to begin family counselling;

- seek a recommendation from friends who may have used a family counsellor, or from the school principal;

- as a last resort, open the Yellow Pages of your phone book to "Marriage, Family and Individual Counsellors."

Family counsellors often charge between $60 and $150 a session, and are not usually covered under provincial health plans. Your employee benefits at work may cover the cost for a limited number of sessions.

Surprisingly, some parents will do anything to avoid admitting that their child has a problem— even a medical one. Don't be part of this group. The teacher will try to clue you in; the school nurse can do some rudimentary tests; but only your family doctor and medical specialists can deal with some of these conditions.

The first step in dealing with any problem is to overcome avoidance. Often your relatives and friends are trying to tell you what's wrong. Some will do so subtly, so as not to offend or second-guess your parenting, and you may not hear what they're really saying. Some will do so aggressively, like the mother-in-law who knows just what to do to solve George's attention problem. It's important to listen to these criticisms, even if they hurt. In raising children day by day, we can easily overlook problems that are developing over time. Friends and relatives who get just snapshots of development are often in a less emotionally involved position to observe your child. All you have to do is ask "Do you think most kids act like that?" "Does George's reading seem okay to you?" What you get back is only an opinion, but it might be sufficient to move you to get some serious testing done.

Having said all that, let us caution about being overly anxious. We have seen parents of grade one students who want their child's IQ tested, as if being designated gifted will make any difference at that stage. We have seen parents drag a child from doctor to doctor, convinced that the poor kid has attention deficit disorder just because he won't sit still for reading time. For every four families that deny a problem, there's one who wants to put their child's health and behaviour under a magnifying glass.

If there is a problem in your family that needs some outside help, the school is often a good place to begin asking. School principals have lists of community organizations, church groups, self-help groups, psychologists and family counsellors who can help you deal with problems before they've gotten out of hand.

Hidden Agendas

In families we frequently live *our* lives as if our normality were *everyone's* normality. We assume, since we all went to university, or we all worked on the farm, or we all got locked in the closet for being bad, that everyone lives like that.

Not so. Often it takes an outsider, a friend or relative or even a passing acquaintance to point out that our habits and ways of thinking might be a little bizarre in other people's eyes. Because some attitudes are hidden, they are exceedingly powerful.

- A friend in New York had two parents who were doctors and his three older siblings all became doctors. Although no one ever said out loud that Frank should become a doctor, he understood the expectation. He fought against it—studying Chinese civilization rather than biology, turning to alcohol and drugs— but finally gave in and went to medical school, only to find that his hands shook too much for him ever to be a surgeon.

- A mother in New Brunswick read regularly to both her children, a girl and a boy. The girl loved the nightly reading, quickly learned to read herself and continues to be a fine reader to this day. The boy resisted the reading time, learned to read reluctantly and rarely opens a book. The mother is disappointed, but the boy's father never reads either. Why's that? "Oh, he doesn't read," says Mom. "He's a man."

- The new-Canadian parents wanted the best for their children, and spent time supervising their homework and extolling the importance of education. But when the teenage daughter

Psychologists: What They Can Do for You and Your Child

Psychologists (Ph.D. level) and psychometrists (M.Sc. level) provide counselling and "insight-oriented" sessions that seek to get at the root of problems in the family. Techniques and length of treatment vary with the treatment orientation and training of the psychologist. Often these same individuals offer both family counselling and individual treatment, depending on the needs of the family.

If the problems in your family are long-term, or go back to how you were brought up, or seem more serious than what can be handled by short-term counselling, then you need to begin seeing a psychologist.

You can access a psychologist through your employee assistance plan, or by recommendation from your family doctor or school principal, or by calling the provincial psychological association. Fees range from $80 to $150 a session, depending on the psychologist's qualifications and experience. Some employee assistance plans cover a limited number of sessions. In addition, many hospitals provide psychological services on an outpatient basis, which are covered under the provincial medical plan. There is often a long waiting list for these services.

Counselling Can Help: The Story of Joan and Dave M.

The official problem wasn't supposed to be Joan or her husband Dave; it was supposed to be their son. Both the children were having trouble in school, but the son was acting out and a speech impairment made him the butt of schoolyard jokes.

Initially, the conference with the principal was to discuss their son, but then the talk broadened, and it became clear the family needed more serious counselling. After two visits to a psychologist, Joan admitted that she was often beaten by her husband and the children were literally terrified by violence in the home. Two months later, Joan left Dave and took her kids off to a shelter.

Family counselling continued for another year before Joan and Dave got back together, acknowledging the part each of them had played in the earlier family violence.

The children returned to their former school and their marks steadily improved. Within two years the son's speech impediment had essentially disappeared. And Joan M. went back to school to fulfil a childhood dream—she wanted to become a teacher.

began to balk at hours of study and had trouble in math and science, Dad would beat her for falling marks. The girl hated the beatings—and her marks did not improve as a result, no matter how hard she tried. But when asked how she would bring up her own children, her answer was simple: "If they were having trouble in school, I'd spank them until they got their marks up."

Our point is this: the patterns that we learn early on—usually from our own families—are remarkably powerful in determining our behaviour as parents and adults. Is it any wonder that we frequently pass these on to our children?

Sometimes these attitudes can be a real spur to achievement. Nothing has greater impact on a child's achievement than the expectation that he or she will do well; nothing does greater damage than the anticipation of failure. Often these messages are communicated by offhand phrases and comments made to someone else, but overheard by your child. If you regularly say, "Of course George got an A on the project. He always does," the message to your son is very clear. So long as he can keep pulling off the As, he'll do so to live up to your expectations. But if you even once or twice whisper, "Jane is so much like Aunt Ethel. She'll get pregnant and drop out of school by age sixteen," don't be surprised when Jane announces the incipient bundle of joy.

These days, it's almost customary to blame the school for how well a child does in life. If George drops out, buys a Harley and starts living in a shack on the beach—then it was the school's fault. Of course, if George gets a B.A. or makes Canada's Olympic swim team or wins a YTV achievement award, then Mom and Dad take a share of the credit. The truth is, credit and blame both need to be shared. It is unlikely that the schools—on the basis of six hours a day, 185 days a year—will determine the course of your child's life. But your child will act out your unconscious attitudes and he will attempt to fulfil your own frustrated dreams. As the psychologist Carl Jung said, "Children are driven unconsciously in a direction that is intended to compensate for everything that was left unfulfilled in the lives of their parents."

We don't think there are perfect families anywhere, or that perfection is even a reasonable goal. The British psychologist D.W. Winnicott wrote about the virtues of "good-enough" parenting. In attempting to be perfect parents, we're likely to make all sorts of egregious errors along the way, but in striving to be good-enough parents, we can do ourselves and our children a real favour. Part of doing a good-enough job is to look at ourselves and our families, especially if some problem becomes obvious at school.

CHAPTER 6

Early Childhood and Preschool Programs: Daycare, Nursery, Junior Kindergarten

The reasons parents choose certain preschool programs are as varied as today's families: some parents are looking to start education early; others want their children to have a wider range of playmates; many require daycare so they can continue work and careers. The decision to arrange for daycare or enrol Geoff in preschool is always fraught with difficulty: Is the situation good enough? What will Aunt Ethel say about my going back to work? Is Geoff ready for preschool yet? Should the school be full-time or part-time or co-op? How will we ever get over our guilt?

Let's deal with guilt first. Almost 70 percent of children in Canada go into a preschool or daycare

A Few Facts on Kids and Daycare

- In Canada there are 4,600,000 children twelve years of age and younger.

- Of these, 3,000,000 (about two-thirds) are looked after in some kind of child-care arrangement: daycare, after-school care or regular baby-sitting.

- In Ontario, more than 60 percent of women with children under age six work outside the home.

- The least expensive provinces for licensed daycare are Manitoba and Saskatchewan (about $320 a month).

- The most expensive are the Yukon ($450) and Ontario ($510). Some licensed daycare spots for infants in Toronto cost as much as $1,200 a month.

- Some provinces used to provide day-care subsidies for low-income wage earners, but most of these have been cut back, so you have to be unemployed or in a job-training program to qualify. Everyone else, please pay cash.

- In Ontario, there are 125,000 licensed daycare spaces; the province provides 67,000 family daycare subsidies.

arrangement sometime before they enter regular school at age five or six. Parents who feel this amounts to virtual abandonment of their child should be comforted by research that shows that high-quality daycare and preschool really do help children learn to work with one another, get ready for kindergarten and sometimes acquire basics in reading and in math. But parents who feel preschool will give their child a leg up in real school are probably deluding themselves. Current research draws no connection between future success in school and sending a three- or four-year-old middle-class child to preschool (though there seem to be real benefits for disadvantaged children). The choice of preschool education versus learning at home really depends on the child, the home environment, the needs of the family and the learning situation at the prospective school.

As a parent, the statistics won't help you much in deciding whether preschool or learning at home is the best approach to meet the needs of *your* young child, *your* family and *your* specific situation. Having a child stay home with a parent or guardian who is tired, irritated or bored provides the worst possible experience at this crucial age, despite what well-meaning grandparents, maiden aunts and even politicians may say. A good daycare or preschool program is probably a better bet than a resentful mom or a dad who blames baby Geoff as the bank threatens to foreclose on the house. To put it simply: many families have no financial choice but to arrange for daycare and nursery school. Even for families who do have a choice, most will opt for some form of preschool at age three or four, and do so for very good reasons.

The Options

Learning at home. Those families who are able to have a parent stay home with preschoolers (and happily there are more dads taking on this role) always say they prefer this type of education. They generally feel that they can provide the nurturing, stimulating environment which can provide for their child's education. By using neighbours, play groups and other community opportunities, these parents can outfit their child with social skills equal to those of children in even the best preschool. Later on, learn-at-home parents might opt to provide a more formal school experience for their child by having Geoff attend a preschool program for two or three half days each week.

Before then, learn-at-home parents have a variety of options for exposing their preschoolers to other children and meeting with other parents. One inexpensive option is community programs run by recreation centres and public libraries. Both you and your child will participate in swimming, crafts, play groups or story times coordinated by a trained leader. These kinds of activities encourage your Geoff to socialize and participate with other youngsters and also provide a chance for the caregivers to meet and share their own experiences and problems. Often these are linked with family service programs and can be accessed through the local family service bureau or the local recreation department (call city hall or your town office). These agencies are particularly helpful for families who are new to the community.

Learning at home should not involve lessons and other formal mechanisms to try to turn Geoff into a child genius. These desperate measures rarely have much effect; nor are the "educational" claims of companies that manufacture crayons or mobiles or modelling clay much to be believed. Nonetheless, little kids need stimulation and attention and access to a wide world of experience. Learn-at-home parents are in a wonderful position to give their child the attention he deserves: a focus on baby Geoff's interests, a

Daycare Costs

The *Financial Post* compared the costs of commercial daycare across Canada for a three-year-old child.

The following figures represent the cost breakdown in November 1990:

Location	Weekly Cost	Yearly Cost
Toronto	$127	6,612
Yellowknife	111	5,760
Ottawa	110	5,712
Whitehorse	93	4,824
Saskatoon	91	4,740
London, Ont.	87	4,512
Montreal	84	4,392
Quebec City	84	4,380
Average	**82**	**4,284**
Vancouver	80	4,152
Regina	78	4,080
Halifax	77	4,020
St. John's, Nfld.	76	3,948
Calgary	73	3,804
Winnipeg	71	3,684
Victoria	70	3,636
Edmonton	64	3,348
Saint John, N.B.	57	2,940

These costs are for standard daycare and don't necessarily reflect the costs that are associated with specialized programs provided by some nursery schools or private "learning centres."

Baby-sitting Options ... From Best to Worst

- Your mom.

- Dad, Aunt Iris and all the other relatives.

- A family friend you've known for some years, preferably with young children of her own.

- A nanny, if you can afford one.

- A neighbour, preferably with young children of her own, whose references you've checked.

- Commercial baby-sitting or daycare centres (usually available only for children more than eighteen months old).

- A mom with a number of children already in her care, recommended by another mother you trust.

- Someone who advertises in the newspaper or with an ad on the supermarket bulletin board.

- The teenager next door (even if you sometimes get her boyfriend at no extra charge).

quick response to his questions or comments, a time to play with other children, a regular quarter or half-hour to experience a book or a story.

The efforts of the learn-at-home parent can be augmented by what's out there in the community: play groups, library story hours, regular visits to friends, park and playground visits, riding the subway or bus, going to the museum or art gallery, working in the garden or out in the barn. No one knows just how much of any experience actually gets through to a small child, but research shows that the absence of such experiences and attention from parents can be a real handicap.

Child care/baby-sitting. We know—your mom is a great baby-sitter, maybe even better with Geoff than you are. After all, the proof of her excellence as a parent is quite evident—it's you. And you came out perfect, or almost perfect, or at least mostly perfect. But frequently your mom has her own life to live and may be unwilling to devote the time or energy that a young child demands. Even if she's willing to help you out, you'll still have to have backup baby-sitting available should she become ill. And there's always the danger that she or Grandad will win a lottery and buy that palace in Monaco, which will make the baby-sitting drop-off quite difficult.

So you have to consider second and third choices: other relatives and private home care with an individual you're willing to trust with your child. If all the aunts and uncles are busy or a thousand kilometres away, and you've decided to opt for someone not in the family, be sure to check references carefully. The caregiver you choose plays a very personal role in the raising of your child while you're at work.

Mothers with one or two children of their own will often take in another for the companionship and a little extra cash. These moms will arrange outings and activities to stimulate and expose their own children to special experiences, just as you would do if you were at home. Your child may benefit a great deal from the creativity and personalized care provided, as well as the contact with other children his age, but the quality of the experience for your child will be very dependent on the mom who's in charge. Check references carefully, ask around the neighbourhood and be prepared to spend from $50 to $150 a week, depending on where you live and the length of your working day.

Licensed home daycare. Licensed private home daycare provides many of the same advantages as good baby-sitting but also offers the benefit of government supervision. These commercial daycare operators must comply with health and safety regulations and submit to inspections of the premises, but the regulations as a whole are none too strenuous. While provinces set a limit on the number of children by age level, there is little or no direction as to program or activities. Once again, it is the quality of the "operator," or mom in charge, that makes all the difference.

Real preschool. Parents who are concerned about a real educational program generally look for a nursery school that is licensed and operated by teachers trained in early childhood education. While this is not an option for a one- or two-year-old (who would not be toilet trained), it may well be the decision of choice for a three- or four-year-old. Maybe even a better option than your mom, who deserves a break by now anyway.

Choosing a Preschool

When selecting an early childhood program or preschool there are some general things to think about for both you and your child.

Learning in the Crib and Crawling on the Floor...

One consistent finding in early childhood research is the importance of stimulation. Young children don't need organized lessons or expensive "educational" toys, but they do need lots of attention from Mom and Dad (and other caregivers) and access to a wide variety of different experiences.

Some of the most important parts of early learning are among the most obvious:

- talk to your baby—not just baby talk, but adult talk, and lots of it;

- respond to your child's interests—make sure there's time to chase the butterfly or play with the toy car;

- sing, chant, tickle, giggle—together;

- go to the park, the zoo, the supermarket, the library—infants pick up far more than we can see;

- read a story—way before a child can talk or even understand the idea of "story."

However gripping *Barney* and *Sesame Street* may be, no television program can ever provide what you can: real love and real life.

Canada and the Rest of the World

In some countries the provision of daycare and preschool programs is virtually controlled by government employment and social policies. In the former East Germany the female labour force participation rate of 90 percent required government programs to care for children who were not of school age. In the former Czechoslovakia the government's generous paid-leave plans encouraged mothers to stay at home and care for their children. In Scandinavia both paid leaves and government-funded daycare allow parents to make choices that are based on their own personal circumstances and preferences rather than family financial constraints.

In Canada, social support for both child-care leaves and subsidized daycare varies according to the mother's employment situation and family finances and where she lives. Some tax and child-care-expense credits are available in some provinces for working mothers. In many provinces, mothers on social assistance can qualify for daycare at no or very low cost. But there will be little opportunity for choice regarding how children are cared for as long as mothers of young children are required to take employment to keep their family afloat.

Purpose: Why do I need to have Geoff in a preschool program? You may require full- or part-time care in order to continue your career— in which case your hours and the hours of the centre are very important. You may be looking for an opportunity for both you and your son to meet others—so you should be checking into co-op nursery schools and community programs. You may also feel that you would like Geoff in preschool to give him a head start in a more formal educational setting. A preschool can get him used to other adults, group routines or language and intellectual experiences that extend his thinking. In this case, you should look carefully at the educational component of the program. You may just want opportunities for Geoff to play with others kids and learn to get along if you don't have another child at home or live in a neighbourhood where there aren't children in his age group. For this, you really want a part-time or drop-in program rather than full-time preschool. Or you may just need a break from parenting to enable you to pursue a hobby, a class or just get the shopping done. After all, parents need time to recharge their intellectual and personal batteries. A regular, daily baby-sitting arrangement might be better for this than formal preschool enrolment.

Transportation: How far do I have to go for this program—and is it worth it? Your preschool options may well be governed by your ability to get Geoff to a particular location at a specific time. If you must rely on public transit or carpooling you'll want to explore those options before selecting a program. There's no point in getting your and your child's heart set on a particular preschool, only to find that the logistics make it impossible to get Geoff there and back. If you are using public transit, try it out at the actual times that you would be travelling to give you a realistic idea of the time and potential problems you might encounter. Winter weather can also throw a wrench into the works if you're travelling with a stroller and bag of supplies.

Hours of operation: How much will that dinner meeting cost me? Nursery school programs generally operate on a half-day basis and serve children from ages two and a half to five years. In some cases there are combination programs where your child can be part of the nursery program for the half day, then return to the daycare group for the remaining time. Where these two types of programs run simultaneously, Geoff will have the opportunity to meet other children who are in the half-day program, as well as different teachers who may provide additional variety to his day.

The hours for daycare and nursery schools often vary in different communities. In metropolitan areas where shift work and commuting put additional demands on parents, the hours are generally from 6:00 A.M. to 6:00 P.M., though the real program probably finishes at four or so. You'll want to check out the policy (and charge) on late pickups to ensure that you have covered all eventualities.

Cost: How many dollars for what Geoff will actually get? Screen your choices on the basis of cost, then add in the transportation and any hidden charges for snacks, lunches, etc. Licensed and trained early-childhood educators are probably the most poorly paid professionals in education, but they still charge more than the mother with no credentials down the street. Quality costs. If quality costs too much, you may inquire at your local family services office to see if you qualify for a place in a subsidized daycare setting. Some employers are beginning to provide access to subsidized preschools right at the work site, a wonderful choice if the program is well run.

Preschool Staffing

These are the teacher-to-student ratios required of licensed Ontario preschools and daycare providers:

Age of Child	Maximum Group Size	Ratio Adult:Child
0 - 18 mos.	10	3:10
18 - 30 mos.	15	1:5
30 mos. - 5 yrs.	16	1:8
5 - 6 yrs.	24	1:12
6 - 9 yrs.	30	1:15

Strangely enough, once an Ontario child enters formal public schooling the ratio for four- and five-year-olds doubles to 1:25, then drops to 1:20 for six- and seven-year-olds. In an ordinary public school, it's not unusual for there to be twenty-eight or more eight-year-olds with one teacher, giving a 1:28+ ratio.

Checklist for an Excellent Nursery School

❏ Most teachers have completed early childhood education (ECE) training.

❏ The pupil-teacher ratio is between one to five and one to eight.

❏ The staff obviously love young kids.

❏ The school is used to train students in early childhood education.

❏ There is a program emphasis or philosophy governing the school.

❏ Field trips are scheduled once a week.

❏ Some of the teachers are men.

❏ Facilities are available for both indoor and outdoor activities.

❏ There is a corner for reading with books and comfy chairs.

❏ There is a quiet time to read or hear stories.

Children's age range and socioeconomic group: Who are those other kids? Some child-care operations look after children right up to school age and even provide after-school care for kids up to twelve years old. When you look at these, you'll want to find out how many children are in each age level and how they're grouped for their programs. Programs that always have Geoff playing with children one or two years younger than he will not necessarily provide the language stimulation and challenge you were counting on. Community preschools that bring your Geoff into contact with kids from other areas may well lead to *surprising* vocabulary before he ever gets to kindergarten. Families for whom *shucks* is a strong expression may well be shocked by what Geoff brings home from school. Be prepared, or choose another option.

Philosophy: What do they believe about what they do? Not every preschool has a philosophical approach to what they do, but many have an emphasis on one facet or another of children's development. Montessori schools, for instance, follow the ideas of Maria Montessori, who saw constructive play as an educational tool. Waldorf schools see musical education as central. Other schools may emphasize experiential education (lots of field trips), or skill development (sports, swimming, games), or academic development (regular reading and story times), or the visual arts (drawing, painting), or the environment (using a natural surrounding to enhance the school experience), or a particular religious faith. Obviously you'll want to make sure that the preschool's emphasis corresponds to your own value system.

Once you've decided what you require in a nursery program for your child and you've screened to determine what programs meet your needs, you'll want to take a closer look at the particular schools to find the best one for both you and your child. This second level of screening will involve more than a phone call or reading a brochure. You'll need to make an appointment to visit without your child so that you can talk with the director and actually see the facilities and staff. Here's where some recommendations from neighbours and friends can pay dividends in screening out the schools that are just not appropriate for you. Once you have your notes complete, sit down and consider what you're looking for in the following areas:

Program. A stimulating preschool program should provide many opportunities for Geoff to engage in language with adults as well as with children. Adult modelling of complex language extends both the thinking and the vocabulary of young children, so avoid preschools where baby talk seems to be the norm. The preschool program should give Geoff lots of practice imitating real tasks such as driving, cleaning, cooking, reading, digging and building, as well as provide experiences that get him to use his senses to learn about his environment. There should be quiet times for listening to stories and noisy times for chanting and singing favourite songs. Interactions with adults should be about ideas, things and activities, not simply getting the rules right (although there should be some of that, too, so that he learns routines). Drama, movement, games that involve small-muscle skills, as well as running, jumping, climbing and balancing, are all part of a well-planned preschool program. Lots of time for doing and creating through colouring, drawing, "writing" and painting will help develop Geoff's fine motor skills as well as give him a chance to express his ideas on paper. An effective preschool program should include problem solving, concentration tasks, group activities, partner play and tasks to do alone. Mathematics concepts

❏ The kids seems to be happy and healthy.

❏ There are a number of activity centres: with sand, water, blocks, dolls, etc.

❏ Conflicts among kids are handled as you would at home.

❏ You are welcome to be involved.

❏ The program is organized into theme units coordinating activities, books and trips.

❏ Kids can stay late for a reasonable extra charge.

❏ Food-preparation areas and washrooms are clean.

❏ The school seems to have some purpose besides making money for the owners.

Scoring: award 5 points for each check. An excellent school will score 80-90; a good school 70-75; an adequate school 60-65.

Your Preschool Child

Three years old

- likes people, wants to please, cooperative
- can negotiate with others—"Let's do this, then we can play with the cars."
- learns routines
- is aware of the environment around him—"That's the moon, Mommy."
- is able to solve problems and make decisions
- plays alongside and sometimes cooperatively with other children
- enjoys listening to stories and pretends to read by holding the book and telling a story from the pictures

Three and a half

- starts to become unsure, anxious and demanding
- exerts independence, can be noncompliant
- sensitive, can get upset easily if things go wrong or are too hard
- enjoys doing grown-up things and mimics these through dramatic play
- shows interest in familiar stories and chimes in with the reader
- uses writing tools to draw and "write" (often on newly papered walls)

should be developed through games that involve sorting, matching, grouping, counting, designing, building, measuring and problem solving. Emphasis on writing numbers at an early age takes time away from the "doing" with objects that is so essential to understanding. Similarly, programs that are preoccupied with flash cards and rote learning of isolated letters or words miss that essential step of hearing the language of print when a story is beautifully read aloud.

Programs that focus on rote counting and letter recognition are responding to the demands of parents who feel that pushing their children early on will propel them for twenty years right into successful careers. Unfortunately, many of these well-intentioned efforts create children who can "perform" the rote task when asked, but have little real understanding of the concepts when solving problems and who don't know that reading is about making sense. These children may start kindergarten and become bored with the formal program, yet not really know how to explore their own creativity or initiate play or activities without being directed. While they feel great about being able to do things that make their parents happy, they quickly find out that other children in the early grades are catching up to them.

We've seen children who arrive in kindergarten able to recite the words in a book, but who never choose to pick one up to read and enjoy. Reading has become work. These same children perform academic tricks at home because they know what's rewarded with smiles from Mom and Dad. Seldom do parents drag Aunt Ethel outside to see the tunnels and the mud roads that their little ones make, but when Geoff counts to fifty or reads the word cards labelling the furniture, he gets oohs and ahs all round. This peculiar adult distortion of childhood curiosity and exploration won't serve Geoff later on. He needs a balanced preschool program.

Facilities. When you're visiting a prospective preschool, observe the facilities and safety practices. Is there enough space for the children both inside and in the outdoor play area? Is the play equipment well maintained and free of dangerous pieces or loose connections? There should be a licence displayed to show that the centre has met the requirements of the health and safety regulatory board for the province as well as the criteria for space and staffing laid down by the Community and Social Services Department. Food-preparation areas, washrooms and rest spots must be clean. Ask the director about first-aid training and find out how emergency situations are handled. If your child has a particular health or developmental need you'll want to explore what provisions will be made for him.

Evidence of the program can also be seen in what's physically available at the school. A quick look around should reveal books, tools for drawing, painting and writing, building blocks, wheeled toys, sand and water tables, measuring tools and lots of "junk" to take apart and put back together. There should be climbers and balance beams both inside and outside and painted lines on floors and the playground for making up games. Equipment needn't be expensive, but it should be sufficient in quantity to ensure that all children can get involved.

One simple measure of both program and sanitary conditions is the "runny-nose index." Take a look around at the children: How many with runny noses? How many with visible impetigo? While any preschool can have a run of diseases, by and large the better the preschool, the healthier the kids will be.

Staffing. Each licensed preschool operator must staff according to a formula set by the province. There must be a qualified early-childhood educator in charge of the programming at each age

Four years old

- active, impulsive, exuberant
- asks questions constantly
- runs and darts around
- is very uninhibited, sometimes embarrassingly so
- enjoys activity, but still enjoys being read to or playing games with language and words
- enjoys his own books and takes them out at will
- is starting to act "grown-up" and resists anything that seems babyish
- takes care of dressing and personal needs himself
- shows pride in his independence

Four and a half

- may show some uncertainty and lose some of the bravado
- behaviour is inconsistent
- starting to settle and become calmer
- begins to share and show consideration for others
- may show an interest in the print and letters in the books as they're being read, even recognizing and naming some
- shows personal taste in books and chooses his own books from the library

Child-Parent Resource Centres

These centres charge a modest membership fee that entitles a family to make use of a toy library, a resource library, play programs, miniworkshops for caregivers, parent breaks while children are at play with a group leader, workshops provided by other agencies and a newsletter outlining the events. Members of these resource centres are generally required to volunteer about two hours' time to the centre. Tasks for volunteers involve helping out with the play program, maintaining and signing out materials in the toy and resource libraries, preparing the newsletter, fundraising, sewing, preparing promotional flyers or reviewing new toys or resources for inclusion in the library. One side benefit: parents who participate in these programs become part of a mutual support group as their children grow through the early years.

level and there is a maximum group size allowed. When checking out the staff there are a number of considerations that will determine if you really want to entrust Geoff to their care. Observe how they manage child behaviour and misbehaviour. You want them to be sensitive, loving, caring, accepting, but not overprotective or totally indulgent. Your child's safety must be ensured by the way the staff keep order and require children to play safely and fairly.

Plan to arrive at a time when parents are either dropping off or picking up children, to see the kind of relationship there is between the staff and the parents. Asking the parents themselves often produces useless information—*of course* they're happy with the school, their child is still in it! Unhappy parents wouldn't be there. Nonetheless, if you watch the interchange of parents and staff and look at the responses of children as they leave, you may learn far more about the school than any set of licences and diplomas will tell you.

While the school is operating, you should observe how conflicts among children are handled to see if the process falls within the range of how you deal with these situations at home. If you find that the staff interactions with the children are too different from what you view as appropriate you'd better look elsewhere for Geoff. Then again, if you feel the strategies that are used are appropriate—if only you had the courage and knowledge to use them—then this may be a chance for you to alter your own approach and become a better parent. Who says preschool education is only for the kids?

The single most important aspect to check out is the staff attitude toward young children. Because of the terribly low wages there is often low morale and considerable turnover in child-care settings. We can't imagine any teacher sticking with that job if she or he didn't like little kids, but strange circumstances sometimes put people in jobs for which they're not suited. Keep an eye open.

Parent involvement. You may wish to be more involved in your child's program and have enough time to participate in the operation and direction of the school. Co-op nursery schools have been developed by parents like you who have the time, energy and ingenuity to give guidance and support to the paid professionals. In a co-op preschool, this is done through a board of volunteer directors and by parents spending time to work with groups of children. The required volunteer time varies with the staff and the cost of the program, but two hours a week seems fairly standard. For some parents the mix of lower cost and more direct control through active participation provides an ideal answer for the education of their young child.

For any preschool, the nature of parent involvement is very important. You may not have the time to invest on a regular basis as required by a co-op, but you may wish to participate in other ways. Make sure that you ask other parents, as well as the director, what kinds of things parents are encouraged to do to be part of their child's school. Are you invited to join in for parties, field trips, special activities, or is the preschool hermetically sealed? As we've said throughout this book, parent involvement is an essential key to effective education.

Specific Types of Preschool Programs

One of the most famous and widely respected early childhood programs is based on the work of Maria Montessori. Started in Italy in the early 1900s, the program emphasizes developing independence in the children. There are variations among the many Montessori schools, but integral

Learning to Read at Home

Most children begin learning to read before they attend school. Here's how to get them started:

- Read with your child daily, at a regular time, for fifteen to thirty minutes.
- For very young children, be prepared to stop making dinner and read when they bring a book to you.
- Make sure there's a shelf of "favourite" books to be read again and again.
- Turn off the TV so you can both concentrate on the reading.
- For young children, repetition is more important than variety. If your daughter wants the same book five nights in a row, indulge her.
- Little kids enjoy joining in on repeated phrases or memorized rhymes. Encourage this—it's not reading, but it's a step along the way.
- Be sure the reading and listening are a part of any preschool program.
- Make sure that Dad reads, as well as Mom—and encourage other relatives to become "guest readers."
- Don't pretend that a story tape with a Fisher-Price tape player substitutes for you. It's a great toy, but not a real reading experience.
- Make sure that reading is full of hugs and laughter and games and questions and talk and silliness—that's what makes reading fun for little kids.

to all are self-teaching materials that encourage the development of coordination, the senses and language. There is some focus on early reading, writing and arithmetic, but the stress is on developing and encouraging the individuality of the child. Montessori schools take students from age two and a half to five and some include a full kindergarten program.

Religious-affiliated daycare programs and preschools are nonprofit and often have, as part of their philosophy, the religious teachings of the operating group. These are frequently run as co-op programs and provide a full day for two-and-a-half to five-year-olds, as well as some after-school programs for older children. Religious-affiliated programs have a natural advantage in the facilities available in meeting halls and the manse, often designed for ambitious Sunday-school programs, sometimes even including a gym. Some programs can use this advantage to trim their fees well below commercial daycare or preschool offerings.

Early childhood education programs run by community colleges to train ECE teachers usually have a laboratory school attached to them. These lab schools run from six to eleven hours a day and take children from eighteen months to five years. The child-to-adult ratio is usually low due to the numbers of student teachers who require practical experience as part of their training. The most up-to-date methods and programs are likely to be piloted here, though using your child to train inexperienced teachers does have its drawbacks. Strict regulatory controls are in place in these "model" schools, and the master teachers usually are masters of their trade. Where available, a lab school is probably the preschool of choice. The real trick involves meeting the requirements to get your child enrolled (sometimes the schools are restricted to student and staff children) or getting in early on a long waiting list.

Y nursery schools ordinarily operate half days and take children from two and a half to five years. Some Y programs are also in place in local schools to provide before- and after-school care for older children. These nonprofit (often subsidized) programs can also be run as co-ops. They are licensed and provide an excellent lower-cost program for young children, though they rarely have a particular philosophy or strength.

These days, when new public schools are built, they often include a preschool setting or classroom. The program in operation may or may not be run by your local board or district, but it will have some reputable local organization behind it. When daycare or preschool programs are located in a high school, they are used almost exclusively by young student mothers who are continuing their education. These innovative programs encourage visits by the young mother (and even her friends) in between classes and at lunch. Sometimes there are additional spaces available for parents from the surrounding community. It's worth a phone call to your local high school or board or district information office to see if such a daycare or preschool is located near you.

Junior Kindergarten

Many school systems are now providing junior kindergarten programs for four-year-olds. These programs provide an option to parents who have their child in nursery school or who wish to have their child begin schooling in the formal setting of a big school. While attendance by a four- or five-year-old is not mandatory, most parents clamour for the chance to get their child registered in these programs. To start with, they're usually free. The programs run for only half a day, but allow your child to develop independence and become comfortable in the classroom. They also expose Geoff to the school library and many of

Readiness for Regular School...

To be ready for kindergarten, by age five your child should be able to:

- retell a simple story in sequence and keep the characters straight;
- hear and identify the beginning sounds of words;
- hear and repeat rhyming sounds;
- follow rules for simple games;
- ask clear-enough questions to get information from adults;
- sort and classify common objects;
- observe living things in his environment and be able to talk about them;
- explain when common events happen during his day;
- talk about how he feels and how others might feel;
- organize his toys and put them away in a specific way;
- know his colours;
- recognize the labels and logos of common products or stores (Big Mac, Eaton's, etc.);
- draw, cut and paste with some precision;
- print some letters from his name;
- count objects to five and recognize the numbers;
- match objects and shapes;
- recall events of the day and talk about them.

the activities that are part of a school life that older students enjoy. The only down side to these JK programs seems to be in the instruction. While nursery and preschool instructors are trained in early childhood education (ECE), many JK teachers are trained in basic elementary school teaching. They may or may not be comfortable with the less-formal structure of school before the primary grades.

Obviously the best educational or learning environment for your preschooler is one that is supportive, loving, safe, stimulating, exciting, yet calm and consistent. Some families are in a position to provide this at home. For many others, the task is to find a preschool where someone else will do all this for you. With care, you probably can.

CHAPTER 7

Kindergarten and Grade One

Your daughter Sara is starting kindergarten and she's scared. In all likelihood, so are you. You are about to deliver your child into the hands of a school you may have visited only once or twice. You may have heard some horror stories from the parents next door about what happened to their son Josh in his first year of school. You weren't terribly impressed by the principal when you went to visit and don't know which of the two kindergarten teachers Sara will end up with. Unlike her nursery school, Sara's new school seems big and impersonal. And perhaps your own experiences early in elementary school weren't all that wonderful; you cringe just remembering the way Mrs. Brown used to make you stand in the corner with your nose pressed to the wall.

So that first school day in September is an upsetting one for you—and all that just makes it more frightening for Sara. The solution is that basic rule of parenting: DON'T PANIC. Chances are, your anxiety about the new school will be far greater than your child's. Try to keep that anxiety under control.

Kindergarten Stress for You

At a very real level, more of the anxiety about kindergarten probably belongs to you than to your child. For your daughter Sara, this big new school and new teacher are part of growing up and mastering the world. For you, both kindergarten and regular school seem very different from your previous experience with nursery school.

- Nursery school settings look more like home playrooms—even down to nap areas.

- Nursery school had more adults visible to work directly with children and to talk to parents; it was more like daycare than school.

- You see your "baby" being swallowed up in a large institution, and you worry about your child's contact with all those other BIG kids in school or on the playground.

- You understand the kind of activities that go on in nursery school, but you're not quite sure what happens in kindergarten.

- You worry that your child won't be able to sit still, or follow the rules, or do the work that may be expected of her.

Our advice is simple: don't worry so much.

Beth Chisolm, a teacher in Vancouver, tells this story about her first day teaching kindergarten. The principal came into her classroom around eleven o'clock to see how things were going, just as Beth had gotten the kids settled in. Beth was annoyed and said, "Where were you when I could have used some help?"

The principal was taken aback. "Help? What was the problem?"

"It was awful," Beth told her. "There they were, holding on to each other, tears streaming down their faces. It was impossible!"

"But the kids seem fine now," the principal responded.

"Kids! It wasn't the kids who were upset. It was the parents who had to leave them here."

If you stop to think, it's obvious that the worst thing you can do for Sara is communicate your own anxieties. Parents can do this in a number of ways, the most damaging being the least obvious. If you say over dinner, "You'll really enjoy your new school," that's well and good. If you then mention at bath time, "But if any of the big kids pick on you, you just tell Mommy," you've given a *real* message of anxiety that is far more telling than your *official* message of encouragement. Give your child a chance to be enthusiastic about her first day in big school; after all, it happens only once.

Assuming that you have read through the earlier chapters in this book, you have already made the best possible choice of a school in your given circumstances. It will not profit your child to hear of your misgivings or to learn that the library is inadequate or the principal wears tacky polyester sport coats. It will help your child to know that her new school will give her the chance to meet many new children, will care for her throughout the day and will help her learn important things like reading and math. Sara's new school *will be* fun: let her know this before she starts off.

When that first morning arrives, go to school with Sara, give her a kiss, explain that you'll be back to pick her up at the end of the morning or afternoon and tell her she'll have a great time. Then leave with no more than one look back. It's so embarrassing to see grown adults with their noses pressed to the window—especially for their own children.

What Actually Goes on in Kindergarten

At one time, before nursery schools and daycare were so prevalent, kindergarten was seen as a transition from a childhood of home and mother to the brand-new idea of school and teacher. Kindergarten was a place to develop "learning readiness," (a concept that was vaguely synonymous with sitting still at a desk and raising one's hand to ask permission to go to the bathroom), while formal instruction and learning goals were put off to grade one. But times have changed.

Your child will already be entering kindergarten with a number of important skills and abilities, thanks to both early childhood education and the effects of programs like *Sesame Street* and *Reading Rainbow*. From reading to math to listening and cooperation, today's kids come to big school better equipped than ever before. The job of the kindergarten teacher is to develop these skills and improve the social interaction of the children. At the same time, the teacher will foster some of the attitudes needed for instruction later on (yes, it is still necessary to sit and listen) and some of the habits (no, Sara cannot go to the bathroom every twenty minutes) that make it possible for school to function (after all, kids outnumber the teacher by twenty to one).

It is also fair to say that kindergarten has a "levelling" function. Some children enter school with grade-three-level reading skills, the capacity to program a VCR and operate a computer and a

Kindergarten Stress for Your Child

Your child has some good reasons to be anxious about starting kindergarten:

- I won't have Mom or Dad around if something goes wrong.

- I won't be able to get along with the other kids.

- My older brother says that school is awful, that kids pick on you.

- I won't be able to do as well as Dad wants me to.

- I might break my new lunch box or pencil case.

- The teacher won't love me the way Mom and Dad do.

- I'll just be one kid in a big class; I won't be special anymore.

- Some bad guy might snatch me from the playground or on the way to school.

You can help by easing up on your own expectations and reassuring your child about the school experience.

What Your Child Can Already Do

The average five-year-old entering kindergarten...

- has a reading vocabulary of twenty to 300 words—not necessarily "cow" or "mother," but functional words like "Big Mac" and "K-Mart";

- has rudimentary math skills, often addition up to the fives, and a concept of money and change;

- knows how to sit and listen to a story being read, then can respond with questions or ideas or further story-telling;

- can work harmoniously with other children for a period of time on a cooperative project.

surprising sophistication about everything from sex to family finances. Other children enter school without much experience in spoken English, with backgrounds of turmoil that have led to serious emotional problems, with home situations that make Osh Kosh B'Gosh as impossible as a new BMW in the driveway. The kindergarten teacher tries to get all of these children ready to learn together, as a class and in mixed groups, for the rest of their school career.

Here's what the teacher does.

Reading. Between a quarter and a third of the time spent in kindergarten will be devoted to reading. Formal instruction in phonics is usually put off until grade one, but that doesn't mean your kindergarten child won't be doing a lot of important work developing reading skills. The first of these is identifying the letters of the alphabet, their names and what sound they usually make. These letters are often introduced in their initial position, as the first letter in a word, so Sara will learn that apple begins with *a* and banana with *b*. Your daughter probably knows all this from *Sesame Street*, but systematic review of the alphabet has been the basis for reading instruction ever since the days of the ancient Greeks.

Probably more important for Sara will be the time actually spent reading picture books. This will take place as a whole class, with the teacher reading; in groups, assisted by the teacher or a volunteer; in pairs, with a reading buddy from an older grade; and alone, with picture books or books with a very simple vocabulary.

In some classrooms, students still do colour in the *b* words on a sheet of paper, just as they did when you went to school and the sheets had that wonderful smell of denatured alcohol from the old ditto machine. These days the sheets are more likely to emerge odourless from the photo-copier, but that doesn't make them any more effective. Unless the teacher is using the time freed up by this busywork to help other students, children gain little in reading and only marginally in small-muscle skills from such exercises.

The goal in kindergarten reading is to make sure that Sara knows her letters and some letter sounds when she enters grade one; that she can sit still to listen to a story for ten minutes or so; and that she sees the basic connection between print on the page, words from the voice and ideas in her mind. If you and your school are both doing effective jobs, Sara will already have begun her lifelong love of books.

Mathematics. In kindergarten, the *idea* of math-ematics is brought home by identifying numbers, by counting and by simple arithmetic of the two-plus-two variety. Again, more formal instruction tends to be left to grade one, so now the activities will be "fun," rather carefully structured. Sara may well count blocks, or arrange classmates by size, or talk about the shapes of something she made with Duplo or Lego. Current educational theory holds that a grounding in mathematical ideas is more important than simply learning to manipulate numbers, so don't be upset if Sara is talking about the relative sizes of "sets" of coloured blocks and still can't add three plus five. These are both mathematical skills, and the first may well be more important when Sara starts working with Lotus 1-2-3 ten years from now.

Theme units. Areas like science and history aren't studied as subjects in kindergarten; they're tackled as parts of a theme unit. The themes your child focusses on in kindergarten will depend on what's current in your community, what resources are available at the school and the

Signs of a Great Reading Program

You can tell even at home whether your child is getting a good grounding in read-ing at school. Look for these signs:

• Books come home with instructions that you are to read them together with your child.

• Your child notices words around her, and tells you what they are or tries to sound them out.

• Your child writes notes and stories without much panic about spelling.

• Your child comes home singing a song or reciting a poem learned in school.

• Your child talks about having been read to by the teacher, or other adults, or older students.

• Your child knows the school librarian and regularly signs out books.

• Your child sees herself as a reader (even if she's still at the pretending or memorizing stage).

Signs of a Great Math Program

- The teacher asks for collections of junk material for sorting, ordering and classifying.

- Many counting and number books are brought home to be read with you.

- Your child is asked to measure items around the house, or find objects with particular shapes.

- Your child plays counting or number games learned in school, trying to improve her skills.

- Your child starts looking for "real" problems to solve: "We need four glasses for us, so how many glasses to do we need if Grandma is coming to supper?" And gives you the answers.

- Math activities are sent home that require your help.

- Mathematics is seen as fun, exciting and easy.

areas with which your child's teacher feels most comfortable. Common theme units include "The Farm," "Animals," "Our Community" and sometimes exotic topics like "Dinosaurs." Often these theme units combine reading material, books, videos and films, hands-on experiments, model building, drawing and field trips. Field trips are one way you can get involved and join in with your child's education. Don't miss out.

Art, music and physical education. Kindergarten kids love to draw, sing, recite along with a book, kick a ball and play tag. Since one of the big goals in kindergarten is to create a positive attitude toward school, it's not surprising that these activities take up about a third of the kindergarten day. As well, developing skills in art and music is important for what happens later on in school and for possible study outside. Physical education is part of the school curriculum not just because some children are underactive and overweight, but because it teaches a great deal about cooperation (playing on a team), organization (your child needs shirts and running shoes on Tuesdays and Thursdays) and the rules of sport. In these days of cost cutting and pressure to concentrate on "the basics," it's important to remember that art, music and physical education are not frills; they are essential in developing your child as a whole person.

What You Can Do at Home

It is unlikely that Sara will be given formal homework in kindergarten, though sometimes parents are asked to help out on an activity or theme unit that begins in school. But this does not mean that what happens in your home has no connection to what happens in school. Increasingly, teachers are beginning to see that habits, attitudes and experiences at *home* are directly connected to the success of children at school. Even in kindergarten, a parent should expect to spend some time backing up what's going on in school.

Read with your child every day. We have suggested earlier in this book that daily or nightly reading should become part of family routine when your child is six months old or even younger.

The importance of a regular, expected reading period of twenty to thirty minutes a day cannot be overstressed. It doesn't matter what time of day you select, or where you do the reading, or how well you read (even parents who have difficulty reading aloud simply can tell stories and help their children's reading considerably)—what matters is regularity and commitment. If you skip a day's reading and Sara does not complain about the loss, then you are not reading regularly enough. Daily or nightly reading time should be *expected* by your child and delivered by you or your spouse or partner with joy and laughter. Remember that family reading time is not instructional time; nor is it a task to be raced through as quickly as possible. Talking and asking questions are as much a part of family reading time as any actual reading of a book or story.

Our companion volume, *The Reading Solution*, goes into much greater detail on what should be read together at any given age level. For a kindergarten or grade one child, the reading material will range from the beautiful picture books of early childhood to the easy-to-read (sometimes labelled "I can read it myself") books with simple words that will support reading instruction in school.

Give structure to your child's day. One important aspect of school is that it enforces a structure on your child's life—and this is not at all a bad thing. Sara will have to get up at seven-thirty to be ready for school at eight-thirty to start her

Getting Off to a Good Start

Here's how to become a real partner in your child's education:

- call the board office to get general information on registration, bus schedules and the school calendar;

- attend any early orientation sessions offered by the school;

- attend an open house at the school *before* you enrol your child;

- be sure to attend any meet-the-teacher nights, open houses, concerts, displays or meetings of the home and school association;

- read all the newsletters and special notices that come home;

- offer to help out on special days where an extra pair of hands will be a lifesaver for the teacher;

- sign-up to be a volunteer: in your child's classroom or the library, as a reading buddy.

A Page from a Kindergarten Daybook

Theme: Animals

8:45 Entry. Attendance, announcements, "O Canada," calendar, poem, story, theme reading (chart and big book).
      Outdoor play routine: Creative playground or free play, or use of small equipment—balls, ropes, trikes, etc.

9:30 General input.
      Math or language lesson.
      Learning centres first, then individual program time.

10:45 Tidy up, snack time.
      Individual sharing time; reading time.

11:00 Story/music/drama
      "Three Little Pigs"

11:20 Hand out finished work, letters home to be put in backpacks.

11:30 Dismissal.

kindergarten class at nine o'clock. That means Sara can't stay up until eleven, or she'll have trouble getting up in the morning and she'll be exhausted at school. Exhausted children can't learn. If you haven't previously set a bedtime and a reasonable wake-up time, do it now.

There is a species of parent who feels that children should eat when hungry, sleep when tired and play whenever it strikes their fancy. We feel such "parenting," however it may be justified philosophically, merely excuses laziness by adults and does serious damage to children. As the psychologist Thomas Szasz has said: "Permissiveness is the principle of treating children as if they were adults; and the tactic of making sure they never reach that stage." Do your child a favour—put her to bed at nine o'clock.

Entering kindergarten is a good time to add or refine another structure in your child's life: *control the TV*. Chances are that your young child, if she were at home or in a home-based day care, watches a lot of television. Some of the educational programs such as *Sesame Street* and *Reading Rainbow* are wonderful adjuncts to a child's life. But too much TV-even good TV—develops a passive attitude and an urge for quick, showy presentation which will not help your child in school. The average Canadian five-year-old now watches slightly more than three hours of television a day. That's plenty. Even more important than the number of hours watched is setting some controls on what's watched and preserving some time when the TV is off. Every household needs quiet time to read or talk or draw or play a game. Any household that uses the television set as a day-long baby-sitter is in real trouble.

Meet the Teacher

At most schools, you'll meet your child's kindergarten teacher at least three different times. Your first meeting will often be at a kindergarten orientation session held before your child begins attending. These sessions vary a great deal from school to school. Often you'll be part of a group that receives a school tour, briefly meets the principal and listens to some talk about behaviour expectations and the kindergarten program. If yours is a good school—or you call to arrange it in advance—you should also be able to get some individual time with your child's future teacher. This should be give-and-take time for both of you. A good teacher will want information about your expectations of the program and what you know about your child. She'll ask about alternate caregivers in case of illness or emergency and the role of ex-spouses in pickup and delivery. She'll want to know about your child's health, diet, development, friends, interests, likes and dislikes.

You will have your own sets of questions. Some will be quite simple: What do the children wear? Is there a place to store extra clothes or running shoes? What about food and gum during school? Other questions will be more significant: What exactly is in the program? Should I expect my child to bring home books or special activities for me to help with? Don't waste all your time with the teacher on purely procedural questions about bus schedules and lunch hours. Try to feel out what kind of teacher she is likely to be— because this affects the kind of support you give at home.

The second time you meet your child's teacher will probably be in October at an official meet-the-teacher day or night. Often these sessions offer much the same information that you should have received during an orientation session, but they add an opportunity to ask questions. This second meeting is also a good time to look around the classroom and at your child's work— a chance to scout out what's happening to her during her time at school. The information you

What to Expect at Kindergarten Orientation

- A chance to meet the principal and the kindergarten teachers.

- Information about the calendar, attendance procedures, the program.

- A school tour, including the library.

- Requirements for clothing, snacks, gym clothes and other equipment.

- An outline of expectations for behaviour and an explanation on how the school deals with behaviour problems.

- Questions of you: phone numbers for emergencies, family doctor, information on diets, allergies, medical problems.

- An invitation to join the parents' group or home and school association.

- An opportunity to sign up as a volunteer.

Kindergarten Report Cards

Many schools combine kindergarten report cards with parent interviews as part of a whole system of reporting on a student's progress. In kindergarten these interviews may be the primary form of reporting. Sometimes there may be no written report card until grade one.

Later in the year, generally around April, there will be a written report or a checklist with comments to bring some uniformity to reporting across the system. This will also allow parents to see specifically how their child is coping with school expectations.

Regardless of when the first report card arrives, it should cover such areas as attendance, social and emotional growth, language skills, mathematical concepts, environmental awareness and physical growth and development. Each of these sections will have a list of criteria and then a scale from "Excellent" to "Needs Improvement" or 1 to 4 to show the level of your child's progress or achievement. Included with report cards may be more detailed lists of skills, knowledge or the units covered by the class.

collect this way and the stories you hear from your child are important for your third and most important meeting.

The third meeting between parent and teacher often comes in November, after the teacher has some impression of what your child is really like (in some schools, after report cards are given out). This meeting will last between twenty and thirty minutes, but can stretch into several meetings if you feel it's necessary. By November, you will have some ideas about your child's teacher and the kind of program your child is getting in school. You will likely have noticed one or two things that you don't much like. Maybe Sara isn't close enough to hear the story during story time, or can't see the big book even when the teacher holds it up. Maybe Sara doesn't like sitting beside Johnny B., who calls her a goof and pulls her hair. These points deserve to be raised, because the teacher is in a position to take action to improve the situation.

Similarly, the teacher may well have observations that would be important for you. *Listen.* If the teacher suggests that Sara might have a vision problem, or is too squirmy, or is causing a problem with the other children, there is more than a fair chance that the teacher is correct. The worst approach is to assume that your Sara is perfect and the teacher is biased against her. If Sara does have some problems adapting to the school environment—whether simple ones like needing glasses or complex ones like acting out—the teacher might help you help Sara. But only if you listen.

Join In and Help Out

Throughout Sara's school career—but especially in the early grades—teachers will be grateful for parent help. If you are available during the day, you can be invaluable as a reading tutor, a library helper, or a parent supervisor on field trips. The advantage for Sara in your participation comes in many ways. Your presence in her new school gives the environment a special value in her eyes. School must be important if Mommy or Daddy spend one morning a week there too. Additionally, your presence gives the teacher the opportunity to arrange special help for children who need it or to organize class trips that enrich the educational experience for Sara and the other children as well.

There are also advantages for you, too, in this volunteering. School is an opportunity for you to see your child in contact with other children, in play and in learning situations. You might find that Sara behaves very differently in these circumstances than she does at home. Your presence in the school or classroom also gives you a chance to scout out what goes on. If Ms. Brown, the kindergarten teacher, pays too much attention to boys, or frequently isn't organized, or really chews out kids for no good reason, you're in a better position to see such things and take action to improve the situation. If there are two or three grade one teachers, you'll learn quickly which one you would prefer for your child. Then you can work quietly to get Sara in that class the following year (see Chapter 4). In our experience, the time a parent spends in school as a volunteer will be repaid many times over in making elementary school a better experience for her child.

Can My Child Be a Problem?

To answer the question simply: yes. You may remember all those problem kids from your own days in school: the bullies, the dummies, the show-offs, the withdrawn kids, the sadistic kids who delighted in torturing turtles or dragonflies, the kids who cheated, the ones who extorted money to go to the bathroom, the kid who stole

If Your Child Is Bright . . .

If your child shows signs of giftedness, or simply advanced development, keep your eyes open for information that will help later in getting her in the appropriate special program.

- What kinds of tasks keep her interest? Open-ended, creative tasks where she can create new problems or stories? Or closed tasks like arithmetic sums and word lists?

- How does she spend playtime? Alone doing school-type activities or with friends in active games or playing roles?

- How does she deal with playmates who change the rules or make up new ones?

- How does she get approval in your house? What activities do you applaud—and what activities do you pay no attention to?

Danger Signs

If you notice two or more of these danger signs, it would be best to have a serious talk with your child's teacher. Your child might have personal or learning problems that will interfere with enjoying school.

❏ Your child is frequently "sick" or doesn't want to go to school.

❏ Your child complains about being picked on or talks about the other kids as "goofs" or says they are all "stuck up."

❏ Your child gets into physical fights—either on the winning or losing side.

❏ Your child hasn't made any new friends at his school.

❏ Your child says she is "bored" by math or reading.

❏ Your child regularly "forgets" her gym clothes, or library books, or school equipment.

❏ Your child is frequently kept in at recess, or says that she hates the teacher.

your baseball glove in grade five. All *those* kids, some of whom made your life difficult or embarrassing or at least hemmed it in. In fact, thinking back, how many good kids were there? You and your friends, of course . . . and even some of them look pretty questionable in retrospect.

While we would like to report that schools today no longer have problem children, that would be a lie. In fact, the experience of teachers and studies by the Vanier Institute indicate the number of kids with serious problems is increasing. Depending on measures and definitions, that 20 percent contingent of kids with problems is probably up to 30 percent today. Children often have problems such as divorce, poverty, "quality time" substituting for parents in the home and the increasing violence of television and video games to contend with, problems that were not as severe or didn't exist thirty years ago. The kids didn't cause these problems, but they certainly act them out in school.

Even, perhaps, your child.

It is difficult for most parents to see or acknowledge that their child could be causing problems at school. A child's behaviour is frequently different at home than it is in class or out in the playground. What passes for normal behaviour in some homes might be quite antisocial out in public. And to admit all this calls into question our parenting, our lifestyle choices, even our genetics. Sara just has to be perfect.

Which is why you have to work hard to listen. What you hear about Sara in kindergarten from the teacher, and perhaps from the principal, is worth noting. If the same comments come back in grade one and grade two, from other teachers and again from the principal, we're not looking at a school conspiracy. Schools and teachers are too busy to bother with conspiracies, despite what some kids may claim. The truth is more likely this: Sara has a problem. You might want to review Chapter 5 and then talk with the teacher about what steps both of you can take so Sara's first year at big school turns out to be a good one.

From Kindergarten to Grade One

The change between kindergarten and the first grade is a significant one. Kindergarten probably lasted only half the day; grade one is a full day. Kindergarten worked primarily on social skills and learning tasks that seemed much like play; grade one involves some instruction and achievement expectations. Kindergarten felt like an extension of nursery school; grade one feels like real school—including lessons, report cards and homework.

Grade one programs vary from province to province, school to school, but all have certain items in common:

Reading. A grade one child is expected to develop a sight word vocabulary of 200 or more words by the end of the year. She is expected to have mastered some rudimentary phonics rules (unless your school has taken the bizarre step of banning phonics): vowel sounds, consonant sounds, some diphthongs (groups of letters). She will read books—some primers in a graded reading approach (especially in a phonics-based program); some works of children's literature (especially in a whole language program); some easy-to-read books provided by the teacher. Approximately one-third of classroom time will be spent reading aloud, in reading instruction, in reading silently and in writing, related to reading.

Grade one is a crucial age for developing reading skills and attitudes. In a single year, Sara's sight-word vocabulary will grow from a handful

How to Help Your Troubled Child

If your child is having trouble adjusting to school, it frequently helps to change some aspect of life at home. Try these ideas:

- provide some special individual time to be with your child—for reading, playing cards, cooking, playing ball, whatever;

- create a family quiet time for reading or schoolwork;

- praise your child's successes and don't dwell on the problems;

- focus on areas where your child can be successful—then give these time and family energy;

- set rhythms for family life: regular wake-up times, bedtimes, mealtimes, reading times;

- be clear in setting limits on unacceptable behaviour—and keep punishments reasonable;

- speak regularly with your child's teacher: ask for strategies, signs of progress;

- remember that times of family stress affect the children too.

of words to hundreds; she'll learn two-thirds of the word-attack skills anyone needs to know; and she'll develop an attitude toward reading and listening to stories that will be essential throughout her life. You should be part of all this. In a good school, the librarian will be sending books home with Sara for her to read—and books for you to read to Sara. In a good school, the teacher will be sending project work home involving reading and writing that call for your help. In a good school, Sara will finish grade one already convinced that she is "a reader." And then there are those other schools. We'll talk about them and what you can do at home despite them later on in this chapter.

Writing. We've included a range of writing samples to show the range of abilities that students display in grade one and the range of topics that they want to write about. Teachers and students alike know that everyone writes best about things that are real and familiar to them. For instance when Chi-Ling and her grade one classmates did a unit on sound, her teacher asked the students to do an experiment on vibrations.

Chi-Ling was excited enough and confident enough to record the findings of her experiment in writing. Her work shows the many skills some grade one children already have: organization, sentence structure, spelling and punctuation.

Obviously Chi-Ling is already an exceptional student. The next two samples show more ordinary writing at the grade one level: iffy or phonetic spelling, inconsistent writing, little sense of sentences or punctuation. At this early stage, children will differ enormously in their development—and not much of this will affect how well they'll ultimately do in school.

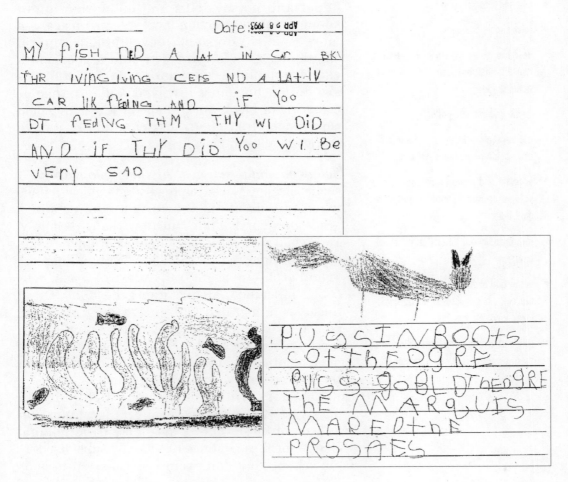

By the End of Grade One: In Math

By the end of grade one, most children will be able to . . .

- count and write numbers to 100;

- match numerals to groups of objects;

- add and subtract up to ten;

- solve simple problems;

- describe, sort, classify and construct two-dimensional and three-dimensional shapes;

- create and describe patterns;

- use vocabulary to show position (e.g., over, behind, in front of, etc.);

- estimate and measure distance, mass, volume using nonstandard and standard units;

- recognize special times (lunch, school, bed);

- name and organize items in a collection (e.g., baseball cards, shells, miniatures, keys, etc.);

- sort and arrange items according to a specific pattern (e.g., cars, animals).

Mathematics. The basic tasks in grade one involve number concepts (just what are numbers anyway?) adding and subtracting (up to ten), counting money (a quarter plus a nickel equals?), constructing patterns with objects and numbers (1, 0, 2, 0, 3, 0 . . . what's next?), measurement (how many metres to the blackboard?) and learning about geometric shapes. All this will take up about a quarter of the day. Techniques for teaching mathematics have changed considerably in the past thirty years, with the emphasis greater now on "concepts" such as size, measurement and problem solving. Rote counting, paper-and-pencil drills and memorization of addition and subtraction facts still take place, but more time is now spent developing a general "math sense." We wanted to find a good math exercise to show you what grade one students are doing, but most involved folded paper or colouring or block work—none of which we could reproduce on a page. Next chapter we'll have more visual examples.

Science, social science, history, geography. It seems strange to use sophisticated subject names when talking about the content subjects in a grade one curriculum, but they really do apply. Your child will work on a number of theme units (common choices: "Animals," "Native People," "The Farm," "Seasons") that develop basic concepts in science, history and geography. Often these are integrated with the reading program, so the grade one day looks quite seamless. In fact, your child's teacher is following a set of provincial guidelines and a specific curriculum set down within your board or school.

Teachers will probably plan field trips to places like the zoo, or a farm or a local museum as part of these units. There may be a nominal charge for these outings (frequently subsidized by the school), but don't refuse permission to your child to go along just because family finances are tight. If you can be honest about your financial situation with the teacher or principal, most schools have funds to make sure your child can take part in special events at no cost to you. These trips are an important part of learning and provide material about which your child can write. The trips are also a great opportunity for you to get involved as a trip helper. Generally, these trips are planned far enough ahead for you to make the necessary arrangements to take a day off or find a sitter to help out with children at home. You'll have an opportunity on the trip to observe your child with his friends and peers and to see how the teacher handles day-to-day problems. You'll also have a great time.

When the field trip is over, the teacher will use the experience to lead the kids into books, filmstrips, videos and magazines at the school's resource centre. Grade one children are taught the skills necessary to find many of these materials on their own, often by using the library computer. The final outcome is usually writing, drawing or a presentation of some kind, and you may well be involved in getting it ready. There's nothing wrong with helping your child to organize her booklet, or proofread her writing, or practise her presentation. In fact, your involvement shows just how important it is to do top-quality work for school. Just avoid taking over the whole project yourself. Sara needs you for inspiration and spelling and practice. She needs you to set up a time to work at the project, or start up the computer, or buy the coloured paper. Sara doesn't need Mom and Dad showing off how much *they* know about dinosaurs.

Art, music, physical and health education. Art development in young children shows a great deal about how they see the world and parallels their development in reading and math. Often the

By the End of Grade One: In Language Arts

By the end of grade one, most children will be able to . . .

- recall and retell information or a story;

- ask questions about new words or ideas;

- take part in conversations and discussions without baby talk;

- recognize that reading must make sense;

- know and name the letters of the alphabet;

- recognize commonly used words (total sight vocabulary runs 500 to 1,000 words);

- know the sounds represented by most single consonants (phonics);

- read familiar, predictable books for herself;

- use context, pictures, prediction and phonics clues to figure out new words;

- use letters and words to label and write down ideas, messages and stories;

- spell some frequently used words correctly;

- use consonants and simple vowels to write new words (e.g., *snd* for sound, *travld* for travelled).

On the Value of Homework

Even in grade one, homework can be...

- an indicator of status, of becoming a real student;

- a reminder of interesting learning experiences in school;

- a way to reinforce concepts, to practise and make automatic such things as the addition tables or counting money;

- a way of communicating between school and home about what's going on in class;

- a good alternative to the parent's question "What did you do in school today?" and the sometimes mumbled response, "Nuthin'." Asking "What work did you bring home for us today?" provides a better focus and better information;

- a chance to develop a habit that gives structure of some of a child's after-school life, like regular mealtimes, daily reading together and bedtime routines;

- an opportunity to learn the importance of applying work to a task.

art activity can provide a focus for interesting discussions between the teacher and your child, as well as a rehearsal of ideas that she may want to write down. A solid grade one art program gives Sara a chance to try out a wide variety of materials like clay, Plasticine, paint and papier-mâché. There should be some talk about different ways of expressing ideas through colour, shape and texture—often motivated by the beautifully illustrated picture books in the classroom and library. As in any good school program, art isn't just an isolated subject, but part of the larger program in reading and theme units.

In a similar way, a good music program is connected to the rest of the curriculum. Your child will still learn little songs by rote, but also spend time developing skills in rhythm and movement. Music is connected here with patterns in mathematics and with small-muscle skills in physical education.

The physical and health education program in grade one takes in fitness, cooperative play, large- and small-muscle development and the idea of wellness. While most children love to run and play—and do so with seemingly limitless energy—there are still parents who protect their children to the point that they are reluctant to participate in physical activity. Phys. ed. will assist in turning this around. And every parent can help their children by making physical activity part of family life—walking, hiking, biking—and packing healthy food for lunch.

Homework in Grade One

When children start "big school" they have expectations about it that are sometimes not fulfilled. One of these is about homework. Your child may have seen older brothers and sisters sitting down doing homework and been shooed away because they needed to concentrate and the work was important. Young children learn from this what school is supposed to be like and often can't wait to do important things like homework for themselves.

A good school provides it. There is no reason why five- and six-year-olds can't take part in some well-designed, pressure-free activities at home to reinforce the learning that takes place in the classroom. There are any number of advantages in doing so, from developing work habits, to showing the importance of school, to letting you know what's going on in class. In most schools, there is probably a homework policy in writing that you can ask to see. With a good teacher, homework activities should be much more than just simple review and practice on photocopied sheets of paper. Effective homework gives parents and children a chance to talk about what the child is learning and apply that learning to bigger tasks. You should be able to expect some of this for your child as early as grade one.

Speaking with the Grade One Teacher

You will be invited into the school at least twice during the grade one year to meet with your child's teachers. These meetings are important, especially so if you do not spend any other time in the school. At these meetings, it will be possible to have some substantive discussions about your child and her capabilities in school.

The first meeting is ordinarily in October or November, either before or after the first report card. Increasingly, these report cards are "anecdotal," meaning that the teacher offers written comments without any of the traditional letter or number grades. For parents, such reports can be frustrating—especially so if the teacher has used benign language to disguise real problem areas. Other report cards use checklists or ratings like "not seen," "developing" and "highly developed"

Some Points for the First Parent-Teacher Interview

You need some honest information—and should also be offering the same—about your child. So here are a few questions to get you started.

- How is Sara getting along with the other children?

- Have you noticed any special problem areas for her?

- Sara is having a problem with Johnny B. Can she be moved?

- Have you seen Sara's special ability in reading/writing/math/gymnastics?

- Did you know that Sara is busy after school with Brownies?

- Is there anything more that we can do at home?

Homework Calendar for Grade One

This is a sample of a February calendar. Parent and child are asked to take on three of the five activities each week.

Week 1

M: A genie has granted you a wish. Write a story about how you'll use it.

T: Math problems.

W: Print five words that have "oo" in them.

Th: Read a book about something red.

F: Write a menu with your favourite food.

Week 2

M: Do five sets of ten jumping jacks. Count them out.

T: Using a rule, measure the length of your shoe, hand and thumb.

W: Read a story from the newspaper.

Th: Make a Valentine for someone special.

F: Write a poem and read it to someone.

to describe your child's skills. This first parent-teacher meeting is a chance to talk face-to-face about your child and make sense of what's on these report cards. Teachers frequently have more confidence telling you about problems in person—"I'm afraid Sara's having real trouble with counting money"—than they are in writing such information down on a permanent record.

It is foolish to expect a teacher after two months of school to be able to discuss Sara's achievement in detail, or to tell you how Sara ranks compared with the other students in grade one. These more specific questions should be saved for your second parent-teacher meeting, usually scheduled after the second report card in February. This is the meeting to ask whether Sara might be gifted, or need special help. This is the meeting to discuss whether or not the reading program seems to be working. And this might be a meeting where the teacher could really tell you how well Sara is doing compared with her peers.

What About the Not-so-good School, the Not-so-good Teacher?

In any given year, your child probably has a fifty-fifty chance of ending up with a teacher who isn't terribly good for her or in a classroom that doesn't really meet her needs. Your child and her learning will both suffer. Try as you might through parent-teacher conferences and gentle persuasion, there may be little you can do immediately to improve the school or teacher in question. So what can you do as a parent to help your child?

Maintain enthusiasm for education. Even if the particular school or teacher may not warrant much approval, you have to keep up your enthusiasm for learning or Sara will lose her natural enthusiasm. As parents and educators, we have seen assignments and lessons that are enough to make us cringe—but children can still profit from these if given enough support at home.

Try to make up for what is missing. If your child's school has thrown out phonics in some misguided understanding of the concept of whole language, spend some time on phonics at home. This doesn't necessarily mean you must pay $19.95 for a phonics instruction kit you see advertised in a magazine (or over $200 for Hooked on Phonics), but it might mean you spend a little of your family reading time breaking down the big words in a way that can be fun. If your child's school has no money for field trips, then you should make a point to take your child to the museum or the travelling dinosaur exhibit.

Get some help. You can sometimes get alternative textbooks from parents who have children in other schools, or even from board administrators at the level beyond the school. Some bookstores sell learning materials appropriate for home schoolers, which parents can use to augment a weak school program. In later grades, professional tutoring is sometimes an option. At the grade one level, it probably makes more sense to turn a bad school year into a great personal learning year—a year to take up Suzuki violin, or sing in a choir, or enrol in a weekend activity program at the museum, or start a personal reading program at the library.

And work to fix what's wrong at your child's school. Reread chapters 3 and 4, then take the steps necessary to improve education for the children who will follow yours. Not-so-good teachers need help to improve, or pressure to leave the profession. Not-so-good schools frequently need a new administration and some dynamic staff people. Your child and future children at the school deserve your action to make this happen.

Week 3:

M: Make a chart and record the high temperature for each day.

T: Visit the public library and check out two different types of books.

W: Act out a part of a story.

Th: Tell Mom or Dad about the funniest book you've read this month.

F: Count and write the numbers from 51 to 101.

Week 4

M: Put five new words in alphabetical order.

T: Tell Mom or Dad how we made pancakes in class.

W: Math problems: Take your collection of cars or dolls and sort it into

sets. Explain to Mom or Dad how you sorted them.

Th: Listen to a piece of music and clap your hands to the beat.

F: Look in the mirror and count your teeth. Then draw a picture of them.

CHAPTER 8

Grades Two and Three

Michael is entering grade two now—and you think things are getting easier. He seems to enjoy school and has made a whole group of friends, both boys and girls, whom he sees at school and sometimes plays with after school and on weekends. At age seven, he's showing all sorts of confidence you didn't see a year or two ago: he wants to go to school by himself or with a friend; he wants to tie his own shoes and print his own letters; he wants to read to you—to show just how good he's getting. But Michael is still fairly easy to deal with. You can distract him from an urgent need for some new Nintendo game with the promise of a Popsicle. You can tell him "No, you can't sleep over at James's house two nights in a row" with no real complaints. By now Michael is beyond temper tantrums, constant head colds and all the other irritations of early childhood and you ought to be enjoying two very good years.

In school, grades two and three are called the end of the "primary" grades, a term that goes back to the Middle Ages, when students studied the *primarium*, a collection of prayers, hymns,

Games for Family Reading Time

Of course you'll want to spend a lot of your family reading time doing just that—reading. But here are some valuable activities to give variety.

- Tell a story. A family monster is a good bet. A story with your child as the central character always works well.

- Trade a page. "I'll read one page and you read one page. Deal?"

- Hot dog. Throw in a silly word every so often—"hot dog" is one; "dirty ratzumfatz" is another. Your child will cry out, "No, Mom, it's—" and then fill in the blank. An easy way to see if he's following along.

- Join in. Many easy-reading books have a repeated set of words. Ask your child to join in, or to "read" a favourite story along with you.

psalms and lives of the saints. When the English king Edward VI issued the first nationwide ABC in 1545, it was in response to the same cries for standards that we read about today; nor were the kids very different in their response to educational innovation. Primary students would be given a "horn book" to aid their studies, basically a wooden paddle supporting a single printed page covered with a thin sheet of horn to protect the paper. Students quickly learned that their horn books were effective weapons going to and from school and suitable for all sorts of batting games in those days long before baseball.

Your Michael will probably never see a horn book in his entire life, but that doesn't mean that what happens in our computer-assisted, high-tech schools is much different from education in schools throughout history. The tasks are the same—learning to read, write, do math, understand geography and history and our culture—only our educational tools have changed. A child who is encouraged at home, who is supported by parents who devote a little time every day to reading and school work, who is fortunate enough to have a good teacher—that child will master the essentials for further learning in these two years, whether he has the Macintosh advantage or just a pencil.

What Actually Goes On in Grades Two and Three

Reading. Development of reading skills is the single most important task in grades two and three. Why? Because our society expects every student to have mastered the rudiments of reading by age nine. Collectively, we'll make allowances for weak math skills, or the inability to read a map, or failure to master the F-major scale, but we panic when a child "can't" read at the end of grade three. The truth, of course, is that children learn different skills at different rates. There is no particular advantage in Michael's learning to read at age four and five rather than at age seven or eight (schools in the most literate country on earth, Finland, don't even *begin* formal reading instruction until age seven). And even students who say they "can't" read at age nine usually "can" read a great deal that they find useful or interesting, but won't bother with boring reading textbooks.

Nonetheless, teachers and schools pay attention to public expectations. Michael's grade two teacher will read daily with the children from a variety of mostly picture books—Dr. Seuss to Franklin the Turtle to Curious George. By grade three, Michael and his class will be tackling longer "chapter books," like *Amelia Bedilia*, with fewer pictures and longer pages of text. Michael will be taken to the library once a week, or more often, to exchange books for personal reading.

Actual classroom practice in reading varies from school to school, from one section of Canada to another. The old practice of students reading out loud, stumbling over words while their classmates made fun of them, has thankfully been put aside by teachers. While this torture was a tremendous ego boost for the handful of good oral readers, it did much to permanently discourage many, many others. These days, reading is often done by the teacher, with children following along in their own books; or by volunteers with small groups; or by a reading buddy, who both reads and listens to Michael read.

Some schools are still using graded "readers" that set up a careful development of phonics skills and increasingly complex vocabulary in a systematic fashion. This approach has been popular since the sixteenth century because it takes the truly haphazard nature of learning to read and seems to make it sequential and scientific. The truth, unfortunately, is that our language is

One Kind of Shared Reading

Reading together out loud can give Michael confidence and help him to get the sound of print language in his ear. Select a book that he should be able to read and talk briefly about the story, using pictures and some of the key words. Explain that you'll read the book together and he can help you by reading with you as much of the story as he can.

Then start reading out loud at a normal pace, encouraging him to say the words along with you. After he gets the idea that he is not going to have to "perform the print" alone and that you really are going to read the story—not just the words—he'll relax and mutter along with you. If you keep the pace slow, you'll find Michael initiating words and saying them more clearly as you continue reading.

Your model of rhythm, intonation and expression will help Michael to focus on making the words make sense. This kind of reading together is much like the help you gave when he was trying to skate or to ride a two-wheeler. Eventually Michael will have to read, skate and ride by himself—but don't stop holding on too quickly, or he'll just fall down and get hurt.

In the Classroom: A Reading Centre

This is where a wide selection of interesting storybooks, "fact" books and collections such as basal readers are available. The books may be colour-coded by difficulty to help children select independently. Children should have many opportunities during the day to visit the reading centre to choose material, read alone or share material with a partner.

In the reading centre, there should be a number of books and pictures, even maps and charts, related to the theme that is currently being studied. Ideally, books that have been written, edited and "published" by children in the class should be available for others to read. Often the centre will include a carpeted, comfortable area where children may just sit and read. Some teachers include cushions, soft chairs or stuffed animals to enhance the cosiness of the setting and replicate the comfortable "nests" to which real readers retire to immerse themselves in a book.

too complex to be mastered in however many discrete lessons—and that real readers usually learn to read outside the lessons, not through them. Of course, there's much to be said for systematic reading instruction, including whole class instruction in phonics or word-attack skills or spelling. We'd far rather see that kind of planned activity in classrooms than no instruction at all. But parents and newspapers that make a fetish of phonics and "direct instruction" should remember that Rudolf Flesch's *Why Johnny Can't Read* became influential in 1955, but many Johnnies were no better off by the time he wrote *Why Johnny Still Can't Read* in 1981.

The competing approach, called "whole language," simply throws tons of print at a child, combining reading, writing and some specific skill development into units based on pieces of children's literature. This approach assumes that children are naturally curious, which they are, and that reading effort and attitude are more dependent on interesting material than on technical matters like syllable count and sentence length. To some extent this is also true. A good teacher in a whole-language classroom will probably get great tested reading scores from Michael and the other children. So will a good teacher using a phonics program.

What does matter in learning to read does not make headlines in the popular press—it's you, the parent. Statistically, the two most important factors in determining how well a child reads have nothing to do with school. They are the attitude of the parents toward reading and school and the amount of print material in the home. In looking at school reading programs around the world, we find that the particular type of instruction is much less important than other factors: educated teachers, access to school and community libraries, the amount of time spent by teachers reading aloud to children and the amount of time kids actually spend reading books. Many of the factors that seem so important to the newspapers—class size, age of first reading instruction, the specific reading program, length of the school year, frequency of testing—just don't make any difference at all.

Language arts. "Language arts" covers everything else we do with words—writing them, speaking them, playing games with them, even animating them on a computer screen. In grade two, Michael will probably have mastered block-printing words, using upper- and lower-case letters. Then he'll go on to tell small stories using a vocabulary several steps ahead of his spelling, probably making a spelling, punctuation or grammar "error" every five words or so. Here's a sample of "good" grade two work:

In the Classroom: A Mathematics Centre

At this centre, materials related to old and new topics are set up. Equipment may include counters, tens and hundreds blocks, centimetre cubes, pattern blocks, attribute blocks, geometric solids, straws, toothpicks, measurement equipment, balances and play money. In addition, problem cards will be set out for independent and group activity.

Games and practise activities to develop automatic recall of number facts are included for individuals and partners. Children can learn valuable math skills from bingo, Monopoly and chess, just as children can pick up reading skills from playing the junior version of Trivial Pursuit.

Teachers try not to inhibit "creative spelling," and rightly so, because the urge to communicate in print shouldn't be stifled by an immediate necessity to get everything correct the first time. Nor should you be too insistent at home about correctness—at the first-draft stage. What's important, as early as grade two, is that your child learns to polish work before it gets handed in, to redo the "creative spellings" with our language's real words. In school, the emphasis will be on "writing process": brainstorming, outlining, writing the first draft, revising ideas, then rewriting and polishing up the work. Your job at home is both to encourage Michael and to make sure the writing process doesn't stop after the first draft.

Some schools make use of computers to help your child polish his work. As early as grade three, Michael may be using a computer spellchecker for some assignments, while he's still learning to use the dictionary on others. As reading has moved from picture books to chapter books, so writing has gone from simple, unformed quasi-sentences to real stories with real sentences. By the end of grade three, it's not unreasonable to expect that Michael will:

- spell most simple words correctly;

- know how to use a dictionary to look up words he doesn't know;

- use the period, question mark and exclamation point (sometimes many of them!!!) correctly.

One important, new development for Michael will be cursive writing, a skill that will increase his writing speed and lead, years later, to an illegible scrawl that will likely force him back to printing. Initial cursive writing is clumsy and difficult to read, but most children enjoy sticking out their tongues in effort and working hard to develop this adult skill. Teachers rarely teach penmanship anymore—as if there were ever only one way to hold a pen or make a z—so some of Michael's letters may well look bizarre. There's probably nothing wrong with this, since Michael later on is more likely to be producing reports and documents on a computer than in laborious longhand. Increasingly, our society is demanding keyboarding skills far more than beautiful handwriting—a boon for all of us with poor small-muscle control.

Here's a sample of grade-three writing on a dinosaur theme. It is one page from an eight-page illustrated project.

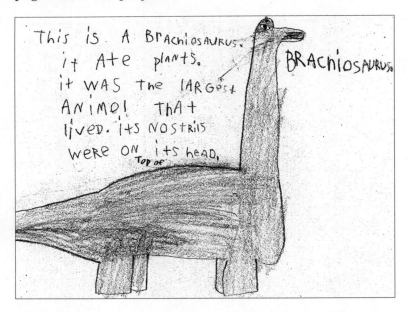

Mathematics. Math in grades two and three is a combination of creative ideas to develop math concepts and rote work to build the old, basic math skills. The creative ideas may well be in a special centre in the classroom: a table, some chairs and a range of equipment from blocks, straws, play money to balances, rulers and Cuisenaire rods. Good teachers start doing problem solving as early as grade two: If Jane has two apples and Rhoda has seven apples, how many do they have together? The problems get slightly more complex in grade three: If Jane has six apples and wants to give them away to her friends Tommy, Alex and Rhoda, how many apples should Jane give to each friend? Here's an example of average grade three work:

Date ___Dec.14___ **Volume**		
Find as many things you can that compare to 1 L.		
greater than 1L	**about 1L**	**less than 1L**
Ocean water table	Ice cream jar milk carten	mini milk carton
buket	measuring up	container
pool	jug	balloon mug
	Deanut butter jar	mouth cup
bath tub	Jam jar	
pond	Cokakola glass bottle	Soup can
sea	picter	marger in jar
river		Small bowl
lake	ketchapbottle	glass
sink	water bottle	tooth paste
fleecy bottle	Soup bottle	Yougart containers

Learning math "facts"—addition, subtraction, multiplication and division—is still a rote activity involving drills, memorization and repeated practice. In grade two, addition and subtraction are the big focus, up to ten; in grade three, multiplication goes up to ten times ten and division is introduced. The dull nature of all this can be spiced up with computer games, flash cards, contests and partners working together, but don't be surprised to see memorization and repetition as part of the homework. They're still important.

Despite the teacher's best efforts, Michael will probably never master mental calculation quite as well as you did, and certainly not as well as your parents did (a generation who learned tables up to twelves, fifteens and twenties by memory). The reason is simple: the calculator. In a calculator- and computer-based world, it's far more important for Michael to understand the *range* of a correct answer or the way to get to a solution than it is to do number crunching in his head. This doesn't mean that simple number facts like seven times six are unimportant, only that Michael won't be as fast at coming up with an answer as you were. Your parents may well shake their heads at declining standards for the upcoming generation; but Michael will be manipulating computer programs when his grandparents are reluctant to touch a keyboard.

Science, social science, history, geography. In grade two, emphasis stays pretty close to home in theme units around animals, baby animals, the community, seeds and plants. Other popular units involve the sun, the moon, planets and special holidays. It's gotten so that a gerbil, a terrarium and a baby chick in the spring are almost mandatory in the grade two classroom. Look in your child's classroom for an interest centre focussed on science or nature. At this centre there may well be magnifying glasses, microscopes, magnets, specimen jars and reference books that your child can use to pursue individual or group activities.

In grade three, Michael will start developing mapping skills, usually using the playground or neighbourhood around the school. Other frequent topics include the weather, transportation (yes, cars!), technology (yes, Nintendo!) and sometimes local geography. In history, topics such as pioneers and First Nations are sometimes begun in grade three—though some schools wait until grade four for these topics. Many English-speaking schools will begin a more systematic core French program in grade three, building vocabulary and conversation skill through practice. In grade two, French is often introduced using rhyme, stories, chants and pictures.

How to Read a Primary Report Card

Primary report cards rarely have marks anymore to let you know how your child is doing. Instead, the teacher writes "anecdotal comments" that can give you an honest portrait of how your child is doing—but only if you get by the public-relations language.

This may help:

- "has improved, but..." Your child was doing poorly, now is doing better, but still has a ways to go.

- "becoming aware of..." Your child hasn't figured out how to do something, but knows he should.

- "creative speller..." Your child spells poorly.

- "attention problems..." Your child wiggles during storytime.

- "some difficulty with other children..." Your child is a bully, or gets picked on by the other kids.

- "interactions are spirited..." Your child is causing trouble in the classroom.

- "difficulty dealing with authority..." Your child mouths off to the teacher.

- "progress has been disappointing in..." Your child just isn't learning this material.

What Your Child Should Have Mastered by the End of Grade Three

- Reading poems, stories, simple nonfiction and chapter books by himself.

- Practising reading a simple text silently, then being able to read it out loud clearly and smoothly.

- Interpreting pictures, simple maps and diagrams.

- Explaining clearly what he has read and making some inferences about it.

- Locating authors and topics in the resource centre.

- Writing ideas in simple sentences complete with capitals and periods.

- Recording ideas he has heard or thought about using lists, notes, important words and diagrams.

- Spelling commonly used words correctly and using phonics to help him record the sounds of less familiar ones.

Art, music, physical and health education. The primary art program is sometimes tied into the production of "books" containing Michael's stories, illustrated by the author. Michael will also paint using watercolours, draw people with some detail, use Plasticine and modelling clay, make block and potato prints of his own design and construct three-dimensional objects with paper and wood scraps. Music programs vary greatly in the early grades, depending on the expertise of the teacher. If Michael is lucky, and he's in a school where music is valued, he'll have lots of singing, rhythm activities, opportunities to see written music and listening experiences ranging from classical to folk. Any primary program should at least offer some work with percussion instruments; a strong music program will give opportunities to play recorders, synthesizers and other melodic instruments.

Grades two and three are excellent examples of why there should be daily physical activity—if not formal gym classes—for all students. Kids of this age abound in energy, and a program geared toward learning partner and group games is just the way to channel it. Ball skills, running and jumping, balancing, sequencing movements, moving to rhythms and music all develop physical coordination and fitness. Some schools also organize intramural games at this age, but real competitive sports should come later.

What You Can Do at Home

Your role when Michael is in grades two and three hasn't changed that much from when he first entered school. The most important task at school, and your most important time at home, is in developing reading. So let us reiterate the key point: *Keep on reading with your child every day.* The preposition "with" is very important here. Back when Michael was in kindergarten, you probably did most of your reading "to" him. Now he'll want to do a fair amount of reading to you, just to show off his developing skills. Chances are that your twenty to thirty minutes of daily reading at home will see Michael reading as much as you do. Just don't fall into the three traps that can snare parents of developing readers.

- ***Don't teach.*** It is not your job to teach phonics or word-attack skills; all that belongs in school. It is your job to encourage reading and the love of reading—by keeping family reading time fun and loving and stress-free. Mothers, especially, have a tendency to make children "sound out" words they don't know, a process that can interfere with the flow of the story. While there's nothing wrong with showing Michael how to sound out a word, or taking time out to look up a word in a dictionary, or stopping to talk about complexities in the plot—remember that the story comes first. Nothing could be worse for Michael's developing confidence than to have to work at every other word on the page, or answer comprehension-testing questions from Mom.

- ***Don't rush.*** Take your time listening to Michael read. Fathers, especially, have a tendency to rush through books without taking time to listen or talk. Remember that there is no set number of pages that have to be finished in family reading time. Nor is there any ideal speed for Michael to read out loud. Our rule of thumb is this: if Michael is still stumbling over a word after five seconds, help him out. Help him out faster if he looks to you for an answer, or if a word coming up is obviously too difficult for his skills. When you read aloud to Michael, slow down a little so he can follow along. You might purposely want to make a mistake every so often, just so he can "correct" you, instead of you always helping him out. You might want

- Reading, writing and comparing three-digit numbers.

- Adding and subtracting two- and three-digit numbers in real situations.

- Using addition and subtraction facts to eighteen and multiplication facts to the five times table.

- Naming and matching geometric shapes to real objects such as balls, boxes, cylinders.

- Constructing and using combinations of geometric shapes to create strong and interesting structures.

- Measuring using metres, centimetres, litres, kilograms.

- Telling time to the nearest five minutes.

- Making change up to a dollar.

- Making picture or bar graphs to collect and explain information.

- Using different ways to solve problems in every subject.

Rule of Thumb ✏]
Avoid the split-grade class.

In many schools, some teachers will teach a split-grade class. There will be, for example, two teachers who have straight grade twos and one teacher with a split grade two-three.

Everything else being equal, choose one of the straight grade twos. The teacher will be under less stress, the lessons will be more coherent, there is less likelihood of bullying and behaviour will be more age-appropriate.

Two cautions. First, everything else is rarely equal. A split-grade class is not a terrible thing and, with a gifted teacher, can be a wonderful experience. Second, bright and mature children frequently do better in a split-grade class with older children than in a single-grade class with their agemates. If your child is going for a three-grade/two-year acceleration, than a split-grade class will be essential.

to use your finger to show where you are in the text, though this can be overdone. Remember how important it is to reread those favourite books of Michael's over and over again, even if they almost drive you crazy. It's the repetition that builds Michael's reading skills, even if you get bored.

- *Don't quit.* Some children develop quite fluent reading skills early on, but that's no excuse to stop family reading time. Just because your child can read many books to you or read along with a tape is no reason to stop your involvement. Try some more difficult books. Try some "information books" instead of reading stories all the time. Try telling stories instead of reading. But don't cut Michael off from your love and approval just because he's become a competent reader.

How to handle homework. There should be homework in grades two and three—math assignments, books to read, reports to write, projects to complete. It's probably a good time to start making use of that most successful tool for encouraging children's school work: the kitchen table.

The kitchen table is the perfect place for Michael to do homework because it keeps the two of you at a proper distance. Michael can work away at his assignment, tongue dangling, pencil firmly gripped, and you can be busy with something else. If Michael needs a quick answer, or more paper, or a marker, or help—you're right there. Even more important, if Michael wants approval for some great story he's written, or for those twenty math problems he's completed, you're there to offer praise.

Let us be clear. Michael does *not* need you to do the math homework, or look up the vocabulary words, or write out his story. As Miss Manners would say, we assume that you have already mastered the skills of grades two and three, so there should be no need for you to display your ability. Michael, however, is still working through his times tables and spelling lists: he needs time, repetition and praise. He doesn't need Mom or Dad to complete or correct his homework before it's turned in. He does need Mom or Dad close by to show how important homework time is and to be available for help if he gets stuck.

Your child's teacher probably has a homework policy or calendar to let you know when Michael will have work to do. If you haven't received one, ask for this information. Make Michael's homework time a part of your daily schedule, either right after school or right around supper. A little discipline will help you get over the "Aw, Mom, I'm too tired" or "Dad, I just want to go out and play" routines. Then set Michael up in the kitchen while you work on cooking or dishes or whatever. If you start Michael's homework habits early, the payoffs will be big later on.

Stay involved with the school. In the last chapter we talked about the importance of your involvement with the school. It certainly hasn't lessened any in grades two and three. If you have the time, find a way to volunteer. Always attend parents' nights and information evenings. Don't be afraid to call the teacher or the principal for information. Always call in when Michael is sick so the school secretary can let the teacher know when Michael is likely to return. Probably the biggest issue you'll have to deal with this year and in the next few years will be finding the best teacher for the *following* year and avoiding a split-grade class.

Remember that education is more than just schooling. The learning that takes palce in Michael's school is very important, but what happens outside can be just as valuable. Grades two and three, ages seven to ten, are the time to begin many outside activities that will enrich Michael's

Education is More than Just Schooling

Grades two and three are a fine time for:
- music lessons
- Suzuki violin
- the church choir
- Little League baseball
- soccer
- hockey or figure skating at the arena
- learning to swim
- 4-H Club, Young Farmers
- Scouting
- karate or judo lessons
- starting gymnastics
- ballet, highland, modern-dance lessons

life. Few schools, for instance, have a music program that can equal a weekly piano lesson, or Suzuki violin lessons, or singing in a church choir. Few schools have an athletic program that can compare with community gymnastics, or swimming lessons at the local pool, or basketball at the YMCA. Few schools have a civics program that can come close to regular attendance at church, temple or synagogue. Few schools have a nature program as good as Scouting or the 4-H Club.

For too many children these days, the time after school is a void to be filled with food, television, video games and unsupervised play. A recent survey in New York State, for instance, found that a quarter of the nine-year-olds there spent *six* hours a day watching television. Six hours! Surely there is something else for those children to do besides having their eyeballs glued to the set.

What we're seeing in schools in Canada is a real split between children who do very little learning outside of school and those who benefit from a wide range of activities and experiences. This doesn't mean that your child should be run ragged, dragged from practices to lessons with such incredible parental planning that there is virtually no time left for Michael to be just Michael. But we feel that every child can benefit from two or three organized activities outside of school—and that means you have to help set these up. As with almost everything else at this age, the payoff comes later on.

What if My Child Is in Trouble?

Teachers used to say that one child in twenty had some special difficulty that affected his learning at school and his development at home. A few years ago, that figure went up to one child in ten. Now, in some jurisdictions, teachers and social workers talk about 20 percent of the children in school needing some kind of special attention: gifted kids, reluctant learners, attention-deficit children, physically challenged students...the list is long.

Actually, we think that *every* child deserves some portion of a teacher's special attention, but we doubt that a fifth of the school population should be designated "special needs" cases. Many children go through ups and downs as they grow, suffering in school from childhood illnesses, family dislocations, divorce and increasing poverty affecting young families. A temporary setback of one kind or another is no reason to go running to your school principal to demand that Michael be tested for learning disabilities. But a parent should pay attention to children having difficulties. By grade two—and certainly by grade three—it is time to get professional help if you suspect your child is in trouble.

Let's go through the steps.

You probably already suspect there is a problem. Children with learning problems often show evidence of their difficulty in infancy. Some families, because of outside pressures to have a "perfect" child, will tend to ignore evidence right in front of their eyes. Don't. Some 15 percent of children have vision difficulties that require glasses; another 1 percent have hearing problems that will affect their ability to listen to stories and learn in school. About 5 percent of the student population have intellectual limitations that affect both their rate of learning and their capacity to master the material at school (see Chapter 13 for more details on this). A child who is intellectually challenged develops more slowly than others: walking at two, talking at three, struggling with addition at seven. Not every child who seems slow to tie his shoes is intellectually challenged, nor does every squirmy child suffer from ADD (attention deficit disorder), but a careful parent pays attention to the early signs of larger problems.

Danger Signs for Your Child

How can you tell when your child might be in need of special attention at school? Look for these signs.

Physical:
- squinting to focus
- inability to read signs at a distance
- failure to hear ordinary conversation
- slurred speech

Intellectual:
- frequent attention shifts in play or conversation
- difficulty listening when read to
- late development of walking, speech

Behavioural
- failure to make eye contact, to engage with other children and adults
- inability to cooperate with other children
- frequent periods of withdrawal, isolation
- aggressive attitude, bullying

Any of these are worth discussion with your child's teacher and your family doctor.

Learning Luggage

Good schools have built cooperative home reading programs into their primary grades in order to provide essential one-on-one daily practice and also to keep parents aware of the skill level and reading interests of their child. These programs generally have a tracking sheet where the child records what book and pages were read, to whom and a collective response to how it went. In some cases parents are encouraged to make comments or observations about the child's reading and interpretation. Parents who have the opportunity to be part of such a program should jump at the chance, but also be prepared to ask questions and discuss other strategies for helping their child at home.

A variation on this kind of program is one in which a book (or some other resource material) and a task card are brought home for the child to work on with the parent. This is not simply busywork that must be completed, but a chance for parents to work and learn cooperatively with their child. It will also give you an opportunity to observe the strategies and skills that your child uses when he's working. Often the materials are thematic and a number of these collections rotate through the class. They may arrive at home in a special backpack, a carry bag or a miniature suitcase; hence the name "learning luggage."

You should discuss your suspicions with your child's teacher—or listen seriously when she brings up the matter. Teachers have an opportunity to know how your child's behaviour at a given age level compares with that of many other children. You can make use of her experience and wisdom to get some perspective on whether Michael has a real learning problem, or whether he's going through a particularly tough time, or whether you're just worrying too much. If you want another opinion, the principal at your child's school will probably be willing to help. If any of you still have strong suspicion of a learning problem, call in the experts.

Get ready for testing and discussions that may last for several months. Depending on the nature of the problem, you and your child's school will call on a number of professionals for evaluation and guidance. In case of vision difficulties, the route will be through your family doctor to an ophthalmologist for glasses or eye exercise or sometimes corrective surgery. In case of hearing problems, the route will be through your family doctor to a medical audiologist or—if your school board can afford such staff—through your school principal to the board audiologist. Correction might be as simple as a new position in the classroom or as complex as wearing an FM receiver to amplify the teacher's speech.

Students with attention problems usually get a psychological evaluation either through the board or through your family doctor. Visits to a psychiatrist for possible medication (Ritalin is still the favourite prescribed drug, though some therapies now involve changing diets or establishing new family routines) can be arranged by your doctor. Often attention problems are short-term and disappear by adolescence, but that won't make school and childhood any easier for your child if you refuse to take action.

A "general learning disability" is probably the most serious and lasting problem for your child. GLD indicates below-normal mental functioning over a wide variety of skill areas, while SLD (specific learning disability) indicates problems in just one or two areas. In order to determine whether this designation applies to your child, an individual assessment is usually done by a board psychometrist. This person will use an intelligence test, often a WISC (Wechsler Intelligence Scale for Children), or an achievement test like the CTBS (Canadian Test of Basic Skills) to get an intellectual portrait of your child's strengths and weaknesses. The psychometrist will then make recommendations to you and your child's school about changes in the program.

You will be involved in one or more special meetings at the school before your child is designated for "special education." The actual process varies from province to province, but generally speaking, schools can take little action to offer special help to your child without first designating or identifying your child for special education. In the old days, schools could simply designate a child "retarded" or "handicapped" and place the child in a special class or school without consultation. That led to some real abuses and sloppy diagnosis of difficulties, so now the whole testing and consultative process takes months. It involves you, your child, your child's teachers, the special resource teacher at the school, the principal and often one or more school-system officials. The outcome of all this varies enormously. Sometimes your child will end up in the same classroom with a slightly modified program. Sometimes your child will be removed from class for an hour a day, or a day a week, for work with a different teacher. Sometimes the recommendation will be for a special class to deal with your child's difficulties—though more and more parents fight this approach and prefer to "mainstream" their child in the neighbourhood school. We discuss all of these options more fully in Chapter 13.

What If My Child Is Just Fine?

Then this is a golden age. From grade two to grade six, ages seven to eleven, most children are healthy, loving, curious about life and happy to be in school. The diseases and diaper distresses of early childhood are over, the acne and irritation of the teenage years yet to begin. For your child, the whole world is opening up. You are still an important part of that world; so is your child's school. The basic habits of reading and study that you begin now will prove important for the rest of your child's life, so don't neglect them. Then take the time to enjoy the rest of your child's expanding universe: take pictures, shoot a video, make an audio tape. These are years to remember fondly.

CHAPTER 9

Grades Four, Five and Six

These are the middle school years: grades four, five and sometimes six. In most of Canada, children are halfway through elementary school, not even thinking about junior high, not even close to the problems of adolescence. According to researchers, these are also peak learning years. After the intellectual groundwork has been set in the primary school years, your child is capable of assimilating facts, skills and ideas faster now than ever again in her life. A good school and a skilled teacher will take advantage of your child's natural curiosity to create a program that is rich, exciting and stimulating.

But let's put a caution up front: your child has a greater chance of getting a weak teacher in middle school than at any other time in her school career. Why? Because of the nature of teachers and the way elementary schools work. There is more fulfilment for many teachers in teaching the primary grades, where essentials like reading and math skills are developed and the kids are almost uniformly adorable. There's a real mystique surrounding the teacher who can deal with twenty-to-thirty squirmy little bodies and not only teach

Now We're in Grade Four

- nine years old

- is inconsistent in behaviour: both childish and mature

- objects to being treated like a baby

- is often impatient, but will practise to
perfect skills

- is into many activities—sports, clubs,
lessons, collecting

- is curious about many things

- has strong willpower, developing self
control

- can self-evaluate

- wants greater independence, but needs
security at home and school

- can organize information, but has to
struggle to put it in words

- follows rules, but needs things to be
"fair"

- is strongly influenced by parents, not
so much by peers

them to read but turn them into real students. On
the other end of the spectrum, many teachers find
more intellectual stimulation in teaching senior
elementary grades, where the children are on a
rotary timetable and a teacher can specialize, to
some extent, in an area of interest like science,
music or geography. The teachers who don't fit
into either of these camps end up teaching the
middle grades, or less capable teachers are stuck
there by principals who know that one bad year
won't hurt a middle school child all that much. In
cautioning you about weak middle school teachers, we don't want to smudge the reputation of
thousands of excellent teachers at these grade levels, but we think you should know when to watch
out for your child.

Right across Canada, middle school brings in a
major expansion of the curriculum. Where the
primary grades really do emphasize reading and
mathematics, the middle school offers a much
broader curriculum, more evenly balanced
between various subject and skill areas. Reading
and math remain important, but so are history,
geography, French, social science, health and
physical education, art and music. In some
boards, the big "C" of Curriculum hits in middle
school with a thump—so teachers can be
required to spend some portions of their time on
everything from AIDS education to province-wide
testing to multicultural awareness week. The
resulting intellectual hodgepodge actually serves
the curiosity of the middle school student quite
well, but it may seem very fragmented and arbitrary to parents looking on from home.

Going into Grade Four

When your daughter Kyla enters grade four, she
is likely to be far more willful and independent
than she was in the primary school years. She
will certainly object to your treating her like a

baby—walking her to school, or helping her to read, or doing her homework for her. Her growing independence has both a charm and a value, but it is hardly secure. Kyla still needs you to organize study time, to make sure there's time every night so she can read to you, to drive her to those after-school activities that are an important part of her larger education.

Nine-year-olds like Kyla are frequently devoted to collecting and fairness. The former you can see in the collections of dolls, baseball cards, Lego sets and plastic models that line her bedroom shelves. The latter you'll hear anytime you step over the boundary of what Kyla thinks is fair, a definition she's arrived at through your example and by exchanging ideas at school and with her friends. If, for instance, all Kyla's friends go to bed at 9:30 or have allowances of two dollars, Kyla will find it most unfair that she must go to bed at 9:00 and gets only a dollar a week allowance, despite setting the table every night. The proper answer to this is something like "Too bad—every family sets its own rules"; and the wonderful thing about a nine-year-old is that such an answer is not only good enough, but exactly the kind of security she needs.

You'll find that Kyla can both work and play for longer periods of time, and much of that without parent supervision. We maintain that middle school children should mostly be in earshot when playing and always within eyeball distance when doing homework. That's because of a very definite impatience that Kyla will probably show, an impatience based on her own growing abilities and the fact that a good school challenges those right to the limit of frustration. You should be close by when that frustration point is reached—Kyla will need you.

When Kyla enters grade four, her teacher will make it abundantly clear that the expectations of middle school (sometimes called junior division)

From a Grade Four-and-Five Teacher's Daybook

January 3

8.30–9.15 Prep period.
Parent helper Bonnie E may come in.

9.15 Gr. 4-Begin multiplication.
Oral review, then p. 250, 251
5 x 1,10,100 double digit
4 x 1,10,100 double digit

9.55 Recess

10.10
Crystal, Brian need a note
Spelling, lesson 18
Library—book selection
Cursive writing A, B
Read aloud—*Swiss Family Robinson*

11.30 Lunch.
No duty this week.

12.30
Gr. 5s to library—research
Gr. 4s—read *Young Merlin*, intro to medieval times.
Personal time line; historical time line

1.50 Recess.
Tell kids to bring pencils.

2.05 Music.
Begin theory. Lines, spaces on paper.
Vocal.
Daily work journal.

2.45–3.05 Remedial

What Your Child Should Have Mastered by the End of Grade Four

- Reading short novels, with few illustrations (e.g., Abel's Island), on his own.

- Retelling a story with information about plot, characters and setting.

- Taking notes and recording information, though spelling is iffy.

- Explaining ideas to an audience in an informal setting.

- Writing legibly using cursive script, both stories and factual material.

- Using standard spelling for most simple words and able to look up others in a dictionary.

- Using simple punctuation: period, question mark, exclamation point, comma (erratically).

- Using decimal and whole numbers to hundredths

are very different from those of primary school. No longer will Ms. Jamieson have time to spend on the teddy bears and tug-of-wars and tears that were always coming up in the early grades. Grade four is going to be "hard work."

The truth is, the "hard work" of grade four is probably no more difficult than the work of grades two and three, but the form of it will be different. Information and activities won't be couched in terms of "fun" quite so much: reading will be to study a book or a particular subject; math will be to master a concept; drawing pictures will be in connection to a theme unit. For some children, the change in tone can be quite off-putting and may cause Kyla (and you) a few sleepless nights.

Counterbalancing the teacher's emphasis on hard work is the natural exuberance of nine-year-olds and their energy in practising things to get them right. Kyla will get a sense of satisfaction out of mastering rote activities such as math tables and spelling, and enjoy using these skills to get on with the real work of problem solving.

Reading. In grade four, Kyla has moved from "learning to read" to "reading to learn." Most schools assume that children have learned the basics of reading in grade three, sometimes already assigning special education help to children who have fallen too far behind. The basics, of course, are really limited to a sight vocabulary of about three thousand words and mastery of a few dozen essential phonics rules—about the level of skill a child needs to handle *Amelia Bedilia*. This is certainly not the level that would be required to tackle *Charlotte's Web* independently, nor is it sufficient to deal with, say, daily newspapers, which have a reading difficulty ranging from a grade six level for a typical news story to a grade eleven level on the sports and editorial pages. Since a competent adult reader has a sight vocabulary of over a hundred thousand words and a mastery of the language that far exceeds phonics, we feel that Kyla and other grade three students have a long way to go in developing their reading skills. Most schools and school systems do not.

Actual time spent reading drops from a third of the school day in grade three to not quite a quarter of the day in grade four. One reason is that the rest of the curriculum has crowded reading out; another reason is that more sophisticated reading is hard to "teach," though the skill certainly improves with practice. In the absence of further teaching of reading, actual reading becomes either a tool for studying a particular novel or reading a textbook, or it becomes a filler to be used at late afternoon. No wonder a quarter to a third of the children in grade four turn off reading, a phenomenon we called the "grade four reading slump" in our companion book *The Reading Solution*. For this group of reading dropouts, reading progress continues at a half rate until, by grade eight, they average two years of development behind their peers. Only regular reading at home, if it is absent in school, can protect your child should she fall into the grade four reading slump.

In a good school, reading for pleasure continues in grade four, often with special attention to junior novels like *Tales of a Fourth Grade Nothing*, *Anne of Green Gables* or *Mama's Gonna Buy You a Mockingbird*. Often a teacher will continue the practice of reading out loud to a class, because no other technique is quite as effective in bringing a book to life for students. The library of a good school will provide many other books for Kyla to read as well: fantasy, nature, adventure, sports, romance, the childhood classics. An effective elementary school reading program encourages—if not demands—that middle school readers read a book a week. Sometimes the teacher will

- Comparing fractions, decimals, whole numbers.

- Adding and subtracting three-digit numbers and decimals.

- Multiplication facts to nine times nine.

- Multiplying by three digits, dividing by one digit.

- Creating two-dimensional and three-dimensional shapes.

- Estimating measurements in metres and centimetres.

- Estimating mass in kilograms, capacity in litres.

- Using different problem-solving techniques in math and science.

- Using a system of charts or graphs to collect data.

call for a response (a book report or survey sheet or interview with a character), sometimes not, but reading for pleasure will remain part of the program. If not, that's all up to you at home.

Language arts. Reading is only part of language arts. In grade four, the emphasis turns to writing, both in the classroom and the library. A good library program will offer your child a variety of materials such as videos, filmstrips, magazines, pictures, CD-ROM, encyclopedias, atlases and reference materials, as well as books. Effective teacher-librarians will show your child how to access these for research and report writing. Librarians often teach in tandem with the regular classroom teacher to help students develop the ability to write longer essays and stories. Unfortunately, many schools are cutting back on the provision for a full-time librarian—a budget-cutting decision that leaves the school without an important curriculum leader and may leave your child without regular access to the library. Protest—loudly—if this happens in your jurisdiction.

Here are two pages from a twelve-page project by a "good" grade four student.

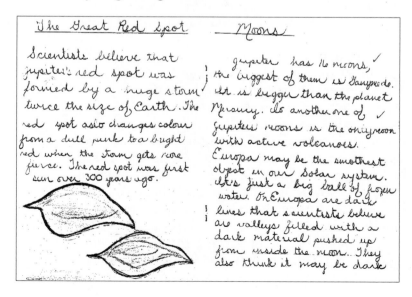

The Great Red Spot

Scientists believe that Jupiter's red spot was formed by a huge storm twice the size of Earth. The red spot also changes colour from a dull pink to a bright red when the storm gets more fierce. The red spot was first seen over 300 years ago.

Moons

Jupiter has 16 moons, the biggest of them is Ganymede. It is bigger than the planet Mercury. Io another one of Jupiter's moons is the only moon with active volcanoes. Europa may be the smoothest object in our Solar system. It's just a big ball of frozen water. On Europa are dark lines that scientists believe are valleys filled with a dark material pushed up from inside the moon. They also think it may be dark

Spelling continues to be taught in many schools through the middle grades, despite press reports to the contrary and some question about its value in a world of computer spell-checkers. The truth is, spelling is probably the only subject area where the whole idea of language can be explored—its roots, its rules, its history, its development—in a way that will be fun for a nine-year-old. A good teacher can turn a spelling lesson into everything from a window on history to a workshop in how the human mind works, and still satisfy the fourth grader's need for practice and immediate success. So much of the value in this, as in everything else, depends on the quality of your child's teacher.

Ideally, spelling and specific writing skills are tied into theme units that connect to other aspects of the curriculum. Grade four students are expected to get beyond the rudimentary writing of the primary years to produce relatively complete paragraphs and sometimes to produce whole books or reports on a topic. These will likely be illustrated and done partially at home. Be prepared to help.

Mathematics. Math instruction and practice generally get slotted in for about forty minutes of the school day. Materials such as attribute and pattern blocks, puzzles, mirrors, geometric solids, balances and other measuring equipment are essential to the learning of mathematical concepts. The use of all these naturally takes time, and so some parents get anxious that their child should be concentrating more on the rules or patterns of mathematics—that famous 'rithmetic of the three Rs.

Not so. The problem with 'rithmetic was always its tendency to trivialize an important set of concepts (size, shape, number, various relationships, manipulations) into an overly simple set of drills (add, subtract, multiply, divide). No

Spelling: Why It's Still a Good Thing

While there are some overly liberal educators who regard spelling as some kind of tyranny, we don't agree. Regular spelling lessons do much more than teach spelling (in fact, "spelling" is rather iffy in developing long-term spelling improvement). Regular spelling lessons...

- reinforce previous word-attack and phonics skills;

- teach the few spelling rules in English that mostly work ("i before e except after c..." and give a sense of what kind of words had better be looked up;

- give a chance for word play—fun and games with our language;

- give a chance to teach history, linguistics, social conventions and sometimes foreign languages—depending on the skill of the teacher;

- provide short, easy writing exercises;

- develop vocabulary, especially through work with synonyms and antonyms;

- provide a sense of accessible "mastery" for those kids who need it;

- teach common word errors (to, too, two) in a way that can be fun;

- say that spelling is an important real-life skill, which it is, even in these days of computer spell-checkers.

wonder so many adults are at a dead loss when confronted with algebra or trigonometry or using a computer spreadsheet. Good teaching these days will equip Kyla with an appropriate number of math "facts," but also help her conceive of ideas, problems and relationships that connect math to the real world.

International comparisons indicate that one important emphasis for math teaching should be in solving problems. While our kids are still working on times tables, Japanese kids are figuring how fast a boat can move downstream. Canadian teachers are still trying to catch up on this. Some schools have developed family math programs that will involve you as a participant and partner in working on math problems at home. Even if there isn't a formal program, you should still be close by when your child is working on his mathematics homework. Rote work isn't worth much of your attention, but more sophisticated math problems must sometimes be talked through with your child. Here's a sample problem and an average answer from a grade four student:

Animal	Mass in Kilograms	To the nearest 10	To nearest 100
Deer	177 ✓	180 ✓	200 ✓
elephant	6387 ✓	6390 ✓	6400 ✓
Hippo	2341 ✓	2340 ✓	2300 ✓
kodiak Bear	768 ✓	770	800
Moose	364 ✓	360	400
Rhino	3562 ✓	3560	3600
Walrus	1753 ✓	1750 ✓	1800 ✓

Animal	Thousand		
Rhino	4000 ✓		
elephant	6000 ✓		
hippo	2000 ✓		

Project work, science and the social sciences.
Kyla will spend about forty minutes a day, or
more, investigating topics in history, social science, science, the environment and other contemporary issues. Grade four is sometimes the
first year for heavy-duty project work: science-
fair projects, history or civilization displays,
sometimes experiments in plant growth. These
projects will begin in school with readings and
discussion, then come home for final work on the
project or presentation. Often these projects are
done in groups, so you may well have two or
three young people busy with cardboard and glue
sticks at your house on Saturday morning. You'll
have a natural urge to help out—which is fine—
just resist the tendency to take over.

French. In many school districts in Canada, the
study of French becomes a daily subject for
English-speaking schoolchildren in grade four.
Conversely, French immersion students begin to
study and write in English at about the same
time. Elementary school French programs have
not been an unqualified success in English
Canada because the kids who didn't take French
immersion sometimes have parents who undercut
the value of the French program. This is a shame.
As a parent, you do not have to speak French to
Kyla to help her build her language abilities, but
you should be willing to listen. And never, ever
indicate that mastering Canada's other language
is lacking in value; Kyla will internalize your offhand redneck attitude much faster than she'll
learn the *passé composé*. Students in many other
countries master not only their own language, but
two other languages that may not even be spoken where they live. Surely in a bilingual country
like Canada we should expect all our young people to read and speak more than a smidgen of
the other official language.

How to Help Your Child with Projects

The first step is to read over the assignment sheet with your child so that you *both*
understand what's called for. Then discuss
the topic in general terms to find out what
your child already knows about it.

Some schools ask children to make a
chart or "web" to explore areas for research. If so, encourage your child to make
one. If not, talk to her about organizing
the research and presentation.

Allow a day or more for your child to
reflect before beginning work on the project.

Help your child access the material
that's needed to do the research or prepare
for the presentation of the project (e.g., go
to library, buy cardboard, markers, etc.).

Then leave your child alone. After
all, it's not *your* project.

When most of the work is done, volunteer to help as an editor, advisor or test
audience. Be gentle with suggestions—
writers are often thin-skinned. Remember
that the goal is not perfection, it's learning.

How to Read a Middle School Report Card

Don't expect the report card to tell you how well your child is doing in comparison with other children. More often the marks are "criterion referenced" (How well does Kyla do what I ask her to do?) and not "norm referenced" (How well does Kyla do in comparison with the average child?). A teacher can usually give you an estimation of this, but only if you ask.

Some report cards include as many as forty different items—attitudes, achievement, outcomes, work habits, etc. These take teachers up to an hour each to prepare and make for a parental nightmare. Try to sort out what counts ("reads with understanding," "applies problem-solving strategies") from what doesn't.

On the left side of the report you'll find listed a number of subjects or skills or attitudes, not all of which will apply to your child. Look for a description of the subjects on the back or in fine print.

On the right side you'll find the grades, one for each subject, or skill, or outcome. Most middle schools use letter grades. At one time, C was average. These days, the ordinary student tends to get a B, the very good and excellent students get As and C might well indicate a problem in effort or attitude. Only serious problem areas get marks of D, E or F. See the teacher.

Physical education, health, music and art. Often middle school students have each of these subjects for two or possibly three periods a week. Depending on the resources of your school and school board, some of these may be handled by a specialist teacher. Your child Kyla may find this variety either exciting or worrisome, depending on her ability to adjust to different teaching styles and on the quality of the teachers involved. As your child gets older, the necessity of teachers who specialize in a subject area keeps increasing. In grade four, it's still possible for a single teacher to handle most of the activities in these more specialized fields. By grade seven, when Kyla has moved from the recorder to the trombone, from markers to oil paints, she'll benefit from the expertise that a specialist teacher can bring.

What Happens in Grades Five and Six

When Kyla goes into grades five and six, she'll be in the last years of childhood before adolescence. For girls, especially, this is a time of rapid physical growth and the beginning of sexual maturation. Kyla will likely become more awkward playing with boys, just as boys tend to retreat to their same-sex peers for play. No one knows if this pattern of behaviour is caused by society or by nature, but it certainly happens. Unfortunately, other kinds of sex-role stereotyping also take place, so many girls suddenly lose interest in math, while some boys lose interest in any book that's not about sports or cars. Neither of these are natural, and both can be counteracted with good teaching and good parenting.

In grade five, the program becomes quite demanding. The day includes virtually the same allotment of time to various subject areas as we outlined for grade four, and there may still be time for the teacher to read aloud, but the nature of instruction tends to become more rigid in these years. While it might be acceptable in grade three or four not to get through all the pages in the math book, by grades five and six teachers have a feeling that every inch of the curriculum just has to be covered.

This can be a problem for some children, perhaps for yours. If Kyla requires a great deal of discussion and some time to work through her ideas, she'll often find the pace of grades five and six doesn't allow for this. Many teachers simply present ideas in the form of a lesson or in print and then give a number of written assignments related to the content. In the worst cases, the program ends up looking like a correspondence course, with the teacher responding to students only after work has been completed. All this can be compounded in many provinces, because elementary school finishes at the end of grade six and junior high school or high school looms on the horizon. Teacher panic at this prospect sometimes augments child panic—an urge to tie up the loose end of elementary school learning before moving on to the next division.

Our response is simple: school level and grade divisions are highly arbitrary. While it is not true, as Robert Fulgham suggests, that everything you need to know you learned in kindergarten, it is true that the teaching methods that worked in kindergarten and the early grades also work quite well later on. Involvement, investigation, discussion, creative play, independent exploration of a wide variety of books and other materials—all these techniques work as effectively as the dull "lesson-homework" model. The threat of junior high school is no excuse for lousy teaching.

Language arts. By grade five, reading has ceased to be a subject in and of itself. Books in class are not read so much as studied, hence a division develops between intensive work on a handful of "core" novels at school and a kind of lip-service

What Your Child Should Have Mastered by the End of Grade Five

- Making a brief formal presentation: a speech or report.

- Reading novels of more than 100 pages, without illustrations.

- Writing reports of a page in length, stories of two pages (spelling and paragraphing will often be iffy).

- Editing his own writing to improve spelling, grammar.

- Recording information in notes using cursive writing, diagrams.

- Reading widely on his own: magazines, books, parts of the newspaper.

- Using whole numbers up to 99,999.

- Adding, subtracting and multiplying simple fractions.

- Adding, subtracting, multiplying and dividing decimals.

- Understanding and naming angles, shapes.

- Using systems of measurement for area, volume, mass, speed, money, temperature and time.

- Collecting and organizing data using charts, graphs, etc.

paid to the virtues of reading at home. For children whose parents value reading and preserve time for it to happen, grades five and six will see the kids polishing off a book or two each week, often including some adult science fiction, fantasy or horror novels. For children whose parents don't care much, the three mandatory book reports will be repeated each year until grade ten—on the same three books—while real outside reading will give way to *Wrestlemania* magazine or the television set. If you want Kyla in the first group, make sure that family reading time continues.

The core novels studied in grades five and six vary from province to province, school to school. Some of the popular titles include *A Wrinkle in Time*, *The Root Cellar*, and *The Lion, the Witch and the Wardrobe*. Often the teacher begins by reading a chapter or two out loud, but further reading will be done silently at school and at home. Class discussion leads into various kinds of writing activities, from reader-response logs, to character diaries, to time lines, to character sketches, to rewritten endings. These assignments will vary in length (50 to 300 words) and presentation (handwritten to computer printed) depending on the teacher. Here's a sample of average (B level) grade six writing on a "reader-response" assignment.

> Dear Mrs. Robins
>   This fantastic book is called <u>The House With a Clock in its Walls</u>. I'm not quite sure why I liked the book but it has excitment all the way through the book. I found that unlike most books this book had a short climax. At some points in the story I felt as if I were feeling the same way the characters did. I think that is the reason this book was so scary. This book was the kind that you just have to keep on reading because it is so exciting. This book had a lot to do with magic, I liked that.

In middle school, students should learn that writing always proceeds by stages. Teachers refer to this as "the writing process" and are supposed to apply it to writing in every subject area. Classroom teachers are expected to allow enough time for each of these stages, as well as the "conferencing" and "peer editing" that come between them. Sometimes work at each of the stages will be assembled into a writing folder, taking some of the emphasis off the finished work.

The good news about this shift toward process over product is that students are far less likely to hand in "one-draft wonders" than in years past. The bad news is that writing process takes up a great deal of class time to accomplish in school what used to be started in school and finished at home. The net result is that fewer projects and essays are expected of students. Parents still have a role in supporting the writing of their children, but don't be surprised to hear your child tell you, "We're doing the editing in class, so I don't need your help." You'll have to respect the process— but *do* eyeball the finished work before it gets turned in. Student editors frequently turn a blind eye to what any adult would find an egregious error or omission.

Mathematics. Grades five and six math instruction becomes more individualized as students who excel widen the gap between themselves and their less competent peers. This tendency requires careful grouping of students to ensure that each child is being challenged and provided with the necessary help. Students will often start off with a large group lesson, then move to a small group for some problem-solving activity, then proceed to an individual or team project. For instance, Kyla's group might be involved in an ongoing evaluation and graphing of the running times for the school track team. This could be set up on a computer speadsheet, with opportunities

Now We're in Grade Six

- eleven years old

- is beginning a rapid growth spurt

- can persist in tasks to complete them

- can produce neat, well-organized work

- can see others' points of view

- is often an enthusiastic learner, interested in many topics

- has improved coordination and physical strength

- enjoys competitive games

- prefers to play with kids of the same sex

- resists authority—requires explanations for rules and decisions

- looks for opportunities to be with his friends

- can be argumentative

- is influenced by what peers are doing

- wants to be older and have more privileges

to update information, make personal-best comparisons and print out goal sheets for each student. Other students in the class might be keeping stats on their favourite sports teams and then spend some time each day making comparisons that require them to analyse the figures and draw some conclusions.

Textbooks will still play a large part in Kyla's mathematics program. The current ones are written with a technologically sophisticated generation in mind, offering problems that may be handled by computer. Use of the calculator is encouraged by many schools as early as grade four, when most of the arithmetic "facts" have been learned. By grade six, most teachers expect students to use a calculator to deal with large numbers or large decimal fractions, but it may be forbidden for simple arithmetic drills.

Here's a sample of typical grade six problem solving:

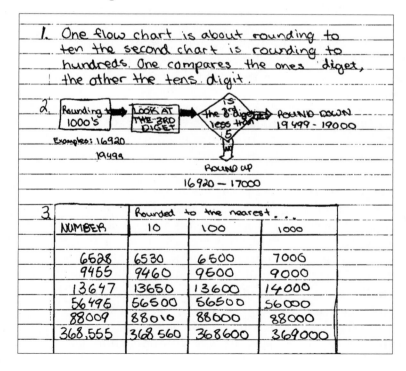

1. One flow chart is about rounding to ten the second chart is rounding to hundreds. One compares the ones diget, the other the tens digit.

2. Rounding to 1000's → LOOK AT THE 3RD DIGET → IS the 3rd digget less than 5 → ROUND DOWN 19 499 – 19000

Examples: 16920 / 19499

ROUND UP 16920 — 17000

3.

NUMBER	Rounded to the nearest...		
	10	100	1000
6628	6530	6500	7000
9455	9460	9500	9000
13647	13650	13600	14000
56496	56500	56500	56000
88009	88010	88600	88000
368,555	368560	368600	369000

History and social science. Grades five and six, ironically, tend to focus on locations closer to home than the exotic "Egypt" and "Jupiter" topics popular in the earlier grades. History and geography often deal with Canada: the voyageurs, Confederation, building the trans-Canada railway. As citizens, our children are expected to know about Canada's history and geography. Unfortunately, the presentation of these topics is frequently less exciting and less "fun" than the exotic locales of grades three and four. Some would blame our Canadian history itself for being boring, though Pierre Berton would obviously say otherwise. More likely we need some inspired teaching to go along with the improved textbooks that have only recently been developed for Canadian history. Too many teachers focus on the dull and dreary political items that dominated their own education, ignoring the excitement of Riel, or the 1837 Rebellion, or Banting and Best and a whole history of Canadian invention. Don't be surprised if Kyla suddenly declares that history is "boring," but it doesn't have to be that way.

Social science will be related more to contemporary issues, at least partially because children in middle school are becoming increasingly concerned about their planet. Kyla may well do units that focus on logging, fishing embargoes or the destruction of the rain forest. Students take a passionate interest in these areas if they feel they can do something to help. Social science programs capitalize on the social concerns of ten-year-olds for projects on pollution and the environment. Students will often read newspapers, write to editors, contact government officials and interview people in the community involved with environmental issues. Then get ready for the project to end all projects, often involving a videocamera, cardboard, glue sticks, Letraset and five of Kyla's friends in a marathon production session that will devastate your kitchen or rec room.

What Your Child Should Have Mastered by the End of Grade Six

- Researching a topic at the library and preparing an oral or visual presentation for an audience.

- Reading longer novels (150 or more pages) with no illustrations (e.g., Hardy Boys, Gordon Korman titles).

- Reading for pleasure various magazines (e.g., *Mad*, *Nintendo Power*), some of the newspaper.

- Writing stories, reports, summaries, notes, experiments.

- Creating paragraphs with a topic sentence and three to six sentences.

- Revising to improve spelling, punctuation, grammar.

- Talking about an idea and responding in a group discussion.

- Estimating answers to math problems.

- Solving multistep math problems.

- Measuring accurately.

- Recognizing geometric figures including parallelograms.

- Manipulating fractions and decimals.

- Finding area and perimeter.

- Using experiments to answer questions.

Science Fairs

There are traditional science fairs held in many schools and school districts. These are quite valuable for the gifted students at senior grade levels, who do well in such competitions, and they have some value for the other students who take part in them.

One new type of science fair is non-competitive: no prizes, no "winners," just public display and applause for every child who completes a project. In one K-8 school of 275 students, more than 200 students worked on a voluntary project and displayed their work in the school gym. Students were still able to get feedback from outside experts on their work, and there was an opportunity for parents and the community to come in and visit.

For ideas on science fair projects at various age levels, see Carol Amato's *Fifty Nifty Science Fair Projects* (Lowell House, 1993).

Health and physical education. Sooner or later sex education has to start; often grades five and six are the time. The girls are certainly ready for information on reproduction and essential topics like menstruation; the boys, fortunately, giggle at such topics less than they used to. The nature of your school's sex education program (or "Family Life," as it's euphemistically called) varies enormously depending on locale and school-board policy. Some grade five students learn quite explicitly about venereal disease and just where the penis goes during intercourse. Others receive this information only in a more general sense. In either case, today's children are better off with a factual presentation at school than learning about sex through an X-rated video or one of the porn magazines at your local variety store.

Your own discussion of sex and sexuality is best begun at this time, too. It's far easier to discuss such highly charged topics before adolescence than later, when your child will pretend to know it all or feign disinterest in the topic. With girls, there's a natural timing for such discussions; with boys, you'll simply have to decide on one.

Science. Often serious science instruction begins in grades five and six, with students moving out of their regular classroom into a special "laboratory" outfitted with gas jets and sinks. The basic topics are the same—simple chemistry, physics and biology—but the equipment gets more sophisticated each year. Typical grade five topics include electricity, magnetism, bridges, weather and conservation. Grade six science often covers simple machines, space and the solar system, energy sources and field studies of plants and animals.

Kyla will be expected to do writing in science as well—experiments, reports, observations. Here's a sample of a typical science report at the grade six level.

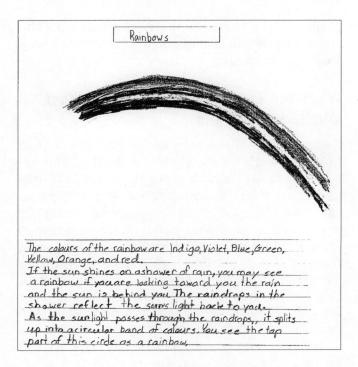

Rainbows

The colours of the rainbow are Indigo, Violet, Blue, Green,
Yellow, Orange, and red.
If the sun shines on a shower of rain, you may see
a rainbow if you are looking toward you the rain
and the sun is behind you. The raindrops in the
shower reflect the sun's light back to you.
As the sunlight passes through the raindrops, it splits
up into a circular band of colours. You see the top
part of this circle as a rainbow.

Art and music. Art programs often stay quite consistent throughout the early grades, but music programs becomes more specific over time. The simple singing and clapping of grade three usually turns into music with drums, recorders and xylophones in grade four. Wealthy boards of education can sometimes begin offering "instrumental music" as early as grade five, giving your child an opportunity to learn an instrument—usually a band instrument, but sometimes the violin—on school time. If such a program is available, take it. The nominal fee is more than worth your money, however stretched the family budget may be. For a few dollars, your child will get group instruction in the trumpet or trombone or clarinet, will get a chance to play in a band or orchestra and may just develop a lifelong love for music. These in-school classes are rarely as good as private lessons (if your child has real talent, you really *must* arrange for a private teacher), but they're much better than no instruction at all. The ancient Greeks regarded music as essential a subject as mathematics; we would not disagree.

What You Can Do at Home to Help Your Middle School Child

Some aspects of the parents' role do not change much throughout elementary school. You must continue to set rules about bedtime, reading time and study time. You must provide comfort and care even as your child develops her independence. And you should make efforts to arrange for outside education: Brownies, Cub Scouts, Sunday school, music lessons, power-skating classes, Suzuki violin classes, a neighbourhood baseball league. These are peak learning years for your child—time to start the activities she'll be involved in throughout her life.

Because both homework and project work will take up more of Kyla's time, it's important to set some regular routine for study. Your child needs a half-hour to do homework, or review the day's lessons, or just talk to you about what's going on in school. Some parents set that half-hour so it comes right after school; others place it immediately before or after supper. The actual time is unimportant. The existence of that half-hour, though, is as vital as the time you set aside for daily reading. The half-hour study time says that school is *important* for the whole family.

Despite the emphasis in home decorating magazines on a study corner for children's bedrooms, we still believe the best place for homework and study is your kitchen table. The advantages are obvious: homework becomes a visibly important item for the whole family; you'll be too busy to interfere too much, but you'll be close enough to answer questions and eyeball the work; the television set will be turned off; and concentration will be turned on. The kitchen table will make

Does Tutoring Help?

Many parents consider tutoring if their child is having difficulty in school, or sometimes if the marks just aren't up to snuff. Does tutoring work? The simple answer is yes. The average child will show a big improvement in school marks and real skills within a few weeks (Sylvan Learning Centres claims an average two years of skill growth for students in the first thirty-six hours of instruction). Some of this has to do with the effectiveness of one-to-one or very small group instruction, but much of the improvement comes simply because so much family time, attention and money are focussed on improving the child's skills.

Can you do as well yourself? Of course, if you're committed to spending an hour or more, three times a week, working patiently with your child. Since few parents can actually pull this off successfully, professional tutoring is a fast-growing support for kids in trouble at school. Your child's teacher can probably make a recommendation, or check the Yellow Pages under "Tutoring."

automatic many aspects of parenting and home-work supervision that have to be thought through if your child does her homework in the family room, or her bedroom, or in front of the TV. You may have to fight hard to resist Kyla's demands for independence, but your long-term concern is with her learning and achievement. Don't give in.

Having established a time and place for home-work, you should not intervene too much in the work itself. Kyla must make her own mistakes and learn that they have consequences. While we think it is fair for a parent to look over an assign-ment to make sure it is complete or has had a sufficient amount of effort, it is not fair to correct the math answers or fix all the spelling. That only teaches Kyla that Mom or Dad have ability and she doesn't. Let her make her own mistakes and learn how to correct them herself.

Be sure to keep your eyes open for signs that school is not going well for your child. When a nine- or ten-year-old shows signs of stress (see the sidebar, p. 156), you'll have to do some gentle exploration to see where the problem may be. Is Kyla being bullied or having trouble fitting in with the other children? Is she having difficulty in class because her skills are behind those of the other children? Is she having trouble with a par-ticular teacher or subject area? Once you figure out where the problem lies, it's time to go to school and discuss the matter with Kyla's teacher. Together, you should be able to come up with a plan that will make things easier at school.

Special Problems: The Bully and the Gang

You've seen the newspaper stories: as ten-year-old Nancy D. is leaving school, she's taunted by a group of girls who call her names. The ringleader of the group pulls at Nancy's hair, then rips her coat, pushing her to the ground. The group rushes around her, someone kicking Nancy,

Choosing a Tutor

Choose a tutor as you would choose a teacher or a baby-sitter: carefully, check-ing references and reputation. The tutoring options come down to three:

- **Peer tutors.** You can employ a slightly older student to spend an hour with your child, two or three times a week. Payment of $8 to $15 an hour will usually suffice, though senior high students may want more. School guid-ance counsellors can put you in touch with top-notch students who tutor, but remember that they have no teacher training.

- **Professional tutors:** New teachers, retired teachers, moms with teaching tickets looking for extra cash—all these will offer professional tutoring for your child. Expect to pay as much as a good piano teacher would get: around $25 to $40 an hour.

- **Tutoring organizations:** Many par-ents swear by such organizations as Sylvan Learning Centres, which team up groups of two or three kids with one professional teacher in a custom-designed program. The lessons are tra-ditional, but solid, and the fee includes regular assessment of skills. Costs: $300 to $400 a month for twice-a-week sessions.

Signs of Stress

When your child shows some of the follow-ing signs, she may be telling you that there's a problem at school:

- avoids doing homework;

- resists working independently;

- constantly needs assurance that the work is "right";

- seldom completes work at school;

- complains that the kids or teacher don't like her;

- plays with younger students, or mostly by herself;

- complains about ailments that don't appear to be real;

- can't find or remember to bring "stuff" to school;

- relies on "study helps": finger count-ing, multiplication charts, finger pointer in reading;

- can't explain homework;

- thinks school work is "stupid."

Simply telling her to work harder won't be enough. You need to meet with the teacher to form a plan of action that will maintain your child's enthusiasm for school.

someone else grabbing her book bag and strew-ing the contents all over the sidewalk. The gang has had its "fun"; and Nancy is in tears. She tells no one, but the following day a mysterious stom-ach ailment keeps her from having to go to school. Only later does Nancy's mother find out what really happened.

The newspaper headlines delight in announc-ing waves of school violence, as if Canadian schools were desperately trying to catch up to their American counterparts. The truth is that most of our schools—and most American schools too—are about as safe as anywhere on earth for our children. But that doesn't mean they're trou-ble-free. An increasing number of children bring to school the problems of home—divorce, family violence, poverty, unemployment—and are look-ing for an easy target for their pent-up hostility. For too many children, the cartoon-style violence of television turns into real violence just outside of school. Every teacher knows the excuses after-ward—"We were just joking around, ma'am, and then he kicked me..."

How do we stop bullying and gang violence in and around schools? Some of the answers are outside our powers as parents: we cannot elimi-nate child poverty or unemployment or abusive parents, much as we might like to. The best answers focus on three areas: the bully, the vic-tim and the environment.

The bully—a gang is just a collection of bullies and followers—enjoys preying on the weakness of others to prop up her own self-image, which is often quite tottery at a deep level. A bully usually has a limited array of social skills, which are cov-ered up in the act of bullying. The best way for teachers to help a bully, then, is to develop her self-esteem and to practise a variety of other social skills to provide healthy outlets for the bully's inherent frustration. All this psychologizing doesn't help you much, though. You can't very well march over to Ms. Jones's house and demand that her daughter develop a more varied array of social skills. You can, however, speak to the parents (sometimes bullies themselves) about what their child is doing (frequently they are unaware) and suggest that neither you nor your child is prepared to accept any more of it (firmness works). The parents and their bullying child are unlikely to admit to the accusations, but your message will filter down and may make life easier for Kyla, at least for a while.

The victim—we'll assume this is your child—is where the most successful work can be done. Victims are not picked at random; they are selected because of certain attitudes and behaviours that tell the bully *this* person is fair game. To stop being a victim, your child will have to stop those behaviours that lead to being picked on. She will have to:

- learn how to say no, and stick by it;
- learn how to maintain dignity despite the humiliation forced by the bully or gang;
- learn to project a certain self-confidence and assurance;
- learn to avoid being alone with the bully;
- learn to fight back.

If you seek help from your child's school, the principal or teacher will be able to assist with all but the last item. Unfortunately, the last item is sometimes the simplest solution to the problem. Most bullies will avoid people who are likely to fight back, either verbally or physically.

While we wouldn't recommend that you and your child practise kick boxing to deal with bullies, we think it is wise to practise assertiveness and street smarts. You can rehearse a "broken

Quick Tips for Your Child
Beating the Bully

Avoid the danger spots. You know where the bully and the gang are likely to hang out. Don't go there.

Walk away. Don't walk to an isolated location, but walk (don't run) to where you know you can find adults: the school office, the closest teacher, a local store.

Don't talk back. There's no point in getting involved in conversation with a bully or a gang. Keep your mouth closed and walk away.

If you must talk...be firm. "I don't enjoy those names." "I want my baseball back." Do not negotiate with a bully; just say what you must. Repeat yourself—like a broken record—to make your point.

Dignity counts. A bully will keep picking on you only if you react. If you're bored or uninterested, he'll lose interest in you. If you respond aggressively, or cringe, or cry-he'll be after you again.

Speak to an adult. Your parents and teachers can help you deal with bullies, but only if they know what's going on. Bullies rarely "get back" at you—in fact, they rarely know who told the adults about them. There is no prize for suffering in silence—get some help.

record" response to taunts—any variation on "sticks and stones will break my bones..." will do the trick. You can change the route that your child takes to get home, or make sure he travels with two or three friends. And you should always alert the teacher to what is going on, despite any protests from your victim-child, so the teacher can be extravigilant in class and in the school hallways. Some bully-victim relationships go on for three or more years, from elementary to secondary school, making each day unpleasant along the way.

The environment is also key in protecting our children from violence. Some areas seem to naturally invite the worst behaviour—alleys, school buses, secluded park areas, hidden playground locations—while others make bullying almost impossible. British researchers have shown, for instance, that it is not necessary to have teachers surveying every area of the schoolyard—but there must always be one "safe" area under the direct supervision of a teacher. One Toronto school found that violent incidents in its parking lot dropped by 300 percent when changes were made in the placement of parking locations and speed bumps.

Your child is far more likely to be subject to bullying outside of school than within it, but the two interconnect. That's another reason to speak to the teacher and the principal about what you've observed. With information, they can take action to change teacher lunchtime-duty positions, or oversee the parking lot for a few minutes after school. School-bus drivers *are* responsible for behaviour on their buses. In most jurisdictions, they answer to the principal of the school they serve. If your child is being bullied or threatened on the school bus, it is up to the principal and the driver to correct the situation. This can only happen if you speak up.

Remember: you cannot protect your child, but you can help your child protect herself. We've too often seen victims *choose* to join the bully at the back of the bus, or in the corner of the school-yard—almost as if the victim were enjoying the action as much as the bully. Unless this pattern stops, and it must stop with your child, then the bullying will simply move from the school to some other location.

We've always had bullies and victims and violence in schools, but the levels seem to be increasing. Some psychologists have talked about the "pervasive ethic of aggressive behaviour" that seems everywhere in our society, from TV cartoons to Hollywood movies to government foreign policy. Despite all this, as parents we want our kids to feel safe going to school, in school and coming home from school. Perhaps we can begin real action on these matters when we stop seeing schools so much as the easy solution and begin admitting that they're just indicators of what's happening in the bigger world.

CHAPTER 10

Grades Seven and Eight

Grades seven and eight frequently kick off some real changes for your child. Rob will sometimes go to a new school, a junior high school, that introduces him to a whole new assortment of kids and teachers. Even if he continues on at a K-7 or K-8 elementary school, he will almost certainly have to deal with a rotary subject timetable that brings him into contact with four or more different teachers. At the same time, Rob will be approaching adolescence with that mixture of adolescent gawkiness and childish earnestness that can make these years so uneven for both parents and children.

For girls, puberty will begin or already have begun: you will already have had that talk about menstruation, babies and contraception. For boys, the physical signs come later and that ritual birds-and-bees talk may have no particular occasion to take place unless you find one. Rob will develop body odour, pubic and sometimes facial hair and begin to grow in erratic spurts. All of this you expect. What you aren't ready for is the way a twelve-year-old turns away from you and

The "Typical" Grade Seven Student

- Is very influenced by media heroes and heroines/role models—especially in the area of appearance.

- Shows steady growth, often followed by rapid and uneven growth spurts.

- If a girl, reaches puberty somewhat earlier than boys—*vive la différence!*

- Displays feelings of insecurity and anxiety about appearance sometimes by aggressive teasing of others or "acting cool."

- Becomes especially conscious of appearance if a girl and may experiment with diets and makeup to achieve the "model" look.

- Experiments unevenly with "adult" roles: supermature one day, a kid the next.

- May be more influenced by peer group than by you or the school.

- Can rebel against authority at home and at school.

your values and begins to look toward his friends and to the media for role models. If this leads him to emulate the conscientious student next door, breathe easy. Just as likely will be an obvious modelling on Slash or some other rock or movie star, with the accompanying snarly attitudes and bizarre outfits. The rebellious adolescent takes on this identity early, often with the hidden approval of at least one parent.

By grade seven, almost anywhere in urban Canada, Rob will already have had a chance to smoke cigarettes, buy dope and drink alcohol. By grade eight, Rob will probably already have determined whether or not he is "into" dope and whether or not he wants to smoke. Perhaps as many as a quarter of grade eight boys have seen a pornographic movie and have already taken sex beyond the kissing stage. Sorry, we wish these facts were not true, but our experience and the statistics agree: childhood in Canada is shrinking. A combination of earlier physical maturity and an onslaught of quasi-adult television viewing have rolled the adolescent years back to age eleven or twelve. Rob will end childhood earlier and begin his teenage years sooner than you did. He thinks this is wonderful; you and we know better.

The end of childhood is often marked by a rejection of the "childish." If Rob played soccer from age four to age eleven, don't be surprised if he gives it up at age twelve. Early adolescent rebellion against previous activities from piano lessons to doll collecting comes with the territory. So does experimentation with adult behaviour, usually as seen in the popular media. The cigarette companies know when kids start—ages eleven, twelve and thirteen. So do the cosmetic companies, the running-shoe manufacturers and the purveyors of pop music. Rob will no longer shell out his hard-won money for books or models; now it will be for du Mauriers or cologne or a Guns 'N Roses tape. Given the amount of television that Rob has watched by age twelve and his level of intellectual development, he really hasn't got a hope of resisting the combination of advertising and peer pressure. Nor can you do much to help him, with your waning influence. If you're lucky, a further stage of rebellion or cynicism at age fifteen or so may rescue him from the tide of materialism. In the meanwhile, sigh, make sure he pays for a portion of the running shoes and wait for further developments.

What Happens at School

In many areas of Canada, Rob will start at a new school—a junior high school. Portions of the next chapter deal with high school organization and will be of interest to you if this should be the case where you live. In the rest of Canada, grade seven and sometimes grade eight are the end of elementary school, but the day is organized quite differently from the way it was in middle school. Rob will be on a full or partial rotary timetable, moving from a homeroom (where perhaps English and math are taught) to a number of subject specialists who will teach him science, geography, history, French, phys. ed. and whatever other subjects your school can muster up.

The theory behind this is simple: a teacher with real interest in and passion for art or music or history is more likely to infuse students with that same enthusiasm if he or she can specialize in that area. At the same time, grade seven students should be capable of moving from room to room, either as a class or following individual timetables, without getting hopelessly lost in the process. The result for teachers is a timetable where perhaps a third of the day is spent with a homeroom doing basic subjects and the rest of the day is spent in their area of specialty.

The homeroom teacher remains your contact and Rob's ombudsman in the school. This teacher

- Shows the beginnings of social aggressiveness and ganglike behaviour in groups, whether a boy or a girl.

- May feel former clubs, activities and organized groups are too "babyish" and gravitate to groups of friends parents don't know.

- If already established and successful in sports or music activities (teams, bands, choruses) tends to direct focus to these areas and have friends within these groups.

- Works well in groups with friends, but may be intolerant of others for various reasons.

- Can deal with abstract ideas and things that happened in the past, and has a hazy idea of what the future holds.

- Requires support and monitoring of assignment and homework schedule to respond to the demands of various rotary classes and teachers.

- Starts to really understand cause and effect in a way that helps in making decisions.

is supposed to oversee his entire program as well as keep an eye on Rob's social, emotional and academic growth. Some homeroom teachers actually manage to do all this; the others, well, they try as best they can.

The homeroom teacher is the one for you to call if you have a concern or sense a problem, even if it might involve one of the other subject teachers. At good schools, the homeroom teacher also provides some rudimentary guidance: classes in how to study, or do homework, or do speed reading, or organize a complex day. Many twelve- and thirteen-year-olds have a hard time shifting to even partial rotary; for them the homeroom teacher becomes an anchor in a rough sea of changing styles and expectations. The homeroom itself should offer a structure for many in-school activities, from noon-hour baseball to morning assemblies featuring the school band.

Often the school day is broken up into seven or eight periods of about forty to forty-five minutes in length. By creative timetabling, some blocks can be doubled up to offer extra time in subjects like English and math. Shop and art, for instance, often benefit from a double block every second day, so students are able to work at their projects or experiments for a longer chunk of time. Other subjects tend to be taught in single periods, sometimes on an alternating-day basis. Physical education, for instance, is recommended to be taught daily, but many schools have such limited time and gym access that it can only be offered every other day. Despite all this attention spent on timetables, the senior elementary school still has enough flexibility to be able to shift programs for special events. Thank goodness. The rigidity of high school will hit soon enough.

The key subject offerings have not changed that much from earlier grades. Here's a rundown with sample work from average grade seven and grade eight students.

Rule of Thumb ☞

Given the option of a K-8 school or a junior high school, avoid the junior high.

There is nothing wrong with the idea of a junior high school except the basic nature of kids—hundreds of hormone-packed twelve- to fourteen-year-olds, all crowded into one building. They lack the example of mature older students; they lack the responsibility of looking after, and setting an example for, younger students. Too often they become far more concerned with Janey's hair or what Alice did with Frankie last weekend than with learning the difference between a metaphor and a simile.

The break between elementary and real high school at age thirteen or fourteen makes far more sense. The grade seven and eight kids take a leadership role in their elementary schools; then they're properly awed when they enter real high school. By age sixteen, the awe has subsided, but the hormones are more in control.

So, all other things being equal, choose a K-7 or K-8 school over a junior high.

English. Teachers put a big push on writing in grades seven and eight. Sometimes the work will be creative, as in a short story or junior "novel"; sometimes analytical, as in questions on the setting of a story or the effectiveness of its ending; sometimes personal, as in keeping a journal; sometime practical, doing reports on various topics. The ability of students to deal with all this varies enormously in grades seven and eight. While some children have begun to develop their own analytical reasoning and higher-level thinking skills, others are still waiting for the teacher to tell them the "right" answers. Early adolescence is a gawky time both physically and intellectually.

Here's a typical story from a grade seven student. Note the use of paragraphing for structure and quotations to develop characters. The punctuation is pretty much correct, but spelling remains a bit iffy:

> "ahhh!!" I screamed. At the same time giving away where I was hiding. I heard loud thunderous foot steps as he walked up the stairs.
>
> "If you come out right now you won't get in bigger trouble," My dad said in a gentle voice trying to coax me out from my hiding place. His persuading did the trick, and I came out. Guess what he did to me he didn't turn me into a zombie he made me clean my room!
>
> In the evening my dad bought a new model train. While I was playing in the basement the train was sitting on it's rails. I was playing with a soccerball at the time, and I was playing with a friend. My friend through the ball too hard, and I couldn't catch it. It flew right into the new train, and the train fell, and it shattered into tiny pieces

By grade eight, an "essay" is expected to be a page long, somewhere between 200 and 300 words. Short answers ought to be somewhat longer than the begrudged sentence or two of earlier grades. Here's a grade eight response to a question on the problems of adolescence; it's been spell-checked by the student and printed on a school computer:

PROBLEMS

People of all ages have problems, but some of the later problems can begin in the teen years. Teenagers are faced with problems everyday, from the simple problem of passing a test, to the difficult problems such as racism, sexism, popularity, physical and mental abuse, drugs and alcohol, rape, sex and teenage pregnancy. The best way they can stay away from these problems, is to find themselves without the influence of peers, then they can face these problems and make good decisions. Some face these obstacles head on others keep them inside. Both ways work depending on the person. By dealing with their problems teenagers can learn how to avoid them in the future!

Schools often abandon "spelling" in grades seven and eight, since no one has ever been sure what words would be appropriate for grade seven or grade eight spellers. Instead, spelling will be tied into the works of literature that are read in class or to the mistakes students make when writing. Often schools put more emphasis on grammar and sentence errors in grades seven and eight. You'll probably be relieved that your child finally knows the difference between an adverb and an adjective, a phrase and a clause, though such information has never been shown to have any effect on the correctness of student writing. Additional exercises on common writing flaws—comma splices, run-on sentences, subject-verb agreement and the like—can also while away some hours of student time. Bright students can actually learn something from these exercises, but most kids seem to profit more from "sentence combining" exercises or simply by carefully revising and rewriting their own work.

The truth, of course, is that students who read a good deal and who are careful about what they write will *always* write better than students who don't read and don't care. Unfortunately, by grade seven more than a third of the kids do very little reading outside of school and may begin to skimp on the reading required inside those hallowed halls as well. Your involvement with reading and eyeballing of work before it is turned in can make an enormous difference in the achievement of your child. Don't ease up.

Mathematics. School math in grades seven and eight continues to develop and extend the ideas begun in earlier grades. By now, Rob should have mastered fractions and decimals. He should be able to calculate percentages, figure simple interest and mentally estimate the answers to problems. He should be able to measure distances in metric and handle a variety of other measurements, including temperature, volume and weight.

What's new at these grade levels are formulas and graphing. By the end of grade seven, Rob should be able to use mathematical formulas to calculate perimeter, area and volume. Some teachers introduce other problems in grade seven to present the idea of x as an unknown, getting the children ready for algebra in grade eight. In addition, Rob should be able to make and interpret various kinds of graphs (pie graphs, bar graphs, line graphs, etc.) both in math and for his other subject areas.

Here's a sample of a math test at the grade seven level:

Pg 69   _Perimeter_   Nov 22/94

     Find the length of side ab

2a)
Let x rep perimeter
x = 25cm − 5cm
x = 20cm ÷ 2
x = 10cm
∴ the perimeter is 10cm

5cm

2b)
Let x rep perimeter
x = 25cm − 9
x = 16cm ÷ 2
x = 8cm
∴ the perimeter is 8cm

9cm

And here's a typical problem an average student would work it out in grade eight:

Problem Solving	Dec. 5, 1994
Strategy Facts From a Story	Operation
Ben Johnson had four races to warm up, his times were 9.87, 9.80, 9.9 6, 10.01, what was his average time?	9.87 9.80 9.96 + 10.01 39.64
His average time in his warm up races was 9.9 6.	9.91 4⟌39.64 3 6. 3.6 3.6 .04 .04 .00

History and geography. These subjects focus on Canada and your local area, sometimes using field trips to explore both areas simultaneously. By now, Rob is getting sick of restudying the voyageurs and is probably getting into the politics of Confederation, the conscription crisis and Canada's contribution to World War II. He should also be looking at whatever key events marked the history of your city and province, perhaps going off to visit the legislature or a local archeological site. Multiculturalism is a major theme these days, replacing the old emphasis on British settlement with a passing nod to everybody else.

Geography is more than just maps now. Rob and his class may well look at local topics like land development, dump-site location and logging practices with one eye on geography and another eye on the environment. Much of the focus will depend on the teacher and how history and geography coordinate in Rob's school.

All the rest. Schools vary enormously in how much they "integrate" their curriculum. Some schools combine subjects into major theme units, so your child may well be working on history, English and art simultaneously—and being marked in all those subject areas. Other schools treat each subject as a discrete entity, assigning different teachers to handle each one, often not allowing enough time so the teachers can coordinate what they do. This latter mode, while anticipating the structure of senior high school, offers a weaker education for younger students.

In grades seven and eight, some subjects of the earlier years will continue: French, phys. ed., health, art and science. For each of these subjects, the material will be somewhat more sophisticated and the skills somewhat more developed than at the earlier grade levels. The two subjects that change greatly in grade seven are music and guidance.

Reading with Young Teens

Who says family reading time has to stop when your child gets out of middle school? Many of the most successful high school students keep reading *with* (not *to*) their parents right up to university.

How do you read *with* an older child?

- Pick up a book he's reading. Read a page from the middle out loud. Talk about the story or characters or style.

- Go to the bookstore and buy two books or magazines for your child—one that he likes; one that you choose together.

- Read parts of the newspaper together out loud: editorials, Ann Landers, the horoscope, sports columns, news items.

- Create some family reading times: a poem at supper, a story at Christmas, a play at the cottage.

- Ask your teenager to read to younger children in the family.

By the end of grade seven students should be able to:

- listen attentively to a presentation for twenty minutes or more;

- defend a point of view with reasons and convincing ideas;

- read young-adult and some adult novels for enjoyment;

- read the newspaper to find out specific information;

- use various lists, databases, systems in the library to find information;

- skim and scan material to pick out important ideas;

- sort out fact from opinion, in print as well as in radio and television;

- write a three-paragraph essay that clearly states a position;

- edit and revise written work effectively —not just correcting a word here and there;

- solve problems in mathematics and science using a specific inquiry method;

- work with fractions, decimals, integers, negative numbers;

- calculate percentages, read and write numbers from 0.001 to ten million;

- mentally estimate results to problems;

Music programs vary enormously from school to school, a real measuring rod for the level of school finance in your area. A BMW-level program will offer a choice of instrumental, band, string and choral music, often with different teachers for each one. A more modest board and school may have only one of these options. In any event, make sure your child is part of the music program. While there may be a nominal extra cost for rental of an instrument, the educational payoff is significant. We've also found that elementary music teachers are more likely to be "cool" than those in almost any other subject.

The guidance program in grade seven and grade eight is also hard to predict. At the very least, there will be some discussion of course options at the senior high school level, and probably some presentations by representatives of local high schools if your child has a choice of where to attend. At best, some schools offer career days, visits from people who hold various jobs, seminars on learning styles and classes on goal setting and career planning. Part of the guidance program looks at interpersonal relationships and conflict resolution. Some schools also offer individual and small group counselling for students who are thought to require special attention. It might well be worth asking about the program at your child's school on parents' night.

Extracurricular activities. At many schools, the number of extracurricular activities zoom way up in grades seven and eight, on the assumption that the kids can stay a bit later and walk home at, say, 4:30 P.M. on their own. Even schools where the entire population gets brought in by school buses will provide a variety of sports and clubs at lunch hour. Any school should be able to offer the usual array of intermural teams—baseball, basketball, football, hockey—and an assortment of clubs. A good school will have a few other intermural sports—perhaps soccer, lacrosse, cross country, track, field hockey—and quite a few *intra*mural (in-school) sports as well. Club and activity offerings are also expanded at a good school. We know schools that have math clubs, astronomy clubs, foster child committees, chess club, environmental groups, debating societies, dance committees, a school newspaper and a student council. The actual range of offerings is dependent on the staff and the size of the school. In fact, these extracurricular offerings are a good measure of staff involvement and energy. Unlike American schools, where teachers are paid to be coaches and advisors, Canadian schools must depend on their teachers to volunteer these extra services. Many teachers do. At a good school, the level of enthusiasm (not to mention encouragement by the principal) will see almost every teacher active in some extracurricular activity. At a weak school, no one seems to have any time.

To point out that your child will profit from being part of a team or club is simply to repeat what we've been saying throughout the book. *There is no better indicator for long-term achievement than early involvement in extracurricular activities.* Encourage your child to be a part of them.

What You Can Do at Home

By now, your child has probably already developed the habits that will make him a successful student: a regular homework time, a preserved "quiet" time for reading with the TV off, some rules on bedtime, as well as limits on television watching and video-game play. If you *haven't* attended to all of these, this is your last chance to start. Go back and reread the previous chapters to see what you should have been doing early on. If you don't start now, it's virtually impossible to establish major changes in family routine during

- calculate rates, discounts, simple interest and taxes on purchases;

- read and understand measurements —temperature, pollution counts, population;

- convert between common metric measures—1 kg = 1000 grams;

- use mathematical formulas to calculate perimeter, area and volume;

- collect and organize information to explain an idea using graphs, charts, diagrams, models, tables;

- use simple laboratory equipment to replicate experiments and make observations about different substances;

- discuss the effects of different forms of energy use on our environment and resources;

- read a road map and calculate distances;

- read different types of maps to get information about climate, vegetation, physical features, etc.;

- identify important factors that affected the history of his family, community, province and country;

- explain the growth and settlement of Canada, with some knowledge of key historical figures like Macdonald and Riel.

By the end of grade eight students should be able to:

- participate effectively in a conversation or discussion about an issue;

- prepare and deliver a three- to five-minute speech for an audience;

- identify prejudice and stereotyping in print, media and real-life;

- read longer novels and adult fiction, as well as nonfiction books;

- use all reference sources in the school or local library;

- examine a writer's ideas and style critically;

- write an essay of three to five paragraphs on an issue or specific topic;

- use reasonably-correct sentence structure and punctuation in all writing;

- collect information and use it without copying or plagiarizing;

- create a bibliography to support research work;

- turn information into simple (two-step) algebraic equations;

- read and write whole numbers and decimals from 0.001 to a hundred million;

- read and write large numbers in scientific notation;

the high school years, especially those that will seem to constrict your child's "freedom." Rules that simply continue on from earlier stages can be seen as "old-fashioned" or "not fair," but they can usually withstand the increasingly sophisticated arguments put up by older children. Just remember that your young teenager not only needs rules to live by, he *wants* you to lay down those rules. Just don't expect him to admit this out loud.

Our basic advice to eyeball homework continues to stay valid, even if Rob retreats more and more to his bedroom or maintains that he's doing group work with friends and that all the work is at Johnny's house. No piece of work should go into school without your having glanced at it. Sometimes you might even offer more help along the way—but wait for Rob to ask. Increasingly he's going to resent your intrusion into "his" domain, unless, of course, he decides he needs your help. Be around when that decision is made.

For boys, especially, these grades are a danger time in reading development. Many young men reject the "storybooks" (a.k.a. fiction) that they have read earlier on and are still reading in school. They want "real stuff": books on issues like drugs, magazines about cars, the *Guinness Book of Records*. They hook into the new horror genre —R. L. Stine and Stephen King—for the thrills and chills, and because their friends are reading it. While it would be nice if your son suddenly began a personal campaign to read the classics, starting with *Beowulf*, it is far more likely that he'll begin reading books and magazines you don't much like. Don't sweat it: at least your son is reading. Better to keep talking, to keep reading together, and every so often to slip in one of the fine young adult novels that are available today.

Probably the most important aspect of your role at this stage in your child's life is to be the cheerleader, supporter and sometimes driver for Rob's wide range of activities. There will be school sports, band concerts, the school musical, student council and maybe a 4-H meeting after school. Grades seven and eight can be wonderful years for school achievement and for taking a leadership role at the end of elementary school. You should do what you can to encourage this.

But grades seven and eight can also be a horror for some students; they were for at least one child in our families. At no other time is the urge to "fit in" so keenly felt and the sense of being an outsider so terribly painful. Many junior high schools resemble little closed societies where, if your child doesn't fit in, he's a nobody. Other junior highs are painful places for the young where name calling and physical intimidation have a real edge. A child who is small, or shy will probably feel more isolated in these grades.

What can you do? Be comforting. Speak to the homeroom teacher and guidance counsellor to see if they can do anything. Get on the principal's case if the first two don't do anything. Urge your child to get involved in activities that will allow him to make friends outside his classroom.

Keep your eyes open at home too. As we'll point out in the next chapter, the problems of teenagers don't begin in the teenage years, they begin *now*. Rob is already deciding whether to smoke or not to smoke; he will be deciding whether to experiment with drugs or not to; he'll be taking his first drink of liquor and deciding whether or not he likes the stuff; he'll be desperately trying to figure out his relationship to girls. You won't see evidence of these problems—and decisions—until later on, but they are happening now. Watch. Be prepared to discuss what's going on in Rob's life and be prepared to respect his privacy. Keep an eye on the group of friends with whom Rob hangs out: their influence will soon be stronger than yours. If you're lucky, the gang will hang out at your house, so you'll have some idea of what's going on. If you're not, it's a good idea

- solve multistep math problems and apply answers;

- create and read maps, grids, graphs, charts, tables;

- calculate solutions to real-life problems involving area, perimeter and volume;

- carry out simple chemistry experiments with solutions and mixtures and explain findings;

- understand and explain how energy and force are measured and the information used;

- explain how soils, plants and animals affect both where and how we live;

- read locations on maps by latitude and longitude;

- explain how the province's and country's resources are linked to trade in the world;

- read news articles from various countries and identify geographic conditions that might affect the situation;

- explain why and how his or her home community was settled and developed;

- identify the kinds of learning that are required for certain career paths;

- describe specific events that have shaped the course of Canada and the Canadian way of life.

Rule of Thumb 👍
If there's an option to enrol your child in some kind of school music program, always take it.

Acknowledging that school music lessons are rarely as good as private lessons, and allowing that not all children are "musical," the fact remains that school music lessons—even at a nominal cost—are a great value for parents. At best, your child may pick up a love of music and the joy of playing an instrument that will last for a lifetime. At worst, your child will at least have had the experience of playing in a band or orchestra or singing in a choir. Bonus: the music crowd is usually a nice group of kids for yours to hang around with.

to invite your child's friends over so you can see what this powerful influence group is like.

This is a book about schools, but what happens to your child at school often mirrors what's going on at home and in the neighbourhood. If you see sudden changes in behaviour, or mood shifts, or even a strange look about the eyes—all this may be more than adolescent growing pains. If there are hidden problems in your home, there's not much a school can do to shield your son from what's going on.

What do we mean by the phrase "hidden problems"? Just this—your child at this age is substantially influenced not by what you officially announce ("Rob, we don't want you staying out past ten o'clock") but by your hidden attitudes ("Oh, well, boys will be boys"). The psychologist Carl Jung talked about the way children often realize the unconscious dreams of their parents. Sometimes you may have to delve into your own buried dreams to figure out why Rob behaves the way he does.

Schools can be a help in all this. Chances are the homeroom teacher still has pretty good tabs on your child. Sometimes she can spot problems developing even before you do. School report cards, when they're honest, can be a good indicator of changes or problems in your child's life. Often a coach or advisor at school will have more heart-to-heart talks with your child than you do at this age. These people can help you with your parenting if you see problems developing.

If there are no problems, relax and enjoy. These years of pimples and training bras are hard on the kids, but have a certain charm from an adult perspective. Many parents fear the onset of adolescence, but most kids make it through their teenage years with flying colours. If you've laid the foundations of communication, expectation, fairness and family values, your child will thrive in the years ahead.

CHAPTER 11

High School: Grades Nine and Ten

C anada must be the only country on earth so fragmented that we cannot even tell you exactly when high school will begin for your child. In Quebec, Alberta, rural Saskatchewan, the Yukon and N.W.T., and in the Maritimes and Newfoundland, some sort of high school begins in grade seven, but *senior* high school doesn't begin until grade ten. In Manitoba, urban Saskatchewan and Ontario, high school usually begins in grade nine, except for those boards that have junior highs, and where the confusion of Ontario's "transition years" is making the first year of high school much more like senior elementary school. Then there's British Columbia, which begins high school in grade eight, slightly out of synch with every other place in North America.

By the same token, we can't tell you when high school will end. Most provinces end high school programs at the conclusion of grade twelve,

So You Want to Be a Kid Again?

From an adult perspective, adolescent life can seem relatively trouble-free, and for most teenagers it is. But for a portion of the teenage population, adolescence is filled with unusual stress and difficulty.

- 8 percent of teenagers suffer from clinical depression—not just the "I feel miserable" variety, but a depression that calls for medical treatment, often Valium or Prozac.

- 1 percent of teenagers are manic-depressive. Their mood swings are so enormous that they frequently require several medications as well as lithium supplements to stay on an even keel.

- A similar proportion of teenagers become anorexic, literally starving themselves for complex psychological reasons.

Don't confuse ordinary teenage angst (33 percent of teens feel "really depressed" once a month; 19 percent have considered suicide) with more chronic problems, but be prepared to consult with your family doctor if psychological problems persist.

except for Ontario, which has renamed its grade thirteen as Ontario academic credit year and made it so difficult that it now takes most kids two years to finish, and Quebec, which ends high school in grade eleven but then encourages graduates to go on to CGEPs for further schooling. Any and all of this may change by government fiat before the typesetters finish work on this page.

Confusing, isn't it?

Fortunately, the system for any given part of the country will be quite uniform and easy enough to figure out with a phone call to your closest school or board of education. We're going to address the comments in this chapter to the beginning years of high school—grades eight, nine and ten—acknowledging a certain overlap with the previous chapter for children who enrol in junior high school in grade seven.

What's New in High School?

The big difference between high school and elementary school has always been the move from a single teacher to a complex rotary timetable that sends students to a number of different subject "specialists." This distinction has become somewhat confused over time, with a few elementary schools now using partial rotary beginning in grade four to offer subjects such as French, music and general shop, while some high schools hold back on full rotary until grade ten to allow students to get their bearings by taking several core subjects with one teacher in one room. Nonetheless, the general distinction remains.

For many years, a young person could begin teaching elementary school without ever having attended university (though this has become virtually impossible in most provinces since the 1970s), while high school teachers were expected to be university graduates and subject specialists. In Ontario, for instance, every high school teacher must have a university degree, but only those with "honours" or four-year degrees can qualify to teach courses at the grade eleven, twelve or OAC level.

The advantage for your daughter Shannon in this scheme is its insurance that the teacher doing grade twelve physics actually knows enough physics to be more than a few pages ahead of the students in reading the textbook. The disadvantage in subject specialization is that teachers can become detached from the school as a place for learning and from students, who need more than just the content of a subject. A great teacher—elementary or secondary—is committed to the school, to curriculum, to learning and to students. Your child has no more chance of finding such a teacher in high school than she did in elementary school, but at least she'll have a bigger variety to choose from.

Choice is a key word in the secondary schools. Each year, a student is able to make a wider set of choices about the courses she takes. While Shannon's grade eight and grade nine programs will be largely laid down by provincial requirements, her grade eleven and grade twelve courses will depend on streaming, career choices, her interests and her abilities.

Guidance. Certain key people in the school are assigned to help your child make those choices: the guidance counsellors. Guidance counsellors rarely teach, though they are all ex-teachers, and they only sometimes counsel. Guidance counsellors exist in that netherland between teachers, administration and the real world, sometimes juggling their responsibilities with wonderful adroitness, sometimes just sitting in retreat in their private offices. The good news about guidance counsellors is that they can be a wonderful resource for your child; the bad news is that your child will have to compete against two or three

Quick tips for your child 💡
Guidance: A Sidebar for Teens

A note to grade nine and ten students.

- Your school has one or more guidance counsellors. They will be useful to you later if you get to know them now.

- The guidance department has a secretary. If you're reasonably nice to her, you'll find guidance appointments easier to get.

- Guidance counsellors come in various shapes, colours and dispositions. Yours was probably assigned alphabetically. If you want to change to another one, speak to your vice-principal.

- Guidance counsellors want to know about you as a person, not just as a student. The more you're willing to talk, the more they can do for you.

- The guidance office can be a cool place. Check out the university and college catalogues and the bulletin board. You might just find a part-time job, or an award that almost has your name already on it.

Rule of Thumb ☞
Go for the top stream.

If there's any question about which stream your child should be in, go for the top stream. If the placement doesn't work, it's always possible to shift down later on. Very few kids start low in grade nine and work their way to the advanced level.

Choosing the top stream, incidentally, also helps determine who your child's friends are likely to be. Only a few aspiring Hell's Angels members volunteer for the demands of the advanced group. Your child may still choose to hang out with these characters, but he'll have to do so between classes.

hundred other students to get some attention. While guidance counsellors theoretically treat every child equally, the truth is that 10 percent of the students take up 90 percent of their time, while the other 90 percent of the kids get what's left over.

Guidance counsellors are really quite essential to help your child manipulate that maze of bureaucracy that makes up the average thousand-student high school. In group sessions, the guidance counsellors will advise Shannon on course selection, give information on university entrance procedures, make periodic announcements about summer programs, scholarships, and presentations by visiting university and college representatives. For many students, this is all they ever get from guidance. For others, an individual guidance counsellor will tailor-make a program, hand-select teachers even though the whole system is on computer, look after a mentor or a peer tutor or a peer counsellor, offer emotional support, provide psychological guidance and sometimes even utter Polonius-like wisdom.

Make sure your child gets both. Shannon will have to make an appointment to visit her guidance counsellor (she'll have one assigned, usually alphabetically by last name, but she can always appeal for a change), but she really must do so. There are long term payoffs in such a relationship, regardless of whether Shannon gets into trouble with her classes or whether she's a straight-A student bound for Queen's, St. Francis Xavier or the University of British Columbia.

Streaming. In every country on earth, students are sorted into groups sometime during high school. England does this at age thirteen through national examinations; France does it at age fourteen through the *brevet*; Mexico does it at age thirteen through high school entrance exams; and Americans mostly allow grade eight teachers to make the sorting decisions. This sorting process is now called "streaming" because the image of little fish swimming up different rivers is more acceptable than the kind of meat-cleaver decisions that used to be made at school "promotion" meetings. In the past, children were streamed in three directions: the weakest students to vocational schools, the middling students to commercial programs in the high schools and the top students to academic programs that would prepare them for university. With the incredible rise of special education over the past fifteen years, the vocational "stream" has almost disappeared, so now the waters simply divide in two.

You already know the theory behind streaming; it's the same theory that held when you were in school. Smart kids can learn faster and learn more than not-so-smart kids, so by separating the two, we'll have wonderful classes of future rocket scientists and brain surgeons who won't be held back by the future plumbers and hairdressers. We'll also have happier future plumbers and hairdressers, as the wisdom went, because these kids are "good with their hands."

The survival of such errant nonsense over so many years in so many places is really a triumph of the deep-down elitism in human nature. The truth, of course, is that the future rocket scientists and plumbers were learning together fairly happily for seven or eight years before streaming. The future rocket scientists will need shop class to learn to remodel their future basements, just as the future plumbers need accounting and advanced math to run their future businesses. And the future plumbers will probably make more money in the long run than the future rocket scientists. On the other hand, by the time kids reach high school, the relatively small differences in ability and motivation that are observable in kindergarten have become gaping abysses in attitude and skill levels. This unfortunate truth leads

Magic Words to Get Your Child into the High School You Both Want

Many urban boards or districts of education give parents and students a free choice of which high school to attend, often with competing presentations to elementary school students from different schools in the area. But some boards still hold to the old rules—if he's not in our area, the kid can't come here.

Such hidebound administrative rules have led students to desperate measures: fake addresses or going to live with relatives in the appropriate school district. A better approach is to find out which magic words will work in your jurisdiction. For instance, one phrase we know to be useful for getting into highly academic schools is "My child wants to take Latin in grade eleven and twelve." Your son may decide later not to take those courses, but the request gives him a reason to be admitted.

By comparing course offerings, you can usually find one course that is given at your preferred school and not at your local school. Naturally, this is the course your child will *desperately* want to take.

Resource Teachers

Because of special education legislation, most high schools now have special resource teachers to assist students with designated special needs. The key word here is "designated," or "identified"; the resource teachers are usually so busy with students who require help that they don't have time to offer it to a child who may just be having a hard go of it in math. See Chapter 13 for more information about special ed. identification.

The resource teachers work with your child's subject teachers to modify the standard classroom program. In addition, they offer a special room for help (sometimes nicknamed "the rubber room"), equipped with computers, easy-to-read books, course books and even a quiet corner. Designated students can request to write tests and exams in the resource room, sometimes with extra time to complete the work required.

to streaming, ostensibly to provide appropriate education for the children, but actually to maintain teacher and administrative sanity.

Make no mistake: you want your Shannon in the top stream. With very few exceptions, the kids in the top stream get the biggest variety of teachers, the most interesting programs, the perks and awards. They also find themselves hanging out with the "right" crowd, a group that will probably reinforce a lot of your values just when your own voice stops carrying much weight. The labels for the top stream vary: advanced, academic, "01-level," "U-level," but the meaning is always clear. Some schools even have an advanced-advanced stream, called "enriched" or "gifted," to bring together the brightest of the bright (see Chapter 14 for more on this).

If for some reason your child has ended up in the bottom stream, you have two choices: either appeal or make the best of the situation. Clearly there is no sense forcing Shannon into a stream where she'll have to take algebra, history and Latin, when what Shannon really wants is practical math, family studies and just enough French to get her diploma. But children are still very fluid in terms of their abilities and interests at age thirteen—indeed, many of us stay fluid throughout life—and ought not to be limited just because of a bad year in grade seven or grade eight. If your child ends up in the wrong stream, it will become abundantly clear as time goes on.

Special help. With the demise of the vocational stream, the weakest students are no longer clustered in a single group, but end up mixing with a variety of kids in quite ordinary classes. By and large, this has been a good thing. The problem comes when Shannon has trouble with regular grade nine math, or can't read the textbook for grade ten history. Most high schools now have a "resource teacher" or "resource room," where she can go for extra help on the subject and extra time to work on tests and exams (mandated by law if Shannon is designated for special education, see Chapter 13).

This system works well for students who have problems in one or two subject areas and have sufficient motivation to keep up with the extra work required for them to stay even with their peers. It tends to fall apart in dealing with students who have a general learning disability that affects many areas or with students who don't care all that much about high school to begin with. At the grade eight, nine, ten level, when the law requires that your child still be in school and the vast majority of children still want to be there, the resource teacher will probably make it possible for learning to continue successfully.

The social whirl. When kids first enter high school, they tend to respond to the changes and choices in one of two ways. There is a group of kids who just *love* the whole idea of high school: new friends, new subjects, more freedom, a variety of teachers and tons of extracurricular activities. Then there is a group that finds all the changes quite daunting: they miss the comfort and continuity of a single teacher; they don't make new friends that easily; they don't take advantage of the sports and clubs available to them. Most high schools are physically big and tend to make younger, less confident kids feel quite anonymous. Though good schools make an effort through homerooms, mentors, advisors and intramural sports to make the bigger school feel friendly, too many high schools don't bother. As a parent, you must exercise care if you feel that Shannon is lost in the larger school and system. She'll need pep talks at home, and a teacher or guidance counsellor on her side at school.

The other danger, usually later on, is that Shannon will fit in too well. When students are

Fitting In

Your child's response to school will not depend all that much on courses, teachers, school administration or the cafeteria. It will mostly depend on "fitting in."

Unlike elementary school, where kids switch friends from year to year, activity to activity, by high school kids frequently choose a group or clique. These are kids who hang around together at school, go out together after school and spend a fair portion of their free time talking to each other over the phone. The importance of the group to an adolescent is sometimes overwhelming; hence your son's reasonable clothes go into the garbage, to be replaced by ripped jeans and bizarre shirts; your daughter's previously attractive face suddenly appears with heavy makeup and a ring through her nose. It's all in the power of the group—and in the TV images each group buys into.

Checklist for Choosing an Excellent High School...

❏ The principal was in the school the day you visited, or would be in the very next day.

❏ The guidance office had a number of students waiting to see the guidance teachers.

❏ The resource room had kids in it, not just teachers doing paperwork.

❏ The staff room did *not* have a Ping-pong table.

❏ You were given an outline of courses, graduation requirements and school routines.

❏ The library was large and full of students working on projects, not just playing cards.

❏ The course offerings will suit your child.

❏ The school seems to have adequate science labs, computer labs and gymnasiums.

❏ There is a co-op program.

❏ The school's reputation is good and coincides with your family's goals.

surveyed about why they like a particular school, the phrase "a chance to see friends" weighs in much more heavily than learning, career preparation or any other factor. Shannon's peer group can become much more powerful than the adult voices she hears at school and at home. Sometimes the effect of this can be marvelous—kids challenging one another to do better, explore new areas, achieve more. Sometimes it can be disastrous—drugs, alcohol, class cutting, dropping out. A wise parent keeps an eye on the friendship choices being made early in high school. While there isn't much we can do to overtly discourage a friendship (never, ever say "I don't want you to see Johnny again"), that doesn't mean you have to drive Shannon across town to visit her friend Chuck at the local Hell's Angels clubhouse. Subtle disinterest sometimes works wonders: "Chuck's a biker, you say? How quaint."

Despite the conventional wisdom that high school and the teenage years are full of difficulty and family strife, many parents find these years with their children to be warm and fulfilling. The difference may well lie in your attitude and your involvement, as much as in your child and her school.

How to Choose the Best High School

Choosing the best high school for your child reopens all those questions we discussed earlier in Chapter 2, but the choices are fewer. Many rural areas have only one high school—and attending even that one requires busing—so the only alternative would be enrolling your child in a boarding school or sending her to live with a relative in some other location. Even major urban areas may not have a very wide range of choices. Not every Canadian city has an alternative high school, or a private academy, or a Catholic high school located close by.

But if you're among the half of Canadians living in a large city, your child *will* have choices. In cities like Toronto, Vancouver, Calgary and Winnipeg you'll find competing public and Catholic high schools, specialized schools for "trades" education and academic kids, French-language high schools for the French immersion kids, alternative schools for kids who don't fit into regular high schools, private schools of many types and fee schedules, and even high school by correspondence if that's what you decide upon. Many large public systems will offer students a choice as to which high school they wish to attend, the only penalty being a longer bus ride to get there.

There are obviously a number of factors to consider in deciding with your child on the best high school within your family's geographical and financial reach. Let's consider them in turn.

Size. Despite the various studies that have shown that the ideal size for a high school is 600 to 700 students, most schools are either bigger or smaller than this. Small schools suffer because course choices and facilities are limited; hence alternative high schools with only a few dozen students frequently have to borrow access to science labs and gymnasia and may only offer course credit in the most basic subject areas. Bigger schools suffer because some children can get lost, both physically and emotionally, in some of the enormous buildings that were the pride of the Empire back when they were built. Larger schools frequently offer a greater course choice—more advanced courses, more enriched courses, classes in Polish and Greek as well as French—but sometimes at a sacrifice in involvement. You probably know your child well enough to know where she'll flourish, but size is only one consideration.

Semestering. High schools divide into two varieties—semestered or nonsemestered—depending on whether their courses are five months long or

❑ Many extracurricular activities are available.

❑ The technological (shop) facilities seem reasonably up-to-date.

❑ Many different classes use the computer labs, not just the kids signed up for computer courses.

❑ Teachers in the staff room seem to enjoy one another's company.

❑ The school offers trips and exchanges to various other countries.

❑ When you walk down the hall between classes, at least half the kids seem to be studying for something.

❑ The cafeteria is at least halfway decent.

❑ There is a "behaviour" code, or some clear means of dealing with antisocial behaviour.

❑ After class change, the hallways don't smell of smoke.

❑ Your child would like to go there.

Scoring: award five points for each check. An excellent school will score 80-90; a good school 70-75; an adequate school 60-65.

High schools are organized either by semesters or by the full year (a few mix both kinds of timetables). A semestered school generally offers students four courses each semester (September to January and February to June) in seventy-minute periods. A nonsemestered school offers seven or eight courses right through the school year (though the year is often broken up into three or four terms for marking purposes) in forty-minute periods.

Young people prefer semestered schools because the courses seem to go faster, they're stuck with poor teachers or dull courses for only five months and they can sometimes finish school a few months early. For these reasons, semestered schools tend to outdraw nonsemestered schools wherever the two are side by side.

But the truth is this: nonsemestered schools offer a better education. Students spend more time in each course (usually 170 to 190 hours versus the 130 to 140 hours per course in a semestered school). And students in some subjects like music, languages and perhaps math lose both skill and content in the long layoff between semesters. If you have a choice for your child, go nonsemestered.

run the full school year. Semestered schools are more popular with students, who get to change teachers and classes more quickly and who can make up a failed subject the next semester without resorting to summer school. They are also popular with administrators, who have the complex job of satisfying student course choices, teacher timetable requests and complex contract demands on staffing and class size.

Teachers, however, have mixed feelings about the popularity of semestered schooling. Obviously the courses are shorter in duration (five months as opposed to ten), but they are also shorter in classroom hours because the periods aren't exactly doubled in time (hence a semestered course totals 130 hours or so, while a nonsemestered course is closer to 170 hours). While some courses benefit from the longer time span of the semestered period—art, some science courses, technical studies, drama, English if taught by a creative teacher—others are harmed by the seven months kids have "off" before they pick up a subject again, especially music, languages and math. Again, while some teachers can make productive use of a period almost as long as a Hollywood feature film, for other teachers and their students this can be 110 minutes of tedium. Taking all this into account, our rule of thumb is simple: for the serious, academic student, a nonsemestered school will offer a better education.

Programs. The programs and courses offered within a school are the real meat of education. By the end of elementary school, you and your child might have some inkling on future career aspirations and goals. If your child is heavily interested in maths and sciences, for instance, then the nearest specialized "science" high school may be a better choice than a wide-ranging academic school. Most high schools will give you a copy of their option sheets and course selection books to help you sort this confusing matter out—or a few sensible questions to the principal or guidance counsellor can get right to the heart of the matter. Often a keen interest by your child in any one area—music, French, math, the arts, technical subjects—will make a particular school stand out.

Reputation. The reputation of any high school is usually ten years out-of-date. While the talk about a particular elementary school is circulated by parents who have children in the school and can be quite accurate, word of mouth about a high school is coloured by what graduates remember about the "good old days" when they attended. High schools can coast on a reputation for years, despite changes in administration and staff that can turn an excellent school into a weak one in two or three years.

Nonetheless, reputation counts. A high school with a strong academic tradition, or a great football team, or a winning arts program will usually make some effort to live up to its history. School reputations also have some small effect on university entrance. Universities keep tabs on the success of students they admit from many high schools. While these lists are not available to the general public, word of mouth will often let you know which schools in your area send most of their graduates on to successful university careers.

Extracurricular activities. High schools differ to some extent in their offerings of extracurricular activities. For students who get involved—and we certainly hope your child would be among this group—extracurricular activities often define the high school experience. Some can be absolutely key: sports like football, basketball and soccer; clubs like debating, yearbook, newspaper and academic challenge; activities like the band, school musical, choir and orchestra; leadership opportunities like student council and the honour society. Parents should remember that the best

Extracurricular Activities

High schools offer many extracurricular activities before school, during lunch and immediately after school. Your child's attitude toward school will frequently be brightened by participation—and the chance to see teachers as coaches and advisors, not just as guys holding a piece of chalk.

Intermural sports: football • baseball • hockey • soccer • swimming • lacrosse • tennis • skiing • field hockey • rowing • wrestling • curling • water polo

In-house sports (less competitive because they're played homeroom against homeroom): touch football • baseball • soccer • dodgeball • badminton • weight lifting

Clubs: yearbook • newspaper • debating • computers • ham radio • Reach for the Top or Academic Challenge • chess

Organizations: student council • social committee (for dances, etc.) • model U.N. or model Parliament • athletic council • grad committee

For those with talent: band • orchestra • jazz band • choir • art club • school musical

Power

There's a new level of power in high schools: the department head. Unlike elementary schools, where each teacher is individually responsible to the principal, in high school much administration is done by the department head or chairman.

If your child has a problem with an individual teacher, the usual route is to speak first to the department head (the school secretary can tell you who this is) and *then* speak to the vice-principal or principal.

In a large high school, the roles of vice-principal and principal will be very different. The principal can be virtually a figurehead who's often off at board meetings or giving speeches to the Rotary Club. The vice-principal does most of the day-to-day administration, including dealing with difficult kids and chasing down persistent latecomers and truants. Is it any surprise that every V.P. is just waiting his or her turn to be a principal?

Conversely, it is the principal who sets the rules and tone for the school. If you have a problem about your child or a teacher, see the V.P. If you want changes in the school, make an appointment to see the principal.

predictor of success in adult life is not high school marks, but high school participation in activities. You should already know your child well enough to determine what some of her interests are. Others will germinate in high school, often nurtured by a strong extracurricular program. The guidance office should have a list of activities; otherwise you can check out a copy of the school yearbook to see what's available.

The visit and first impressions. You'll probably want to visit the various high schools that are available to your child, but the information you receive by looking around won't be terribly helpful. There are no obvious physical manifestations of a good high school. Architecture and age mean little: we have visited splendid schools in rotting Victorian Gothic buildings and mediocre schools in state-of-the-art physical plants. The apparent signs of a good elementary school—bulletin-board displays, kids pictures, active hallways—are usually absent or accidental in a high school. Your talk with the high school principal or guidance personnel can tell you a good deal about courses, calendars and procedures, but it gives little hint of the real tone of the school. Much of your personal impression will probably be based on the hordes of unruly adolescents who pile out into the halls between periods and then disappear into classrooms as if by magic. If you're standing in one hallway when this occurs, you'll be convinced that the school consists of well-behaved future attorneys; if you're standing in another, you'll hear four-letter vocabulary that will make you vow to keep your child several miles from the front doors. Just remember: it's the *same* school. The information you've gotten, though powerful, is simply incomplete.

Nor is it possible to have a meaningful talk with a subject teacher or department head when you've just walked in off the street. High school teachers can tell you at length about their subject, but often know little about course offerings down the hall, or what extracurriculars are offered, or what the food in the cafeteria is like. If you *personally* know a local high school teacher, and you can get some general opinions on a number of schools over a cup of coffee some weekend, listen hard. But a school classroom visit won't give you much to go on.

The actual decision about which high school your child will attend is one that should be made *with* your child. Shannon will have her opinions; you will have yours. Some talking is in order, not just on this decision, but on many others right through secondary school.

What Actually Goes On in Grades Nine and Ten

When your child chooses courses for grades nine and ten, she'll have to contend with a certain set of requirements. First, there are the *mandatory* courses that Shannon must take—usually English and mathematics, sometimes history, phys. ed. and/or French. Then there are the *optional* courses that she can choose to take from an assortment that often includes art, music, dramatics, family studies, geography, business, computers, keyboarding, French and other languages, general science and shop (or technological studies, as it prefers to be called). Finally, there are the *diploma requirements* that have to be kept in mind so that Shannon can graduate at the end of grade eleven or twelve. The diploma requirements set down the compulsory courses that must be taken over the three or four years of the high school program. Shannon's option sheet—the course selection form she fills out in the spring before she enrolls in high school—will spell out all of this in more detail. If your child attends school in a large board of education,

Quick tips for your child ☼ Writing the High School Essay

- Short is rarely sweet. Always write up to the maximum length assigned.

- Appearances count. An essay that comes in with a title page and an extra sheet for marking has already won extra marks in the teacher's eyes.

- Don't be juvenile. High school teachers are not impressed by pictures, multi-coloured title pages or bizarre type-faces on your computer.

- The first paragraph should be perfect. Use a dictionary. Read the opening to your parents.

- The first-sentence trick: take the question or topic as phrased by your teacher and turn it around to a statement. Then add a sentence or two of your own to finish out the paragraph.

- Computers are handy for spelling and tend to make your essays look professional. Typewriters are almost as good. A handwritten essay can also be quite acceptable—just write legibly and be sure you have margins.

- Never submit an essay unless you have rewritten it at least once. Then read it out loud just before you turn it in, to catch all the mistakes you didn't see the night before.

When Should You Buy a Computer for Your High School Student?

The simple answer is this: as soon as you can. A computer can be very important for everything from presentations, to essays, to doing senior-level math. The capability for checking spelling and printing an attractive document makes even a cheaper, older computer an important tool for your child (just ignore her complaints about outdated technology). A thousand dollars will get you a computer and printer perhaps three years behind today's models.

More expensive and more modern computers can do more tricks: grammar checks, thesaurus, CD-ROM encyclopedias and atlases, modems to connect onto on-line libraries and info sources, video cards to incorporate sound and images into presentation material. None of this is essential for a high school student, but they're fun if you have the four thousand dollars required for these bells and whistles.

Just remember: whatever you buy will be outdated in three years anyway. That's life on the information highway.

she'll also receive a program book for the whole secondary system showing where she can take courses in everything from cosmetology to fashion arts to scientific instrumentation.

One of the major changes between elementary and high school has to do with the responsibility placed on students. While the average elementary school will always call home if your child is not in class, the average secondary school will only try to contact you if your child is missing homeroom. This leads to the phenomenon of class skipping or cutting that you remember from your days in school. There are no longer hall monitors or truant officers to make leaving school in midday difficult, so some students take advantage of lax attendance and computer systems to skip classes they don't particularly enjoy. The result is poor marks and sometimes subject failure. While school administrations try to stay on top of this for their thousand-or-so students, the real responsibility belongs to your child. Your only real clue to the problem will come at report-card time when you see that Shannon has missed six classes in every other subject, but twenty-four classes in computers, where the teacher, she says, is "a goof." Don't be surprised when Shannon fails computers at the end of term.

Evaluation in high school is ordinarily based quite simply on a combination of tests, activities, projects and examinations. Marks in secondary school are rather coldly calculated. Each item has a value or "weight," and these are simply added up at certain times each term to produce a mark. The particular system is usually explained to students on the first or second day of class (they forget) and then to parents on the first parents' night (too quickly for you to understand).

Nonetheless, the mark system is usually fair. If Shannon misses a test and fails to make it up, the resulting zero will sink her mark by two, three or more points at the end of the course. If Shannon fails to turn in a project, the zero could drop her mark as much as ten points. Again, the responsibility is on the student to get work in, to be present on test days and to pay attention to her own marks. Our only caution would be to Shannon: always double-check your teacher's mark book for omission or errors in calculation. Our experience with various high school teachers, for instance, would indicate that you've got one chance in twenty of having a teacher miscalculate your mark simply by making a mistake in arithmetic. It's worth a second look—or keep track of your own marks just to check.

The Courses

English. Everybody has to take grade nine and grade ten English, usually one period each day. This is considerably less time than was spent on English and composition back in the 1940s and 1950s, even though demands on the program— from using computers to accommodating writing process—have gone way up. The net result is that Shannon isn't going to read very much in class: a novel, a play, a handful of short stories, a few essays. If a lightning bolt should destroy all the copies of *Romeo and Juliet*, *Julius Caesar*, *The Chrysalids* and *Who Has Seen the Wind*, half of our grade nine and ten English programs would be virtually without material to teach.

To make up for this, Shannon should be asked to do considerable reading at home. Some of this will be reported back to the teacher in various formats, from the ever-popular book report to the creative videotaped interview with characters from a novel; some should just be for her own enjoyment. Alas, a parent cannot assume that Shannon will do sufficient reading at school to even maintain her current level of skills.

Those Impersonal High School Report Cards

We read a great deal in the papers about lousy elementary school report cards, but at least they give you some sense that the teacher was trying to communicate something. Chances are your child's high school report card will seem even worse—computerized, full of stock educational phrases, with columns of marks but no explanation how the marks were determined. Welcome to the age of computer reporting.

Reading a computerized high school report is quick. The mark gives you the student's current or final standing in the course work. The "days absent" and "times late" column gives you an inkling of whether your child is conscientious. The particular computerized comment was probably selected by the teacher from a list of a hundred vetted phrases. What's missing in all this is any sense of the personal—a real shock after the elaborate anecdotal reports of elementary school.

So how do you find out more? Go to the parents' night. The teachers will be at tables in the gym (or you'll traipse around the school to find individual classrooms), ready with their mark books and perhaps ten minutes to tell you how your child *really* performed in their class.

Most of the time at school will be spent in lessons, discussion and writing. More creative teachers attempt to build in some acting to accompany the selected play, some role playing to illustrate theme issues and perhaps some games to reinforce skills, but most teachers follow a "teach it—talk it—write it" pattern that is fairly predictable. Probably two-thirds of Shannon's mark will be based on what she writes: essays, short answers, projects and exams. Of this mark, about half will be for the substance of what she writes and about half will be for the style and mechanics, things like spelling, punctuation, grammar and paragraphing.

Typical essay writing in grade nine, for English, history, social science and virtually any other subject, will look like the example below:

I remember   Oct. 20

I think that this poem is about an adult remembering the past. Maybe when he lived in his village he must of been having some sort of celebration.

I think the whole point of this poem is to remember the good times, times when a child could run freely at night without wondering or worrying of kidnappers. A time when you didn't need alarms or locks on your windows, and doors.

A time when your biggest worry would be the weather unlike now we wonder which mercedes to take or which car matches your outfit. It was a time long ago.

· When you didn't have the slightest worry.
· When everything seemed perfect, when you could run around the streets.

Grade nine and ten students will be expected to do essays of 300 to 500 words, shorter for grade nine nonacademic; longer for grade ten academic programs. Paragraphing is essential.

Some sophisticated language and style are expected. Spelling mistakes should be limited to more abstruse words, perhaps five a page, and an A student will fix those with the dictionary or computer spell-checker.

By grade ten, Shannon should be building in some quotations from the story or novel under discussion to help prove her point. Parents should remember that the real progress made in writing through middle and high school is not in elimination of errors but in growing sophistication of style. The actual number of mechanical errors stays consistent, but the "quality" of those errors should improve—e.g., while a grade six student might use a comma where a period belongs, a grade ten student would use a comma where a semicolon belongs.

Social sciences. The social science options usually include history, geography or some combination under a title like "Man in Society" and sometimes family studies—not as the old "home ec." but in a course that looks at the family from a sociological perspective. Most provinces require two or more courses in this area, so it's best for Shannon to begin in grade nine.

High school history courses frequently assume that earlier Canadian history has been dealt with in the middle school, so grade nine might well be a "Canada in the Twentieth Century" course that focusses on the two world wars and the social trends from the conscription crisis to the rise of the Beatles (yes, this is history to the next generation). The grade ten course is often a world history course that skims over virtually everything that happened on earth between ancient Egypt and the development of Nintendo (it may leave out one or two items in between, we're afraid). While both courses have an intrinsic subject appeal not found in earlier history courses, real excitement remains in the hands of the teacher.

Quick tips for your child ⚙
Getting Great Marks on a Presentation

A teacher will usually explain just how she intends to mark the presentation (in fact, she may ask other students to do part of the grading). But if she forgets, here's what teachers look for:

- Evidence of preparation: a beginning (introduction), middle (the meat, as it were) and end (often a question period). Tip: refer frequently to some obvious notes prepared in advance, but *don't just read your notes.*

- Evidence of research: a trip to the library always adds ten marks.

- Filling the time: a presentation should last as long as the time allotted; don't expect questions to fill an empty ten minutes.

- A "visual": use of the blackboard (good), an overhead (better), a coloured overhead (wow!); videos can be a plus or a minus.

- Class involvement: Were the other kids interested? Did they ask questions at the end (a smart group always plants a few questions in the audience).

- Rehearsal: one rehearsal in front of a parent frequently does wonders for the quality of a presentation to the class.

Quick tips for your child 💡
How to Ace an Exam

Before the test:

- Study and review not just the night before, but through the whole course.

- Go over all your notes with a friend; better yet, go over all the notes with a *smart* friend.

- Never miss class the last day before an exam. Take notes when the teacher tells you what will be on it.

- Try to anticipate the questions—then practise writing out a few answers.

During the test:

- Take all the time you're given. Ask for more if you need it.

- Pace out the test: figure out how much each question is worth, then give the answer exactly that much time.

- Answer all the questions. When in doubt, guess. A blank is always worth zero; a guess might get you a mark.

- Don't worry about "beautiful"; complete is more important. Cross out mistakes. Add more material with arrows if you need to.

- Check in advance to see if you can use your calculator, or notes, or a dictionary. Then bring what you need.

Geography in grade nine is much more than map making and map reading; it actually goes into questions like Why would anyone build a city here? The result is a combination of geography, history, economics and politics—all at a pretty rudimentary level. By grade ten, geography courses frequently specialize in particular parts of the globe, though the intellectual substance remains the same.

The hybrid courses—"Man in Society" and "Family Studies"—try to introduce sociological ways of looking at humans and human society, but without the historical or geographical focus of the two more specialized options. These courses can be more "fun" than the others, with a focus on current issues like television violence, censorship, parenting and human behaviour.

All these courses will require projects and presentations. In your day, a project was almost always written. You remember the drill: title page, table of contents, introduction, research, bibliography. These days, a project may often be submitted in many forms: wall displays, videos, audio tapes, interviews and presentations. It's harder to find a standard for these more unusual project formats, so teachers frequently make a guess at how much effort went into the research, preparation and presentation. As a parent, try to make sure Shannon is putting in the same hours she would if the project were written.

In the 1970s and 1980s, big business began putting pressure on schools to produce students who could talk as well as write. The result is a tremendous growth in "presentations" done either individually or by a group. A grade nine presentation usually takes five to fifteen minutes of class time (as in written work, the longer the better in terms of marks) and should involve preparation, board work or overheads and perhaps a display or some class involvement. Grade nine and ten students always underestimate the time that's required to put together a presentation and always overestimate the time it will take to present their notes out loud. When you look over the project ahead of time—even better, practise it with your child—remember that a page of notes yields two to three minutes of presentation time. If the assignment calls for ten minutes in front of the class, make sure there are at least three pages of material before Shannon goes up front with her group.

Mathematics. Most provinces require two years of high school math; most universities require three or four years for admission. Grade nine math usually requires a calculator and focusses on problem solving and algebra. Grade ten math moves toward geometry and a slightly more complex variety of problems. Here's a sample for an ordinary grade ten student:

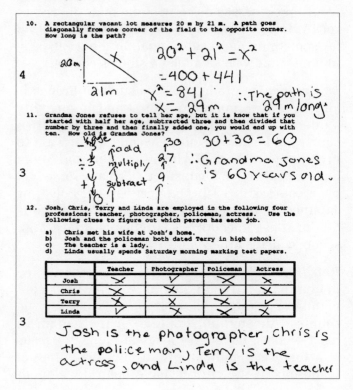

10. A rectangular vacant lot measures 20 m by 21 m. A path goes diagonally from one corner of the field to the opposite corner. How long is the path?

$$20^2 + 21^2 = x^2$$
$$= 400 + 441$$
$$x^2 = 841$$
$$x = 29 \text{ m}$$

∴ The path is 29 m long.

4

11. Grandma Jones refuses to tell her age, but it is know that if you started with half her age, subtracted three and then divided that number by three and then finally added one, you would end up with ten. How old is Grandma Jones?

$$30 + 30 = 60$$

∴ Grandma Jones is 60 years old.

3

12. Josh, Chris, Terry and Linda are employed in the following four professions: teacher, photographer, policeman, actress. Use the following clues to figure out which person has each job.

a) Chris met his wife at Josh's home.
b) Josh and the policeman both dated Terry in high school.
c) The teacher is a lady.
d) Linda usually spends Saturday morning marking test papers.

	Teacher	Photographer	Policeman	Actress
Josh	X	✓	X	X
Chris	X	X	✓	X
Terry	X	X	X	✓
Linda	✓	X	X	X

3

Josh is the photographer, Chris is the policeman, Terry is the actress, and Linda is the teacher

The Library

Despite your child's moaning about the inadequacy of the school library, chances are it's not all that bad. There will be a fair selection of books for adolescent readers, encyclopedias like Compton's and *The Canadian Encyclopedia* that can actually be read by ordinary students, research material on the most popular topics assigned by teachers and magazines for reading when on a spare. Most libraries are open both before and after school—a real plus if your child has reasons to go early or stay late.

The other real plus to high school libraries is the teacher-librarian—sometimes a wonderful, kind adult whom teenagers may turn to in times of stress. As a professional, the teacher-librarian is in a position to help your child do research for projects and presentations far more than the classroom teacher trying to deal with thirty kids at once.

Some libraries come complete with computers for research and typing, video equipment for preparing presentations and audio equipment for doing presentations in class. A few are even connected to computer on-line networks, like Internet or provincial education networks, to hook students up with the most current research and ideas on a topic. Check out your school's library on parents' night.

Art, dramatic arts, music. These so-called artsy subjects are essential for students who have discovered some personal talent during elementary school. And they're not a bad addition to the timetable for students who have at least some interest in exploring them. Some shy students, especially, benefit from the activities in dramatic arts that involve far more role playing than actual acting. Often one or two courses in this area will be required before graduation.

Media studies. This is a hybrid course, partly English, partly drama, partly technology. The hook for teachers is a chance to examine topics related to TV, movies, print and society, while getting some analytical thinking and detailed writing going for students. The hook for students is a video camera: in every course, the students will team up to shoot one, two or three videos ranging from mock-newcasts to pseudo-soap operas to rock videos. Occasionally the camera will be used for something more substantial, but that's usually in the second year of a media studies course.

Languages. In grade nine, the study of French is almost always mandatory for English-speaking students. Graduation sometimes requires two courses in languages, so your child might want to investigate all the offerings in grade ten. Many high schools offer Spanish or German; some will have courses in Latin, modern Greek, Polish or Japanese. For students whose native tongue is one of these specialized languages, these high school courses are usually a cinch.

Religion. If your child attends a Catholic or denominational high school, religion will be a mandatory grade nine course and will likely be required throughout the high school years. In most schools, the course looks at the life of Jesus in a historical context and at how the essential teachings of the church have been developed.

Later courses will link these teachings to the issues of life that she'll encounter as a teen and young adult. The grade ten course deals with the sacraments and other aspects of Catholic doctrine. Any sociological or comparative approach to religion is usually put off to the final years in high school.

Science. Most provinces require two science courses before graduation; many universities want to see four or more. Grade nine and ten science continues to be a hodgepodge, as it was in grade eight—a little biology, some chemistry, some physics. The individual topics gradually become more sophisticated and the lab work becomes more essential.

Shannon will be expected to keep excellent notes during the lessons and make detailed records of her laboratory experiments. Both are carefully marked by the teacher. A wise parent eyeballs the lab book and notes every other week to see how things are going. If the marks aren't good, close down the TV for a half-hour each day and make sure the lab work is rewritten at home.

Business and technology. The grade nine or ten "Introduction to Business" course looks at both business and consumer behaviour, with a little elementary economics thrown in. Most schools also offer a keyboarding course that will save Shannon from a future of two-finger typing— even four-finger typing is a big plus in this computer age.

What used to be called general shop is now labeled "Introduction to Technological Studies" to give it a computer-age attraction. The grade nine course often rotates students through all the school's shops in a smorgasbord approach to the trades; the grade ten courses will offer specialization in whatever particular areas your school is equipped, from auto repair to wood shop and whatever lies alphabetically in-between. Tech

Four Myths about High School

In his book *The Good School,* sociologist Alan King identified four common untruths about high school kids.

- *Students who come from broken homes are less happy with school.* Not true, but they are less likely to participate in extracurricular activities.

- *Students who work part-time do less well in school than those who don't.* Not true…unless the young person is working more than fifteen hours a week.

- *High expectations on conduct and achievement alienate students.* Not so. The more teachers demand, the better the attitude of kids toward school.

- *Many good students drop out.* Good students rarely drop out; kids who have fallen behind are more likely to quit. And two-thirds of those will drop back in later on to try to finish high school.

Warning Signs of the Troubled High School Student

High school students are more secretive that elementary school kids, so sometimes it's very hard to tell when they're about to get into trouble. Nonetheless, here are some things to look for:

- shows a sudden change of attitude or loss of interest in school;

- frequently "sleeps in," often combined with "couldn't get to sleep" nights;

- has a new group of friends—especially kids you don't know and your child doesn't want you to meet;

- shows a sudden decline in marks, or no report card at all—(check with your school if you haven't got a report by the end of October);

- doesn't come home after school as before;

- drops out of extracurricular activities;

- money starts disappearing from the house or your child isn't where she says she was going to be when you called.

courses have been losing popularity in high schools as more and more young people fail to see the connection between school and getting ready for some real work after graduation. That's a shame. As a friend pointed out to us, "What I learned from shop came down to this. There are going to be guys up on a roof hammering down shingles all day long, working like crazy, and there's going to be one guy on the ground with the blueprints and some measuring tools watching them work. I decided in grade ten to be the guy on the ground."

And everything else. Any particular high school will offer up to fifty courses in grades nine and ten depending on its size, teachers and facilities. If your child attends a vocational school or specialized technical school, the offerings will be somewhat different from the preceding. You and your child will want to spend some considerable amount of time examining the choices and completing the option sheet, but there's no particular reason to panic at this stage. Few schools permit life-determining choices at the grade eight, nine or ten level. Even at the senior high level, the worst that can happen is that your child ends up spending an extra year in high school after changing her mind about the direction of her life. For most kids, grades nine and ten are a wonderful, rambunctious introduction to serious school and serious learning.

What If My Child Gets in Trouble?

More young people seem to get into trouble in high school than in elementary school because the trouble is made more obvious: they flunk a course. In elementary school, the principal and staff have to make a decision that holds back a child for a full year, essentially failing her in every course, and they do so only for a tiny fraction of students. In high school, Shannon can fail English or science while she aces math and phys. ed. with no one even raising an eyebrow. Subject failure becomes much more common than grade failure ever was.

At one time, there was an expectation that teachers would fail 10 percent of the students in a course just to satisfy the statistical demands of the bell curve; but these days only about one student in fifteen or twenty fails a subject in grade nine and ten. That failure rates rises dramatically in the senior years of high school.

Few young people fail a course early in high school because the subject itself is so difficult or the demands of the teacher so draconian. Mostly, kids fail because they don't *want* to pass. For Shannon to fail in these early high school grades, she must actively choose not to show up for class and not to complete assignments and tests. Unfortunately, you are not likely to be aware that this choice has been made until the failing mark arrives (and many adolescents have found ways to head off mailed report cards, or simply "forget" to bring home the reports they receive at school). There are signs along the way, of course: "My teacher is a goof," or "Math is sooo boring," or persistent sleeping in to avoid a class, but often these get overlooked. Nor do most high schools and high school teachers look after attendance closely enough to warn you *before* your child is in trouble. The more usual pattern is for you to see a failing mark at midterm and then find out, after asking, that Shannon has skipped eight classes without excuses and failed to complete the major class project. Nice surprise.

So then what? Shannon has failed two courses, and her options at school will come down to three: going to summer school, repeating the course the following year or going to night school. The summer school option offers an opportunity to retake a failed course in fewer hours than the

Dropouts and Stop-outs

The statistics on dropouts are invariably frightening—10, 20 or 30 percent of high school students drop out before completion—but they don't tell us how many kids drop out and *stay* out. Most dropout statistics come from registers of students who choose to stop attending school, for whatever reason, even if they've only shown their faces for a single day early in September. Dropout statistics don't record when these same students re-enroll, and they go wildly askew with students who may take seven years to finish up a four-year high school program or with adults who take a few courses to finally get their high school diplomas.

The truth is, the number of regularly attending students who drop out, and stay out of high school forever, is very small—probably under 10 percent of the current high school group. The real world tends to bring a message home to young people about the value of education, even if they ignore it from you, their teachers and those freebie commercial spots on television.

Part-time Jobs

Part-time jobs can begin as early as grade seven—baby-sitting, delivering newspapers, helping out in the family business—but they become an *issue* by grade ten. By age fourteen, your child will be able to take any number of jobs, from working at the local hamburger joint to painting a house. Something like 10 percent of all the teenagers in North America will work for one company: McDonald's. Most of these McJobs pay minimum wage, but all provide a window on the real world of work.

The only trouble is, that window is distorted. Unlike real life, most kids are allowed to keep their pay cheques while they're housed and fed for free. Unlike real life, the jobs are low level and upward mobility is unimportant. Unlike real life, it doesn't make all that much difference if a teenager is fired or out of work for a period of time.

Is part-time work a good thing? We think so. It teaches responsibility, dogged effort, business expectations and a host of miscellaneous skills. But these jobs lead nowhere in particular—and they're not nearly as important as school. When that question comes up—and it will—make sure you're clear that the upcoming history test is more important than another six-hour shift at the bun warmer.

regular year and with less disruption to graduation timetables. On the other hand, many young people end up taking an extra year to finish high school in any event, so they see no problem in simply retaking the course the following year or semester. The night school option is used mostly by senior high school students. In most provinces, Shannon's failing mark will be deleted from the school record when she later passes the course. The advantage of this approach is to make possible that old "try, try again" ethic; the disadvantage is that our failures in real life are rarely so easily forgotten.

Regardless of how Shannon chooses to deal with the failure, it's time for a serious talk and some serious self-examination, especially in these early high school years. Where was the problem? A group of Shannon's friends? Disinterest in the course itself? The teacher? Failure to set aside study time? Too much part-time work? You shouldn't discount the possibility that drug or alcohol abuse can be part of the problem, much as you shudder to think so. Both problems start at the end of middle school, but their effects become apparent early in high school. Keep both eyes open.

For students who are simply struggling with course material that is too difficult for them, a change in course level (stream), help from a resource teacher or hired tutoring may make all the difference. If not, you'll end up with a dropout.

The school dropout doesn't suddenly decide to leave school at age sixteen; she begins to work on that as early as age eleven or twelve. The signs are obvious early on, when you look back: boredom, lack of commitment, class skipping, subject failure, lousy marks, indifferent attitude. By age sixteen, there's little you can do to stop a child from dropping out unless you began to take action at age thirteen or fourteen.

But dropping out doesn't mean you're child has rowed her boat over some educational Niagara. For most children, dropping out is a hiatus before the kids decide to drop back in. Fortunately, most high schools permit students to come back when they choose—frequently after a desultory few months at work, or when that wonderful minimum-wage job disappears, or when the boyfriend goes off with someone else. Parents should not be too quick to panic or slam doors if Shannon decides she's had enough of school; she'll figure out soon enough that a grade ten credential won't take you far these days. Patience has its rewards.

The Parents' Role

Your role becomes more difficult as your children reach high school age because they'll often tell you that you don't have one. The kids are wrong, of course, about this and many other things; in fact, anyone who takes seriously the wisdom of a thirteen-year-old has watched one television sit-com too many. The truth is this: in successful families, parents continue to be involved with their kids' education right up to the Ph.D. level. Grade nine is certainly not the time to "butt out."

Maintain a structure. A grade nine student should not set her own bedtime, or determine what time she will arise, or be asked to schedule her own homework and reading time. Assuming you have already developed a schedule for all these, stick to it. In grade nine, you child will *average* at least thirty minutes of homework a night; by grade ten it should be closer to an hour. But note the word "average." In high school, there really are some nights when none of the teachers has assigned work, but there will be other nights when your child will have to put in five hours to get a history project finished, and

How to Create a Teenage Monster...

Good parenting is tough, but being a lousy parent is easy. If you want to see your child develop into a monster or end up in jail, try the following:

- Be hypocritical: preach a certain behaviour to your child, then do the opposite.

- Hit your kid: there's nothing like slapping a child to make a teen (a) behave even worse or (b) run away from home altogether.

- When you can't hit, yell: even if your teen won't listen, the neighbours might appreciate your anger, especially if you use colourful vocabulary.

- Don't set any limits: let your child proceed with all the wisdom of her sixteen years, but be prepared to look after the baby and/or drug habit that results.

- Wink when he gets in trouble: sure, your child got caught doing 140 km in a 60 km zone, but boys will be boys, wink-wink, nudge-nudge. Next time you see the police, your son will doing hard time.

- Ignore the good stuff: If your child aces a math test, who cares? Spend your family time yelling about her messy bedroom.

What Your Child Should Know at the End of Grade Ten

As your child's program gets more specific, it becomes harder for us to apply general statements to what he should know. Nonetheless, here are a few basics:

- can identify prejudice, stereotyping and point of view in written and spoken materials;

- understands the concept of audience, both in speaking and writing;

- adapts level of language and style (formal, informal, etc.) to different demands;

- reads widely, both adult and some young-adult fiction;

- can do an effective presentation of ten to twenty minutes with a group;

- can use basic literary terms (e.g., alliteration, metaphor, conflict, theme) to discuss print material;

- can organize and write an essay of 1,000 words, incorporating quotations and research material;

- can discuss the techniques and influence of TV and other visual media;

- uses keyboard to type essays and navigate through computer programs;

there is always time needed for reading and review. Your child should have an assignment calendar to help avoid test and project crunches, but they'll occur anyhow, often just before holidays and a week before exams. Make sure your child has the structure and support ("Well, you can do without TV for one night") that will help her get through the crunch.

Talk together; read together. Statisticians say that the average parent and average teenager engage in four minutes of significant conversation per week. Per week! We suggest that successful families talk more than this, often over breakfast or dinner, even if the kids tend to reply in monosyllables or fill their sentences with "like" and "you know." We also know that many more parents keep reading with their adolescent children than the kids are likely to admit. There is no reason family reading time—that twenty minutes before bed—can't continue. Failing that, you can always open up whatever your child is reading, read a paragraph aloud and ask what she thinks about the book in hand. And failing that, there's the newspaper. Oral reading of Ann Landers and the horoscopes start the day for many families. Nor does the importance of buying books for your child end when her baby-sitting money becomes five times her weekly allowance. Shannon is far more likely to buy a rock tape or expensive running shoes than a book, alas, because of the triumph of North American marketing. You can keep books coming into Shannon's hands by offering to buy one for if she buys one for herself, or by trading novels back and forth after you each read them. Young people who continue to read on their own throughout the teenage years significantly outperform students who stop doing so.

Eyeball the homework. We've written before about the importance of the kitchen table as a study centre; this remains true for high school.

As a parent, you don't want to do Shannon's homework, but you want to be sure it gets done and gets done properly. That means you should be close enough to field the odd question, close enough to offer words of encouragement when Shannon gets discouraged and close enough to just take a glance over the page when Shannon says she's done. The kitchen table is perfect; Shannon's "Private—Keep Out" bedroom is not.

Keep going to parents' night, the fashion show, the musical, etc. High school parents' nights are invariably a zoo, with hundreds of moms and dads crowded into a gym or groping along strange halls to find classrooms for a ten-minute interview. But the interviews are important, both so you'll know what's going on and to show Shannon (and her teachers) that you care about her achievement. High school report cards have always been less informative than elementary school reports and with the advent of computers they've gotten worse. Computerized comments (teachers are given a list of thirty to 200 possible phrases, all guaranteed to be inoffensive) have managed to remove the last area where a teacher could try to tell you how Shannon works, or thinks, or behaves. So the only way to find out what Shannon's "68 . . . trying hard" really means is to ask the teacher, and the best time to do that is at parents' night. (Most high school teachers will return phone calls—but do you really want four or eight callbacks?)

High schools often have an array of other events that parents can attend if they wish—football games, fashion shows, awards nights, music association dinners, curriculum presentations—and involved parents make a point to go to some of these. Your attendance says that school is important; it says that involvement and activity are important; it says that achievement counts. When Shannon no longer seems to be listening to

- knows appropriate history facts from the areas studied and can connect to current events;

- can organize, research and prepare a lengthy report or presentation without teacher assistance;

- can develop and interpret a wide array of maps, graphs and charts;

- recognizes the equivalent forms of a number (e.g., $-1/2 = 1/-2 = -0.5$);

- can use ratios, proportions and rates to solve a problem;

- can handle algebraic equations, including binomial and trinomial;

- can translate verbal expressions into mathematical equations;

- can express large numbers in scientific notation;

- can make real-world use of his math knowledge (building, architecture, tracking the stock market);

- can use coordinates to create two-dimensional shapes, can flip and rotate three-dimensional shapes;

- has mastered area, volume and capacity for most common shapes;

- can construct and interpret scale drawings and maps.

your words, she's watching carefully what you do. Be sure that message reinforces the importance of schooling.

We could go on with further words of advice, like Polonius to Hamlet, but we know full well what happened to that kindly old man. Let's end with these encouraging words instead. The teenage years have gotten a lousy rep. They are rarely as difficult or problem plagued or antagonistic as they seem on television and film. Nor are all teenagers the sullen, foul-mouthed punks we see hanging around the malls. Most children grow up to be fair-to-middling reasonable adolescents, which isn't a bad thing. You've lost a child, but you're gaining a junior partner.

CHAPTER 12

Senior High School: Grades Eleven, Twelve and OAC

Congratulations: your child has made it to grade eleven without turning to drugs, getting pregnant, totalling the car, dropping out of school or becoming the subject of a made-for-TV movie. All these things may still occur, but you'd probably have seen some evidence of grief already if it were about to strike in the immediate future. Chances are that your child Alan has turned out reasonably all right; almost all children do. Your real concerns aren't with disaster anymore; they're with school achievement and Alan's future, two topics that have a lot to do with each other.

Sadly, you are probably not in a very good position to change either. During his first two or three years in high school, Alan will already have established a group of friends whose voices are more immediate than yours. He will have

Send Your Teenager Away, Far Away...

One of the most valuable experiences for a teenager can be an exchange program with a teen from another province or country. Foreign-language facility is not essential, but most programs require parents to handle some of the cost. Here's where to look for a program:

- Rotary Club. This group has been sponsoring exchange programs for years to countries like England, Japan, Australia and Sweden. School guidance counsellors usually have an application form.

- Ministries or Department of Education. Most provincial education departments have some kind of exchange program, often heavily funded by the taxpayer. A call to the ministry or department will provide more information.

- AFS Interculture Canada offers programs that range from six-week summer exchanges to one-year international programs in more than thirty countries.

- EF Education Foundation for Foreign Study sponsors half- or full-year exchanges with Australia, New Zealand, France, England and Germany.

established a pattern of school work and effort that sets a level of achievement (and report card marks) that is hard to change. And he may have decided that any number of things—his car; his girlfriend, Christina; his job at Harvey's; his friends—are more important than his future. All these explain why any parent who begins reading this book now is reading it too late. Sorry.

If you began reading this book earlier, or were doing good parenting without any advice, then you ought to understand what's going on in Alan's high school and the kinds of choices he faces at this point in his life. Your word will no longer be the final one, but it is still an important one to your child. Better that you should be informed about the possibilities and dangers of senior high school than you should have your ideas ignored because they're based on information that's thirty years out-of-date.

How Senior High Schools Sort into Three Groups

In Canada, senior high school is where the kids are finally aimed at work, at community college or at the university. We use the word "aimed" because the system really does aim your child in a particular direction—through course offerings, course expectations, teacher style and guidance procedures. It would also be fair to say that young people and their families usually have some say in choosing where the school will aim them, but only if they want to exercise that say. For the child who is without goals, or for families who don't care much, the school will make virtually all the choices. For more concerned parents—obviously this includes you because you're reading this book—the choices come down to three:

For the child going on to university. Your child may be aimed at university by family expectations, by his own achievement, by native intelligence, by concerned teachers or by some combination of all these factors. Fifty years ago, when not even one child in twenty went on to university, the selection of those students was usually based on the first two items: you got to university if you were rich or you were very, very smart. These days, between 20 and 30 percent of high school students (depending on the province) go on to university, so the criteria have become much less clear. Most Canadian students go on to Canadian universities where access to piles of family cash (still helpful in the United States) is far less important than a strong set of grade twelve marks.

University entrance in Canada varies somewhat from school to school, but is based almost entirely on marks achieved at the end of grade eleven or early in grade twelve. Ontario requires the marks in six OAC courses, formerly called grade thirteen. A top program, like mechanical engineering at the University of Waterloo, requires an average well over 85 percent (A+) for admission. Even enrolling as a general arts major at a nearby university will call for an average of 70 percent (B) or higher. The competition for marks that results has long had an effect on academic senior high school education. Starting in grade eleven, school gets much tougher. Teachers can demand more, cajole less and fail with impunity—and the kids know it.

By the time Alan hits calculus and finite math in grade twelve or thirteen, he may well have failed a subject or two despite his best efforts. Most provinces permit a student to simply retake a course as often as he likes, leading some students to shop among regular school, summer school and night school for the easiest teacher and the highest grade. There are a handful of universities that look at other aspects of student achievement—athletics, leadership, arts background—but these factors make little difference

Grade Twelve Kids Work—But at What?

In 1991, the Hamilton, Ontario, public school system surveyed its grade twelve students to find out about the amount of time they put into paying jobs and into homework in English. Here are the results for "advanced level" students:

- Time spent on part-time employment:
  Did not have a job: 38 percent
  Worked 1-10 hours weekly on a job: 25 percent
  Worked 11-20 hours weekly on a job: 28 percent
  Worked more than 21 hours weekly on a job: 9 percent

- Time spent on written English homework:
  Less than 2 hours per week: 49 percent
  From 2 to 5 hours per week: 46 percent
  More than 5 hours per week: 5 percent

Why Do the Kids Work?

Queen's University sociologist Alan King frequently does surveys of high school students for organizations like the Ontario Secondary School Teachers' Federation. Here a summary of his findings on high school students and work:

Reasons given by senior high students:
(in order of importance)
- to develop a feeling of independence and responsibility
- to buy clothes
- to be independent of parents

Reasons given by junior high students:
- to buy more clothes
- to develop a feeling of independence and responsibility
- to buy a car or motorbike

How many of the kids work?
- 21 percent of kids age fourteen and fifteen have jobs, and average $2,293 in yearly income
- 69 percent of kids sixteen and seventeen have jobs, and average $3,667 in yearly income

to admission. As they say about location in real estate, three things are important in getting into a Canadian university—marks, marks and marks.

This simple fact puts incredible pressure on senior high school students like Alan. Teachers demand serious, mind-numbing study before tests and want to see projects and research papers that could take ten to thirty hours to prepare. At the same time, Alan is likely to find a part-time job that will take up ten to twenty hours a week and he may start spending time with a romantic friend, who will take up endless hours in person and on the phone. The good news from all this is that Alan will finally watch less TV: teenagers log fewer viewing hours at 2.8 per day than any other age group in our society. The bad news is that he will also find less time to sleep.

A fair number of students can't handle the shift in pressure and respond by failing courses, changing career goals or dropping out. The only up side is that failure in high school is cheap and easy to recover from; failure at university is expensive and stays on the transcript virtually forever. With failure rates in some high school courses of up to 50 percent of the class, parents should be prepared for some significant hand holding.

For the child going to work. Despite dire predictions from the business community, there still are jobs for students with only a high school education. Thank goodness. A fair number of our young people get sick of school—any kind of school— well before grade twelve. For them, the goal is to get out, get a job and get on with life. In order to do that, high school has to make them as employable as possible as fast as it can.

The old answer to this—the "vocational" stream—is disappearing in many schools and jurisdictions. The replacement is a "general" program that can aim a student either at work or at community college—depending on both your child's patience and the current job outlook. A good high school will try to offer the non-university student as many technical subjects as it can: drafting, design, auto body, woodworking, building construction, horticulture, auto mechanics—some boards or districts list hundreds of different courses. At some schools, your child will be able to specialize for two or three years in a particular tech subject—say, electrical—and then move on to a job or apprenticeship (especially if you have an "in" in the trade). In Germany, this is the system for *most* high school students, and it works well. In Canada, the connection between high school specialization and available jobs is fraught with problems because of nonexistent apprenticeship programs, closed unions or limited numbers of start-up positions. Nonetheless, for students who want to go to work quickly, there really is no other option but the "general" program.

For the child who doesn't know what he wants to do. If Alan falls into this group, he will be least well served by the average high school. A child without a strong urge to get into university is unlikely to garner high marks in the demanding "advanced" stream. A child without a strong urge to work in a particular field is unlikely to be much interested in technical subjects and may not fit, socially, in the "general" stream. Unfortunately, between a third and a half of our senior high school students fall into this middle group of Don't-Knows and they can end up wandering through the corridors of high school like lost souls.

At one time, the community college system provided an out for the Don't-Knows. They could stay in the "advanced" stream, with lacklustre marks, or decide to go upscale from the "general" stream with Bs or better and be reasonably assured of admission to a community college. Then they'd have two or three more years to get

University Entrance Requirements

University of British Columbia—Arts

High school graduation, including Math 11, Math 12, and (desired) Physics 12.

University of British Columbia—Science

High school graduation, including Math 12, Chemistry 11, Physics 11 plus one of Biology 12, Chemistry 12, Computer Science 12, Geology 12 or Physics 12.

University of Saskatchewan—Arts and Science

High school graduation, including English A30, B30, Algebra 30, Geo-Trig 30 or Math 30, plus two other subjects at 30-level.

University of Saskatchewan—Engineering

English A30, B30, Algebra 30, Geo-Trig 30 (or Math B30/C30), Chemistry 30, Physics 30, plus one other subject at 30-level.

St. Mary's University—Arts

From Nova Scotia: grade twelve graduation, including English 441 and four other subjects at the 44-level.

St. Mary's University—Engineering

Grade twelve graduation, with English 441, Math 441, Physics 441, Chemistry 441 and one other subject at the 44-level.

Co-op Education: A Great Idea

One problem with our mostly academic high schools is that the kids don't get enough real-life work experience. Part-time jobs offer some window on the world of work, but too often it's a window made greasy by bubbling French fries. Co-op education does a better job, by giving high school students a chance to try their hand at (or at least get close to) high-level careers.

This is how co-op works. A senior high school student elects to take one period for a co-op placement. The teacher co-op monitor matches the student to an employer on the basis of mutual interest and compatibility. Then the student goes off daily for that period to work at the co-op job site.

The up side: an honest look at what real employers expect and a chance to explore a future avenue of employment. The down side: usually high school co-op kids don't get paid.

their act together before having to deal with that real and sometimes cruel world out there.

But not anymore. With the decline of instant job access for university students, our community colleges have been jammed full of kids who *ought* to be at university or kids who have finished university with a degree in anthropology and decided, finally, that they want a job that might pay the rent. The community college teachers love these bright, motivated students. Unfortunately, these kids don't leave much room for the high school Don't-Knows with their low-B averages. Sometimes it's harder to get into a top-ranked community college program than into a general B.A. program at university.

There are no easy solutions for parents and the Don't-Knows themselves. School guidance counsellors can sometimes be helpful and encouraging; occasionally they offer group counselling sessions on goal setting and even computer aptitude or interest programs to help kids find a direction for their lives. If these services aren't sufficient, then parents can contact a counsellor or psychologist (look under "Career Counselling" in the Yellow Pages) who can do a set of aptitude or interest tests for a few hundred dollars that may help your child figure out where he wants to go.

If you think back honestly, you'll remember that many of us were quite directionless at age sixteen to eighteen—in fact, some of us are still in that state. The difference between our generation and that of our children is simple: there were plenty of jobs and easy admission to higher education when we were Don't-Knows, but that just isn't true for our kids. They have to make big decisions sooner—or at least decisions that are good enough for the time being. If you're the parent of a Don't-Know, helping with those good-enough decisions is a big part of your role.

Should You and Your Child Choose a Different Senior High School?

In some communities, the senior high school is physically a separate building from the junior high. As such, the change to a new building is a natural time to re-examine school options. Even if your community puts all the high school grades into the same building, grade eleven is usually a good time to rethink the current situation. Try these three questions to begin:

- Is the school good enough?

- Is my child learning and relatively happy?

- Does the school offer what my child will need next?

The previous chapter provides some guidelines for evaluating a high school program that might be worth looking at again. The key difference in senior high school lies in preparation and specialization.

If your child is likely to go directly to a job or apprenticeship, you want to make certain that his high school offers the technical subjects, co-op programs and hands-on experience that will prepare him for the work to come. Another high school in your city or region may well be stronger in a particular trade, and that might justify a transfer. Some high school vocational and technical programs are so good that employers pluck the top students for employment right after graduation. There are never enough nursing assistants, dental assistants, auto-body-repair workers, electricians and plumbers to go around. Good preparation in high school and a good recommendation from a high school teacher is often enough to start a lifetime of work in these areas.

If your child is going on to university, then the quality of education in his last two or three years

Choosing a Senior High School

What your child wants in a high school:

According to surveys by Alan King and his associates at Queen's University, this is what young people look for in a school:
- to be with friends;
- convenient location and/or timetable to fit in work, social life, etc.;
- extracurricular activities that suit current interests.

What you want in a high school for your child:
- high academic achievement and reputation;
- best preparation for university, community college or future careers;
- a stimulating but safe environment for learning.

The differences between these two wish lists make the selection of a high school very tricky indeed. Good luck in your negotiations.

has a direct bearing on his success later on. Universities keep unofficial lists that rank high schools on the past success of students who have come to them and that try to compensate for marking-standard differences (an A at one school might barely equal a B at another) to level the playing field of admission. Unfortunately, these lists are never made public, so parents have little recourse but to rely on "reputation," however unclear that may be. In urban centres, some high schools have long traditions of sending many students on to Canadian universities and sometimes to prestige colleges like Harvard or Oxford. There's no guarantee that such a high school will do a better job educating your child, but at least there's some tradition of success and adequate preparation. Conversely, an *outstanding* student at a less spectacular school is often highly prized by universities. Certainly a university application with a number of honours and awards even from a "no name" high school looks better than a do-nothing application from a prestigious private school.

The Course Work

The course work and options in grades eleven and twelve (and OAC year in Ontario) is similar to that offered earlier, but now there is even more choice and even more specialization. We can't begin to run through the hundreds of possible courses your child might be able to take in the various subject areas, but we can offer a few comments on and examples of some of the more usual courses.

English. In most provinces, English remains mandatory right through high school regardless of whether your child is university bound or job bound. The courses often follow the same pattern as previous ones: a novel, a play (often by

Shakespeare), a handful of short stories, some essays. Students will write essays that are somewhat longer (three pages or 1,000 words is not uncommon) and prepare presentations that may last for twenty or thirty minutes. Here's the first page of a character portrait of Sergius in Shaw's *Arms and the Man*, written by an average grade eleven advanced-level student.

> Sergius Saranoff is a major in the Bulgarian Army. Being handsome and tall, it seems normal to have women gawking over him. His nose is thin but his nostrils are large, his chin demonstrates superiority. Observing his eyes and eyebrows you can conclude that he is a very perceptive, curious man. He is very gallant when in front of the Petkoffs, kissing their hands. He is engaged to Raina Petkoff, the daughter of Major Petkoff, who Sergius was in the war with. He is from a wealthy background and knows good family values. It seems strange that he's so into family values because he's having an affair. He's having this affair with Louka, the Petkoff's maid. Sergius is a proud, arrogant man that thinks he should be placed in higher positions. (wanting to be higher than a major)

The work is competently organized, with specific examples and a few quotations to make the key points. There are still spelling mistakes, colloquialisms and paragraphing problems that keep the essay below the A level, but the student is showing more insight into character and more general sophistication in writing than she would have in grade nine.

Many high schools conduct formal examinations in the senior years, partially to get students ready for university, partially because parents expect these ritual rites of passage. There's no particular indication that exams offer any better evaluation than "continuous evaluation" (meaning a combination of tests, projects, presentations, daily marks and small assignments), but they remain a new and sometimes daunting ordeal for students. In some schools, students can be "recommended" so they don't have to take exams, often if their average is over 70 percent. This is why Alan can spend a week sitting around the house, watching TV during exam period, and perhaps only wander into school for a single exam. He's not kidding when he explains this to you; that's how the system works.

By grades twelve and thirteen, many teachers will expect that student essays will be submitted in a typed or computer-printed format. Here's an average grade twelve piece of work:

"MUSIC SHOULD BE PLAYED TO THE MAX"

informal style

Can you imagine it's about two o'clock in the afternoon and you are just about to take a nap, when all of a sudden you hear the loudest music you have ever heard. Your windows start shaking and you think a tornado is coming. You run to the window to see where all the noise is coming from and all you see is a bright red sports car with a guy sitting inside who can barely see over the steering wheel, waiting for the light to change. Then you think to yourself people have been listening to music in public places without headphones for the longest time, and why shouldn't they? Not everyone has the same taste in music, that's what makes everyone different from each other. There are people with different cultures that like to listen to their own type of music and are not embarrassed about it. Music should be played freely and as loud as one wants to, considering the

not clear why p of v changed?

A typed essay has to be carefully prepared before the typing actually begins, a process that might first require two drafts in longhand. A computer essay can be continually rewritten on the screen, even printed out several times before the final copy is pulled from the machine. Better teachers will ask to look at the work in several stages along the way. So should you. Revising at this level should mean re-thinking, not just cleaning up mistakes.

Finished work still has to be printed out on paper (submitting a computer disc is considered a bit cheap, unless the teacher is very, very techno-hip) and would be relatively error-free if computer spell-checkers and grammar-checkers really did their job. Because they don't, it's still wise for Mom or Dad to take a look through just before the work is submitted.

Mathematics. A university-bound student will have to take two or three senior math courses in order to graduate. That simple calculator you helped buy in grade nine just won't do the appropriate tricks anymore; be ready to spend $20 to $100 on a "scientific" calculator to do the more sophisticated work (especially trigonometric calculations) in these senior grades.

In grade eleven, the topics include ratio, proportion, functions and transformations, quadratic equations, analytic geometry, sequences and series. Topics in grade twelve traditionally include algebra, polynomials, radicals, exponential functions, geometry and trigonometry. In grade thirteen in Ontario—or in "advanced placement" math in other provinces—both finite math and calculus are introduced. These brain-bruising courses tend to divide the future scientists and engineers from the rest of us. Don't be surprised to see Alan pulling out his hair—he still has enough of it—while he labours over his math text. Here's a sample of what grade twelve work looks like in an advanced-level course:

The big change in these subjects over the past few years has been a new emphasis on verbal and written problem solving. Math teachers are looking for more than mechanical ability; they want your child to be able to think through a problem. This is true at both the advanced and general levels, though this example is from a grade twelve advanced-level student.

---

1. Express $\displaystyle\sum_{i=9}^{32} (i^2 - 3i)$ with a lower limit of 1.

$$= 54 + 70 + 88 + 108 + \ldots + 928$$

$\underset{16}{}\ \underset{18}{}\ \underset{20}{}$

$$\sum_{i=1}^{23} (\qquad)$$

2. Express $\dfrac{1}{2} + \dfrac{3}{4} + \dfrac{5}{8} + \dfrac{7}{16} + \ldots + \dfrac{19}{1024}$ in summation notation.

$$= \sum_{i=1}^{10} \frac{2i-1}{2^i}$$

3. Evaluate each of the following:

    a) $\displaystyle\sum_{i=1}^{23} (2i - 3)$ b) $81 + 78 + 75 + 72 + \ldots + 33$

$$= -1 + 1 + 3 + 5 + \ldots + 43$$

$a = -1$
$d = 2$
$n = 23.$

$$S_n = \frac{n}{2}\left[2a + (n-1)d\right]$$

$$= \frac{23}{2}\left[-2 + (22)2\right]$$

$$= 483$$

$a = 81$
$d = -3$
$n = ?$

$t_n = a + (n-1)d.$
$33 = 81 + (n-1)-3$
$-48 = 3n - 3$
$-45 = -3n$
$n = 15$

$$S_n = \frac{n}{2}\left[2a + (n-1)d\right]$$
$$= \frac{15}{2}\left[2(81) + 14(-3)\right]$$

162

Everything else. The other courses offered in the various departments and at the various levels differ so much from school to school, province to province, that it's really quite impossible for us to outline what's happening in history, science, technology, drama, languages, geography, phys. ed., music and the various other subjects. Most boards or districts of education have elaborate booklets explaining all this. In addition, every high school is expected to have courses of study on file for each subject. These are available to parents if you want to spend the mind-numbing hours required to get through the bureaucratic educationalese in which the documents are written. Otherwise, talk to your child. He often has a handle on what's going on. And go to the parents' nights just to make sure your child hasn't grabbed the wrong handle.

What Parents Can Do

Hang tough. There is a nasty tendency out there—fuelled by *The Simpsons* and *Married with Children*—to treat older teenagers as if they were really adults without need of supervision. Your child will have developed sophisticated techniques by now to make you feel totally incompetent as a parent: invidious comparisons to more "liberal" families ("Bob's family lets *his* girlfriend sleep over"); unpleasant references to your old-fashioned values and/or personal hypocrisy ("You drink, so how come it's a crime when I get drunk just this once?"); logical arguments based on phony generalizations and clever redefinitions ("So if it's okay for Bob to drive us to the concert, then I guess I can come back whenever Bob decides to drive back"). There is no obvious solution to the assault that parents face from both the media and their children except to hang tough.

Teenagers need a structure. School can't create one all by itself, the media would rather see

What Happens to Those French Immersion Kids

A great many kids start out in French immersion only to "unimmerse" themselves in high school. This happens for several reasons:

- Course selection in French is always smaller than it is in English, so there seems to be greater freedom of choice for regular students.

- Young people frequently decide that *their* agenda and *their* friends are more important than *your* theory about the importance of a second language.

- And the grass always looks greener on the other side of the linguistic fence.

If you have any influence left as a parent, it would be wise to try to keep your child "immersed" in at least some of his courses. A second language is always an asset—even more in this complex world—regardless of whether Quebec stays in Canada or defines itself away.

When They're Too Old to Spank...

- **Talk to them.** Teenagers don't want to know what they did wrong *after* they did it; they want the rules laid down in advance. If they step over a boundary, talk about it before you take action.

- **Ground 'em.** Grounding (no visits to friends and no friends visiting) is considered a fair punishment by most teenagers. The time period for the grounding relates to the severity of the offence; e.g., if your child stays out an hour past curfew, a one-weekend grounding would be considered fair.

- **Take away a privilege.** This is the second most approved punishment. You can forbid playing Nintendo, driving the car, going to a concert—but always for a limited period of time.

- **Dock 'em pay.** If you're child still gets an allowance, dock a certain amount of money for minor offences against family decency (e.g., 25 cents per wet bathing suit in the hamper; $2 if you have to pick up your teen's room *after* he cleans it).

You don't get out of being a parent just because your child's hit high school; you just have to get smarter at the job.

your child a hog-wild consumer than a functioning adult and organized religion has little influence with most young people. That leaves you, Mom and Dad. Somebody has to set curfews, limits on behaviour and expectations around the house. Somebody has to say that drugs do real damage, that teenage pregnancy is a bad idea and a teenager bringing up a baby is worse, that school and study are more important than ten extra hours at work to buy a new pair of Nikes. That somebody is you.

It is helpful if you're knowledgeable about the world your child inhabits and the one he's about to enter. This book should help you with that. But all the knowledge in the world can't save you if you collapse in the face of arguments and pleading from teens who think they know what life is all about. There's a fair deal to be said about the virtues of being arbitrary—even if it's only to give your teenager something to complain about to his friends. It will be far easier for Alan to leave that Saturday-night party at one o'clock if he can say "My parents will kill me if I come in late" than if he has to explain about reasonable hours of sleep, physical limitations of the teenage body and the fact that he needs eight hours on Sunday to work on a kineseology project. Do Alan a favour—set some limits.

Stay involved. You may not know all the wrinkles about co-op education, apprenticeships and university entrance, but you do have twenty more years of experience with many things than your child. If you find time to talk to a guidance counsellor at the school, you may actually know as much about Alan's situation and the hoops he has to jump through in the near future as Alan does. Don't abandon your child just because he's taller than you are. Go to the parents' night. Attend the open house. Call the school when Alan's sick so they don't have to call you. Keep an eye on Alan's friends. Make sure the boy eats and sleeps and reads a book now and then.

It is unlikely that you can help much with homework in calculus or biology, but you can still eyeball the work to make sure all the questions are complete. You may not remember *King Lear* well enough to offer many ideas on the paper Alan has to write, but you can look through the computer printout to make sure he used the spell-checker and put page numbers on. And certainly you're going to be smart enough to praise Alan for his successes and ease up on the nagging over his failures. We've got faith in you.

CHAPTER 13

Special Education

Thirty years ago, there was a stigma to special education. The name alone meant some children attending "special" schools, or stuck in special classrooms with other kids suffering very serious intellectual and physical limitations. Thirty years ago, a child in special education was subject to name calling in school and often limited to an education that finished off in grade ten and left him with grade-five-level skills.

How times change! These days, special education is like flying first class on a plane where all the other kids are stuck back in the regular cabin: the seats are wider, there's more room to move around and the flight attendant is so much more attentive. The stigma has mostly disappeared, replaced by envy from kids who don't get extra time to write tests, or a room with a computer to type up their projects, or time-out with a teacher who'll listen to their problems. Special education these days is what good education has always been about: individual attention, flexibility, responsiveness to student needs. Should we be at all surprised that kids are virtually lining up to be designated for special ed.?

Back in the 1980s, when money for education seemed to be growing on the nearest tree, special

Does Your Child Need Special Ed.?

If you would check off five of these statements, there's a good chance your child needs special education.

❏ My child seemed to develop more slowly than other children: speaking, toilet training, tying shoes, reading.

❏ My child has difficulty concentrating in school and at home.

❏ My child seems to need my help to do the simplest things.

❏ My child sometimes loses control and gets angry with other children.

❏ My child doesn't seem to enjoy school at all—he's frustrated by the school work.

❏ My child's teacher has suggested that he might benefit from special education.

❏ My family has a history of learning problems.

❏ My child had serious ear infections as a preschooler.

❏ My child is extremely impatient when he can't figure things out.

education legislation was passed in every provincial legislature to guarantee the rights of students to "appropriate" education regardless of disability. What our MLAs had in mind was kids with spina bifida or kids with hearing problems finally being able to go to a local school with children from their neighbourhood. The concept was noble—and the neighbourhood school integration worked. But what we also got was a special education system that now designates between 10 and 20 percent of the student population as having "special needs" and deserving special services. While children with learning problems certainly do need support—specially trained teachers, rooms equipped to help them learn despite a handicap, flexibility in classroom programming—we have some concerns about the 80 to 90 percent of ordinary kids who get left out.

Let's suppose that your son Jamie is having difficulty in school: poor work, acting out in class, not paying attention, obviously unhappy with everything about school. Jamie's teacher will probably suggest some testing by a school professional, to be followed by a conference between you and a team of teachers from the school and sometimes the board or district office. That conference puts together a plan that bends the system or classroom practices to take account of Jamie's special needs. It also teams Jamie up with a special "resource teacher," who can provide one-on-one assistance and counselling when needed. The net effect is usually quite an improvement in Jamie's achievement and his attitude toward school.

Does My Child Need Special Education?

If your child was born with an obvious handicap —vision or hearing impairment or physical handicaps that make movement difficult—there's no question that your child will warrant a special education designation. These days almost all children with such handicaps can be accommodated in the neighbourhood school. Visit any school and you'll see the kind of changes that have been made over the past ten years to make this possible: access ramps everywhere, teachers wearing microphones for hearing-impaired students, special gym equipment, teacher aides who accompany the most severely handicapped children. An early conference with the school principal and subsequent meetings with teachers will devise ways to revise both the program and the routines of the school to accommodate your child. All this will begin early, in kindergarten or junior kindergarten, and continue throughout your child's school career.

For other children, like Jamie, the need for special education is not as obvious. Jamie was always a difficult child: quickly bored in play, finding it hard to cooperate with other children. He seemed bright enough, but even his kindergarten teacher saw the potential for learning problems. By grade one, Jamie was still just identifying letters rather than reading, and he seemed to have trouble listening when Ms. Beamish was reading to the class. In grade two, the teacher said that Jamie was "a troublemaker" and had to keep him after school to complete his work. You were convinced that particular teacher was an ogre and that Jamie was really just fine, until grade three. Jamie still wasn't reading; his math skills were at the grade one level; his behaviour had sent him twice to the office. His grade three teacher suggested a conference to consider a special program for Jamie and, finally, you agreed.

There is a natural tendency for all parents to deny that our children have problems, especially those that are not immediately obvious. It is easier to blame a teacher, or the system, or a bad year than to admit that Jamie might have problems in learning that make him "special." Getting

Many Kinds of Special Education

Special education is not just for students with obvious physical or developmental handicaps (perhaps 3 percent of children). Today's special education programs cover a wide range of students with special needs (often 10 to 20 percent of the student population).

- Physical handicaps: orthopedically handicapped, spina bifida, hearing impaired, vision impaired, etc.

- Development difficulties: slow development, specific learning problems in a particular area, often speech and language.

- Attention problems: ADD (attention deficit disorder) and hyperactivity.

- Emotional problems: aggressiveness, passivity, social adjustment problems.

- Specific learning disorders: (SLD) students normal in most respects but with a particular area of learning difficulty.

- General learning disorder: (GLD) wide-ranging problems in intellectual functioning.

- Gifted and talented education (see the next chapter).

over this initial stage of denial, however, is always the first step in getting Jamie the help he needs. The longer a parent delays recognition, the longer it will take until Jamie's school begins to make changes for him.

The Special Ed. Designation Process

Once someone suspects that Jamie might need special education, a particular process kicks in at school. At many boards and districts, you can get a helpful manual that describes the designation process and the specific names (and acronyms) used in your jurisdiction. Here we'll generalize what tends to happen right across Canada:

Step one: starting the process. A special education designation review can be initiated by a parent, a teacher or a principal. Usually the cooperation of all three will be necessary for further steps to be taken. It is almost always in your child's best interest to go ahead with the special ed. designation process if that has been suggested by a teacher or principal. The information you receive will be useful in any event, and the actual identification of your child for special education can easily be stopped at a later stage if you wish to do so.

Step two: testing. Depending on the nature of your child's problem in school, a number of tests are usually conducted to provide information that will be used later in making decisions on the program. Some schools do their own reading and mathematics tests, often using the Canadian Tests of Basic Skills or the Gates MacGinitie tests. These tests can be administered in sections, sometimes in the classroom or school office, requiring only a few hours of class time. Other boards and districts provide a psychometrist who personally conducts a three-hour-long WISC (Wechsler Intelligence Scale for Children) or similar kind of broad-range

Mainstreaming vs. the Self-Contained Classroom

Mainstreaming (or integration), the up side:

- Children can stay at neighbourhood school with their friends.
- Not much stigma is attached to special ed. kids.
- Special ed. children benefit from being in a classroom with regular children and vice versa.
- Group work and other classroom situations are more like real life with a mixture of kids with different abilities.
- With support from the resource teachers, many special education children do as well as their more ordinary peers.

The down side:

- Program modifications are sometimes only surface adjustments; the real work remains too difficult.
- Not every classroom teacher handles special ed. children well or can individualize programs effectively.
- Regular classrooms may not have specialized equipment or appropriate curriculum materials.
- While class size is often adjusted down to allow teachers to deal with special kids, it remains well over twenty.
- Handicapped kids are sometimes left out of activities in gym.
- Opportunity to achieve real distinction in the school is limited.

IQ test. The WISC can be interpreted by a professional to give you a wide range of information on your child's abilities both in school subjects and in general intellectual functioning.

Unfortunately, the wait for this kind of testing is sometimes months long. It is possible, through your doctor or local mental health organization, to arrange for your own testing, but be prepared for fees of up to $500, which are not covered by provincial medical plans. Even if you do go ahead, school officials often discount such tests unless done by their own personnel.

Step three: the big conference. After the testing is completed, the school principal will arrange a conference to discuss your child and his needs. In most provinces, there must always be at least three school people at the conference—usually a principal, a teacher and the school's resource teacher. We have seen conferences with as many as a dozen people clustered around the table, all talking about a single child: parents, step-parents, subject teachers, guidance people, special ed. consultants from the board or district, the resource teacher, the school vice-principal and principal, the school-system psychologist, a psychologist in private practice, hospital psychiatrists . . . sometimes even the family doctor.

Such a conference can be daunting for many parents: it's just you and all the professionals. Sometimes it can seem like you *against* all the professionals, though theoretically everyone wants the best for your child. If you find such a meeting too overpowering to handle alone, you might ask for a knowledgeable friend or a member of the local Learning Disabilities Association to join you for moral support. It's important that you feel in control of the whole special ed. designation process. If that means you'd like a friend along as an advocate for you or your child, insist upon it.

The self-contained class (or school), the up side:
- There are specially trained teachers in a small class, often with fewer than ten students.
- The program is tailor-made for the needs of special education children, and is not just a watered-down version of the regular curriculum.
- Students can achieve real distinction (sports awards, academic honours) in the context of their group.
- The physical classroom is often set up to accommodate the needs of these children.

The down side:
- Special ed. kids are artificially isolated from their peers; this leads to social isolation and aggravates the stigma of a handicap.
- Some self-contained classes are not in the neighbourhood school, so busing will be required.
- The special curriculum may be too easy or the teacher may underestimate the ability of your child.
- Self-contained special ed. schools tend to have a higher number of children with social problems who sometimes display unpleasant behaviour.

The purpose of the conference is to discuss your child: Jamie's abilities and disabilities, strengths and weaknesses, learning styles and learning problems. By assembling all this information from a number of perspectives, the school will try to put together a program to optimize Jamie's education. As a parent, it's important to remember that the purpose of the conference is not to put a label on your child, but to decide what kind of program modification will be best for him.

Step four: changing the program. Thirty years ago, children who needed a special program were either put in self-contained classes or sent to special schools. These days, schools bend over backward to keep your child in a regular class and provide special assistance with a resource teacher or teacher's aide. There are pros and cons to each approach, but the current wisdom is to keep children with special needs in their neighbourhood school and with their neighbourhood friends if at all possible. In terms of avoiding stigma, this approach has been a tremendous success; in terms of providing individual attention, it does well; in terms of modifying the program successfully, results are iffy. This is why the plans at the big conference are so important— much more important than the label placed on your child's special needs—and why you have to make sure those plans are carried out.

To keep a child with special needs in a regular classroom, schools have come up with a number of components:

- *Resource teachers:* special education teachers, often in their own classroom or office, who are there to assist your child. Sometimes a specific number of hours with the resource teacher are specified in the plan; sometimes the use of such a teacher is left to the discretion of the student.

- *Resource room:* the habitat of the special resource teacher, this provides special curriculum materials that can be substituted for classroom work, a computer for work to be completed, a "time-out" space and—of course—the resource teacher.

- *Teacher's aides:* for children with orthopedic or multiple handicaps, a teacher's aide helps deal with the physical needs of the child: moving from class to class, writing, participation in class trips and personal needs.

- *Program alteration:* just as a wheelchair-bound student cannot be expected to climb ropes, so a slow-development student can't be expected to whiz through algebra. Program alteration can change both the *pace* and the *content* of what's learned in the classroom. Often this must be done through cooperation between the resource teacher and the classroom or subject teachers.

- *Therapists, counsellors and other support.* Some students may need regular assistance from a physical therapist, speech therapist, psychological counsellor or other support person who comes to school on a weekly or bi-weekly schedule.

- *Parents.* The most important component in permitting school success for your special-needs child is probably you and your involvement. Ironically, this is the area that an assembly of bigwigs, doctors and teachers is least likely to discuss. It's important to ask the question "How can I help Jamie at home?" Then you'll get some specific suggestions.

The actual combination of the components, and the types of changes to the program, are what you'll discuss at the end of the big conference. The

Your Special Education File Folder

The first tool of every parent in dealing with serious school problems is a file folder. This is especially true for the bureaucratic morass of special education. Here's what to put in your special ed. folder:

- records of meetings—dated;

- copies of report cards, disciplinary notes and other classroom records;

- copies of test results, medical and psychological reports;

- any outside reports you may have gathered;

- officially signed designation papers;

- the plan or program devised for your child;

- notes on your child's reaction to the revised program—with dates.

ADD: **Hyperactivity for This Decade**

Attention deficit disorder (ADD) has been termed "yuppie hyperactivity," much the way one terms a rich uncle "eccentric" rather than crazy. ADD is a mental disorder of some form—perhaps biological, perhaps genetic, perhaps connected to our frenetic culture—that afflicts between 2 and 4 percent of school-age children. The symptoms are well-known:

- short attention span;
- constant, frantic activity;
- low toleration for boredom;
- easily distracted (but with occasional periods of intent focussing);
- restless energy.

It's also true that these describe the average four-year-old, so ADD is more a matter of degree than a group of symptoms.

Treatment is still likely to be a drug called Ritalin—a stimulant for most adults, but a soothing drug for ADD children at least until puberty. The effect of Ritalin has been described as putting a new antenna on a radio: it eliminates the static.

Parents should also be aware of pseudo-ADD, a culturally driven version of real ADD, which seems to come from too fast a life pace, too many remote control clickers and too much time playing video games. The cure for pseudo-ADD is easier: shut down the electronics and create some quiet time in your home.

plan that you and the teachers come up with is not engraved in stone—in fact, regular review is often part of the plan—but it is where everyone is supposed to begin. If this plan is done well, it can make for a remarkable improvement in school for your child.

Step five: keep an eye on what happens. Many special ed. designation conferences conclude with a wonderful list of changes to take place in curriculum, in the classroom and using the resource teacher. And then—well, you know what they say about good intentions. For a child who's been integrated (or mainstreamed) into a regular class, the success of the plan hinges on the classroom teacher. Given an energetic, caring teacher in a classroom of supportive kids, your child will blossom thanks to the revised program. But if your child ends up with a not-so-good or burned-out teacher in a classroom of thirty kids, three of whom are designated for special education ("Sorry," the principal said, "we're having a problem with staffing"), then the results will be dismal.

That's why you have to keep an eye on what's happening in the actual classroom and how your child is feeling about the situation. The resource teacher should be your ally if the agreed-upon plan doesn't happen, or happens only in bits and pieces. The two of you can go to the principal and try to come up with another approach that might work better for your child.

Your Role as a Parent

As the parent of a child with special needs, you have a very difficult role to play. You must always remain a parent to your child: read with him, help with homework, organize outside activities. But you must also be an advocate to make sure Jamie gets the best education that's possible in your area. Joining a local group of such parents can be very helpful, both emotionally and procedurally, in helping you stand up on behalf of your child.

Sadly, we have observed that some parents cop out near the end of the special ed. placement process. After having your child designated or identified, there is a natural tendency to see this as an excuse for everything Jamie does. Don't fall into this trap. You can't simply shrug and say, "Jamie's doing the best he can," when Jamie himself is looking for support in his efforts to excel. Successful parenting of a child with special needs means setting goals both at school and at home. Follow-through can be exhausting, but the results are worth it.

One of us taught a young woman designated as "trainable retarded" for a number of years. Nancy was obviously slow—in her movements, her speaking, her speed of thought. But Nancy's parents and family never stopped enriching her life and supporting the program at school. The parents read to Nancy every night, so that by grade ten, though her tested IQ was in the 70s, Nancy's reading skills were at the same level as the rest of her class. They took Nancy to theatre and concerts and on a trip to Europe, so that in high school Nancy was more familiar with acting, music and geography than most of her fellow students. They expected that Nancy would one day be self-supporting, so they pushed the school to build her math and business skills. The parents were so successful in all this that after a co-op assignment in grade twelve, Nancy was offered full-time job by that employer. Nancy never officially graduated from high school with the normal diploma, but she received a special certificate from the school and a standing ovation from her classmates when she "graduated" with them. The tribute goes to her—and to a family that didn't cop out.

Join with Other Parents

The Learning Disabilities Association of Canada (LDAC) is organized into 140 local chapters that bring together parents of all "special" children to share ideas and learn about treatments. Your phone book will have the local chapter under "Learning Disabilities Association," or contact:

Learning Disabilities Association of Canada
323 Chapel Street, Suite 200
Ottawa, Ontario K1N 7Z2

The Canadian Council on Exceptional Children (CEC) is a branch of the Washington-based council. It offers workshops and regular meetings in some cities for both teachers and parents.

Many large communities have other organizations dealing with specific disabilities: VOICE (for hearing-impaired children), Head Injury Association, Down Syndrome Association, Centre for the Hearing Impaired, Society for Autistic Citizens, Association for the Mentally Retarded, etc.

Many boards and districts of education have created advisory committees of parents with children in special education. You'll find these committees useful for connecting with other parents in a similar situation and acting as advocates for special education at a local level. Contact your local board or district for more information.

CHAPTER 14

Gifted Programs

A gifted child rarely seems like much of a gift to his parents. While young, Adam may amaze your relatives with early reading, sophisticated language development and stellar achievement at school. He will memorize a book at age three, read *Maclean's* to Grandmother at age four, dazzle Uncle Ralph with algebra at age ten, speak fluent French to Aunt Josée at age eleven. But the price paid for these achievements are all at your house: frequent bouts of boredom and loneliness, emotional roller-coaster rides in middle school, growing argumentativeness in the adolescent years. Aunt Josée and Uncle Ralph may envy you the pride you feel in your child's achievements, but they have no idea of the ups and downs in being Adam's parent.

Nor can most of us fully understand what it is like to be gifted. There are the obvious advantages: school work can be a piece of cake; conversation with adults comes easily; talk around the house is chock-full of puns, witticisms and jokes. But there are the hidden disadvantages. Gifted children are frequently ostracized by many of their peers, often feel lonely and depressed, can be bored senseless in school, frequently exhibit impatience and a nasty edge in talking with "ordinary" people, sometimes become obsessively interested in a particular game or activity. As a parent, you'll have your hands full trying to deal with both the up side and the down side of giftedness.

Schools and teachers should be your natural allies in nurturing a gifted child. They can help you determine whether your child is "bright" or "gifted" or "talented" and then recommend special programs available within the school system. Teachers can sometimes mentor or guide gifted children to remarkable achievements while still quite young. And they can help you deal with some of the trials of parenting such a child. But first things first—you'll often have a hunch that your child is gifted well before he enters school and meets his first teacher.

Is Your Child Gifted?

It is possible to give an IQ test to a child as early as age two, but why bother? The fact that Adam may or may not be gifted hardly affects the way you go about parenting, nor will it have any effect on school programs until much later on. Applying the tag "genius" to your four-year-old does the child no favour. Parents should remember, too, that Einstein did not speak until he was four or read until age seven, so for all the generalizations that follow there are notable exceptions. Nonetheless, here's what to look for:

Early development of abilities. Many gifted children begin reading at a very early age, sometimes real reading (not just memorization) at age three. Similarly, oral language skills develop quickly: talking at nine months, full sentences at a year, expression of some complex ideas at age two. Gifted children frequently have a keen sense of humour that they display early on, with an appreciation of verbal puns at age three or four. Children with a special talent in music will show keen interest and rapid development of technique well before school age. A child need not be a Mozart (who improvised minuets on the clavichord at age five) or a Jeremy Bentham (who could read both English and Latin at age four) to be truly gifted, but early development gives an indication of intellectual abilities that will remain strong throughout life.

A caution here: first children and only children frequently develop language abilities faster than others. This is most likely due to a desire by the child to fulfil your aspirations and to the natural effect of a child's talking more to adults than to other children. One study of gifted children noted that well over half the sample were first or only children, a real statistical anomaly. The researcher went back and gave IQ tests to the other siblings and found, to their surprise, that the second, third and fourth children often scored higher than the officially "gifted" first child. The middle children, however, didn't *act* gifted, so no one had paid any attention.

Intensity of interest. Gifted children, more than others, are marked by an intensity of concentration in areas that interest them. This intensity will appear even in the crib, with serious staring at crib toys or playthings. Mothers of gifted children, looking back, comment most frequently on the long attention span of their babies. Later on in childhood, a young gifted child may play for hours with cars or blocks or in imaginative doll universes when other children would have gotten bored and gone off to Barney. One study in Florida found that gifted young musicians spent seven times as many hours practising an instrument as did ordinary music students. When school begins, this kind of intensity can be wonderful if focussed on a project or a class topic, but frequently the interest will be directed elsewhere. School work will be mastered with an effortless

Is Your Child Gifted?

Here are a dozen characteristics of gifted children. If you're child exhibits more than half of these, have a discussion with her teacher and consider testing for a "gifted" designation at school.

- Extremely curious
- Intensely pursues personal interests
- Very aware of surroundings
- Critical of self and others
- Witty; enjoys word play
- Sensitive to injustice
- Questions statements and ideas
- Understands general principles quickly
- Sees relationships among diverse ideas
- Generates ideas quickly
- Enjoys creative work
- Hates rote learning

shrug—or ignored altogether—while Adam's real focus is outer space, or a fantasy life, or medieval armour, or whatever else has caught his fancy.

Curiosity. "Why is the sky blue?" every child will ask. But a gifted child won't let parents off the hook with a "Beats me" answer; nor will the questions stop even if you offer an explanation about suspended water and light refraction. Gifted children are curious to an extreme, and about a wide range of topics. They see connections between items in the outside world and quickly grasp general concepts, but all this just leads to more questions. "Why does light refrac' through the raindrops? What if it didn't? Where does the water come from? How does it stay up there?" The more you're pestered with questions, the more likely you're dealing with a gifted child.

When your child begins school, experienced teachers will quickly be able to tell you whether or not your child may be gifted. Unlike parents, who should always dote on their children, teachers can be a bit more dispassionate in evaluation and their judgement tends to correlate very highly with IQ tests. At the same time, gifted students frequently become aware that they are somehow different from their classmates—and their classmates that the gifted child is somehow different from them. Experiments with self- and peer evaluation for giftedness indicate that these are almost as reliable as teacher observation and perhaps a better indicator than a half-hour group IQ test.

IQ and achievement tests. Psychologists and guidance counsellors get catalogues filled with intelligence and achievement tests—hundreds of them—each with their scales, norms, strengths and failings. Starting in grade three, some schools regularly put children through a battery of achievement tests, like the Canadian Test of Basic

Raising a Gifted Baby

Dr. Burton White in *Educating the Infant and Toddler* talks about the ways successful parents raised babies who turned out to be bright, if not gifted. Here's what good parents were observed doing to build language skills from infancy:

- they identified the interests of their child and talked about them;

- they engaged in fifteen to twenty verbal interchanges an hour, most lasting between twenty and thirty seconds;

- they rarely "taught" or lectured their children;

- they spoke in full sentences, using words slightly above the child's apparent level of comprehension;

- they read picture books and stories from infancy, even though children rarely sustained attention until age two.

Skills, to see how they're doing compared with a wide range of children. Other schools use quick group intelligence tests that can be done in less than an hour of class time and then scored by a computer. The results of both these tests are about as good as hooking up a car to the engine diagnostics machine at Canadian Tire—you'll find out the obvious and miss the subtleties. Unlike Canadian Tire, however, many schools won't tell you how your child has scored on these tests unless you ask to see the formal school record.

The Gifted Designation Process

The process of designating your child as gifted can be begun by you, a teacher or the principal of your child's school. The first step is usually a battery of tests like those we've just outlined. More reliable results can be had from a full range IQ test like the WISC-R or Stanford-Binet. Schools are sometimes reluctant to do a full WISC or Standford-Binet because they must be administered one-to-one by a trained consultant, psychometrist or psychologist and because the tests take almost three hours to complete. Since these professionals are well paid and often in short supply, some schools may grant the gifted designation without doing a full-scale intelligence test. This can be a shame, however, because a gifted child rarely scores equally in all the subtest areas. A full IQ test yields quite a complete intellectual portrait of your child, one that will be useful later on to tailor-make a program that fits. This information is probably more important than the IQ itself, though that number is often the qualifier to get into the gifted program. Most gifted programs require an IQ of 120 or 125 to qualify—the actual cutoff point depends on the finances of your board or district—but there should be other factors besides simple IQ measurement in making the decision. Your child's behaviour in school, his

A Few Words about WISC

The Wechsler Intelligence Scale for Children is a powerful tool for understanding your child's intellectual strengths and weaknesses. It's probably more effective in evaluating potential than achievement, but it does offer reliable indicators for each category. Here's a rundown of the test:

The verbal subsection is done out loud, one to one, with a psychometrist or board official. It includes defining vocabulary, identifying similarities and differences and understanding oral arithmetic problems. There are questions on general information, passages for reading and a section that calls for repeating a set of numbers forward and backward.

The performance subsection is done with pencil and paper and a few blocks while a professional looks on. It involves completing pictures, arranging pictures in a logical series, doing mazes and assembling wooden puzzles.

What's Wrong with IQ Tests

While a full-range, one-on-one intelligence test is probably the best tool we have for getting information about a child's intelligence, there are still a number of problems with such testing.

- Intelligence scores vary depending on health, stimulation, interest in the test material.

- IQ tests don't correlate against each other that well and can change with a different examiner or different test situation.

- IQ tests mostly ignore creativity, effort and stamina. They reward speed more than thoroughness.

- IQ tests are too individual; they require no group or social skills.

- No intelligence test measures the ability to acquire knowledge.

- Current IQ tests are too dependent on reading and verbal skills; they're also biased toward WASP reasoning and background information.

relationship to his peers and the recommendations of his teacher should all be important in deciding whether or not he will benefit from the gifted designation.

After the testing and paperwork is complete, you'll be called in for a conference to discuss whether or not your child should be deemed gifted, the nature of his abilities and the program options available to you. The conference will be attended by the principal or vice-principal, your child's teacher, the school's resource teacher, sometimes the psychometrist who did the testing and sometimes a representative from the special education bureaucracy. Then there will be you and your partner. If you'd like someone else to join in, you can easily arrange for a member of your school board's special education advisory group to come with you. She can act as moral support, an experienced voice, someone who knows the bureaucracy, perhaps even serve as an advocate for your child.

This conference should not be adversarial. Theoretically, everyone has the best interests of your child at heart. But important decisions will be made in an hour or two that will affect the rest of your child's school career. Best to be prepared. The first part of the discussion will focus on your child's classroom achievement and behaviour; then the results of the testing will come forward. You should feel free to ask questions and take notes during these discussions: what observations took place, exactly what testing was done; what was the opinion of Mrs. So-and-So, your child's grade two teacher?

At some point, the question comes up: to be or not to be; that is, to have your child designated gifted or to oppose such a designation. Hamlet, for instance, was undoubtedly a very gifted young man, but it's unlikely—given the outcome of the play—that his special education in Würtemburg did much besides exacerbate his existential and moral problems. Not every gifted child benefits from gifted education, especially if it means moving from a good, solid peer group in the ordinary classroom to a self-contained class at a different school altogether. For well-adjusted children with "bright" levels of general intelligence (IQs of 115 to 130) who fit in well in class, a gifted program may well be useless. It is always possible, of course, to combine the two approaches by accepting the gifted designation (for possible future use) and rejecting the program options. It is usually not possible to get your child into a gifted program without the gifted designation.

But for many gifted children, the designation and accompanying program are a vital tool for successful education. If your child is bored in the regular class, has trouble making friends, has begun to treat school with cynicism and/or tests at the high end of the gifted scale (IQs of 145 and up, the top one-half of one percent of the population), then he'll likely be much happier in any kind of gifted program than with the status quo.

Program Options for the Gifted

At one time, the usual school approach for dealing with gifted children was acceleration: skipping a grade. These days acceleration is rare. It removes a child from his natural agemates, leads to some incongruity in sexual interest in adolescence and doesn't really provide what a gifted child needs— an individualized, challenging program. The only time acceleration is likely to be recommended is when a child is physically mature for his age or when his birthday is at the cusp of the next grade level (a November birthday, for example, would make your child only two months younger than other students in the next grade). Even if acceleration is decided upon, say from grade two to grade three, a more substantive gifted program may well be necessary later on.

Programs for the Gifted

There are sometimes many school options for gifted students. Here's a rundown:

- full-time (self-contained) enrichment class
- part-time enrichment class
- regular withdrawal for an enrichment program (the once-a-week option)
- extra projects or independent study
- meetings with itinerant gifted teacher or school resource teacher
- after-school or lunchtime clubs (debating, chess, music, science, library, etc.)
- academic fairs or challenges
- acceleration (skipping a grade)
- moderate acceleration (completing three grades in two years)
- schools specializing in science, art, technology, gifted education
- accelerated courses in high schools
- mentorship or internship programs
- special summer courses or camps
- Saturday programs in the community
- correspondence courses, lessons, or independent study
- part-time university credits

Rule of Thumb 🖝
Given the choice of a self-contained gifted class or a once-a-week gifted program, choose the once-a-week option.

There are some wonderful teachers running gifted classes, teachers who enrich the program in meaningful ways, teachers who use the collective intelligence of the class to foster challenging, creative learning. But then there are the problems of putting two-dozen gifted kids in the same room five days a week: a formula for disaster far worse than gum stuck under the desk.

The once-a-week program option gives your child an opportunity for enrichment, a chance to meet and work with other gifted children, and yet he can still maintain significant contact with the "ordinary" people with whom he'll spend most of his life. The gifted teacher may well be able to use her influence to make the time spent in regular class that much more stimulating.

There are really two good options for changing the program to accommodate the needs of a gifted child: the self-contained classroom or regular (often once a week) withdrawal from class for a gifted program. Sometimes a third option is presented—classroom enrichment—which only means that your child's already overworked classroom teacher gets asked to prepare extra assignments for your child. This rarely works well, and you should press hard for something better.

In some schools, the kids in the self-contained gifted class really do get the perks: better qualified teachers, somewhat smaller classes, field trips as part of the program, guest speakers, use of labs and shops at neighbouring schools. If that's the case in your child's school, then the advantages of the self-contained class may outweigh the disadvantages. But the disadvantages are significant. There is a real sense of gifted kids being "different" when they are clustered in one class. This can combine with preadolescent mockery and one-upmanship to make for difficult social situations in the playgrounds of normal life. Moreover, twenty gifted kids in a single room can accomplish wonderful feats, but they can also make life hell for a weak teacher and for one another. If you have a sense that the school is going to recommend such a class for your child, best to speak to parents whose children are already enrolled or to the kids themselves. A solid program with a good teacher may justify such a placement.

The more common option now for dealing with gifted children is regular withdrawal for participation in a special program. In this option, the three or four gifted kids in a given class will be removed one day a week to work with a different teacher in a different classroom environment. This once-a-week program can offer many of the same perks as the self-contained class: a specially trained teacher, access to better facilities, field trips and guest speakers as part of the program.

However, it does so only once a week, allowing your gifted child four days to make friends and maintain relationships in his regular classroom. In theory, the gifted resource teacher will work to bolster the regular classroom program for his charges, so their once-a-week withdrawal will have some connection with what goes on in the regular classroom. This withdrawal option seems like the best of both worlds, and students who have been through such a program are usually enthusiastic.

But there are limitations. It is unlikely that a once-a-week program will lead to real advanced placement in any subject later on, so skipping grade nine French, say, won't be an option when your child enters high school. Once-a-week withdrawal can also seem like an "add-on," especially when your child reaches the argumentative years of early adolescence. He's required to do all the regular classroom work *and* his gifted teacher is demanding special projects and extra homework that cut into his time. While a ten-year-old will thrive on the challenge, a twelve-year old will balk.

By high school, all gifted programs seem to get confused. In large cities, there are sometimes specialized high schools that offer a gifted stream in a particular area, like science or music. Some elite private schools have enrolment so limited that virtually the entire school could be designated as gifted. But in most communities and in most schools, the gifted program will virtually disappear after grade nine.

We realize this is a harsh generalization, so let's admit a few qualifiers. Sometimes—in some schools—there are enough gifted kids to offer an "enriched" level of a course or two. Sometimes the identified gifted kids are brought together for a special program or speaker. Sometimes many of the gifted kids will find themselves together in a club, like debating or reach for the top or young authors. But despite the rhetoric that you might

Evaluating a Gifted Program

Here are a dozen questions that deserve answers before you hand over your child:

- Are there stated goals or outcomes for the program?

- What screening process is used to select students for the program?

- How are parents informed and involved?

- Does the program make use of community resources?

- How are teachers chosen for the program?

- Is there a mix of group and individual work?

- What is the pupil-teacher ratio?

- Do students contribute to the direction of the program?

- Is there continuity from year to year?

- How is creativity encouraged?

- Is there extra funding for program activities?

- How does the program tie into regular classroom work?

Use Your Community

- Museums and art galleries. Most offer Saturday morning or afternoon classes on a variety of topics.

- Universities and community colleges. Some offer special programs for high school students on weekends or in the summer; others make computer or sports facilities available to families.

- Forts, pioneer villages, tourist attractions. Check for special Saturday or Sunday workshops, March-break programs or week-long summer activities.

- Royal Conservatory of Music offers a program not just in playing instruments but also in dramatics, public speaking and music theory.

- Tutoring or volunteer opportunities. Call your communities volunteer bureau.

- Community or heritage language programs. These are often offered in local schools on weekends and after school hours. It's an opportunity to learn Lithuanian or Greek at very low cost.

- The ys. The YMCA and YWCA offer more than just swimming programs.

- Et cetera: 4-H Club, Young Farmers, Toastmasters, Kiwanis, ballet or judo lessons, t'ai chi...keep your eyes and ears open for opportunities.

hear from a principal or board official, very few of Canada's high schools offer a solid gifted program, simply because it's hard to timetable into a school schedule based on course credits. Nor do older high school kids have much impetus to use the school for enrichment. Unlike the American system, where high school students can earn advanced placement at university by taking college-level courses in high school, Canadian universities almost never grant degree credits for courses taken in high school and pay no attention to the gifted designation when it comes time for university admission. Is it any wonder that our gifted high school students disappear into the woodwork in grade ten or eleven, or devote their time to finishing high school faster rather than learning more while they're there?

This is all the more reason for you to explore other avenues with your teenage son or daughter, so their giftedness can be challenged in a wider community rather than hidden beneath the headphones of a Walkman.

Parent, Resource Teacher and Gifted Child

Gifted children are always children at risk. While their achievements may be substantial, they are also more prone to spectacular failure—alcoholism, drug abuse, suicide, depression and other psychological disorders. While they may lead very healthy and successful lives, the histories of child prodigies more often play like horror stories than tales of heroic achievement and success. As a parent, you want to do what you can to help your gifted child lead a challenging, fulfilling life. Your natural ally in this is the resource teacher at Adam's school who will be charged with overseeing his program.

Gifted children are demanding. They are easily bored, consume information and ideas quickly, want more information than you can possibly provide and know how to whine effectively to get what they want. As a parent, you can simply devote your life to your young prodigy (as the parents of many gifted musicians have done since the days of Mozart), help to schedule as many diverse opportunities as you can, pray that a mentor shows up on the scene and hope that your child will carry on when you're no longer in the picture. Most parents, however, are unwilling to sacrifice twenty years of their lives for one child, so the struggle is to balance both sets of needs.

In the nature of giftedness is isolation. The gifted pianist must practise three or four hours a day; the young mathematician must be alone to work on math theory; the young writer needs time on a word processor to work on her poetry. Your job—and the job at school—is to counteract that isolation with normal social relations. A gifted child frequently prefers time with adults to time with children, but she *needs* that time with people her own age. A gifted child would frequently prefer to continue reading, or typing, or practising viola, but you must insist that he go out and play.

Some of the strongest school gifted programs recognize this need. They build in tutoring, or working with handicapped children, or volunteer work as part of a program to widen the experience of a gifted child. You can do the same at home, often with advice from the resource teacher at school.

If there were one single bit of advice for parents of gifted children, it's this: get help. The Association for Bright Children will put you in contact with other parents in the same situation. Your child's school can be the source for mentors who can carry some of the demands for her development. An older professional, a counsellor at the Y, an interested university professor, a distant relative in your family—all of these people can provide some of the guidance and mentoring that

Join with Other Parents

The Association for Bright Children is an advocacy group seeking better gifted programs in every province. They offer workshops for parents and a regular newsletter with information on new books and programs. For more information:

Association for Bright Children
2 Bloor Street West, Suite 100-156
Toronto, Ontario M4W 3E2

gifted young people need. The lessons of history are clear: child prodigies held up to the glare of public performance almost always come to grief. A gifted young person must be shielded from this so his early achievements and his potential— heavy burdens in themselves—don't cast such a shadow that adult life becomes impossible. If you can do so, and bring in the school to help, your gifted child can become an extraordinary adult. Good luck.

CHAPTER 15

Questions Parents Ask

Q: How can I get a class rank for my child. I want to know how he's doing compared with other children.

A: You probably can't. Most schools don't compare student marks until graduation or awards time, so regular class ranking is a pretty rare event. Besides, a measurement of whether your child stands first, third or last in his class may not be very useful in figuring his overall ability, because his class may be streamed to include only one segment of the population in that grade.

Many schools give standardized achievement tests to their students on a regular basis and then bury the results on the formal student record forms kept in the office. We think that parents should always get the results from such testing—with appropriate explanations from the school—to put to rest some deep-seated fears parents have about the accuracy of school evaluation. While there are many things wrong with standardized tests (time limits, skewed samples, arbitrary questions, limited format), they can say quite honestly if your child is in the bottom quartile of his age group—or the top ten percent, if that's the case.

Q: How can I tell if my child's school is really preparing him for the next grade or stage in his school career?

A: Your school probably has a statement of overall goals or outcomes that will give you an idea of what is supposed to be dealt with at a particular grade level—and provide you with some idea for the next grades to come. If your child is planning on attending a new school next year, go to that school's open house and find out what the requirements are for study skills, homework assignments, exams and regular class tests. If these appear quite demanding, talk to the teachers or principals to get some idea of what skills a new student will need to thrive.

Once you have some indicators of what your child will need, look carefully at the program at your child's current school. If careless work and shoddy or inadequate preparation earn your child passing marks, you will probably want to talk to your child about the importance of measuring up to a higher standard. Then let the school know that you expect better. Schools need to hear this more often.

Q: What are the high-demand jobs going to be when my child graduates? I want her to take the necessary high school courses to prepare and get into the university programs.

A: The simplest answer is, who knows? Ten years ago everyone thought that becoming a lawyer was a sure bet for financial success and an exciting career; now lawyers are a glut on the market. The trouble with setting up school entirely for a future career is that most of our children (in fact, many of us) will have three or four different careers. The old wisdom for dealing with this was to sug-

Future Jobs: An OECD View

At least one function of school is to prepare our children for someday getting a job. The trouble, of course, comes in anticipating what jobs will be in demand ten or twenty years in the future. Here are predictions for 1995 to 2005 made by the international Organization for Economic Cooperation and Development:

Fast-growing jobs:
- child-care workers
- systems analysts, computer operators
- food-and-beverage workers
- medical technologists

Shrinking jobs:
- typists, clerk-typists
- truck drivers
- travelling salesmen
- fishing and forestry workers
- machine tool workers

According to the OECD, preparation for the fast-growing jobs won't require specific education so much as strong "literacy and numeracy skills."

gest a strong liberal-arts program. Unfortunately, that solution seems to lead to long periods of unemployment or waiting on tables for kids of this generation. Perhaps a better approach is to urge your child to pursue something she has talent or interest in—accounting, sports, science, teaching—and keep the program and other experiences varied enough that future career shifts won't be too traumatic.

Q: How can I tell if my child's school is giving her up-to-date instruction in computer technology?

A: In a good school, opportunity should be provided for *all* students to use a word-processing program as well as the problem-solving software available for computers. This can happen either in your child's own classroom, where one or two stations should be available for students to use throughout the day, or as part of some regularly scheduled computer lab time, where there would be a bank of computers for student use. If the school uses a computer lab, your child will be able to log on to the system and have her own workspace. Otherwise she will need her own disc, which she uses to save her material. You should also expect your school library to have a computer or two and the capacity to access information on CD-ROM, if not a connection to the Internet. If these basic facilities are not available at your child's school, it's time to ask some pointed questions of the principal and your elected school trustees.

Just remember that even the best computer is really only a classroom tool—like the typewriters and slide rules of ages ago—and any tool is only as good as the craftsman who uses it. Teachers who are comfortable with, and trained to take advantage of, the computer in the classroom can do much more for your child with an old Commodore 64 than can a poorly prepared teacher

Computers: Pro and Con

Boards or districts of education seem to have lots of money for computers. Is this money well spent?

Pro:
- Many kids love to work with them.
- They are great for word-processing because correction is easy and spell-check helps to make the work perfect.
- Clever programs can present concepts in an entertaining fashion.
- Kids can work at their own speed; they can try again until they get a task right.
- Senior students can access research via CD-ROM and the Internet.

Con:
- In groups, one kid tends to hog the computer.
- Some children will play or guess rather than attempt to learn with the machine.
- Teachers can spend so much time getting the system up and dealing with glitches that there's no time left to teach.
- They give a sense that information is always visual or entertaining.
- They provide no *human* love or support or encouragement.

In our opinion, the pros outweigh the cons, but don't expect a bank of computers to work miracles with a weak teacher or a poor school.

with a roomful of Pentium PCs. Teachers need a great deal of in-service training in using computers—and often don't get it from boards or districts, who will put their money into machines but not into developing their staffs. Only insider gossip can tell you if this is the case for your area.

Q: Students in my daughter's grade seven class are harassing her and making sexual comments. These upset her so much that she doesn't want to go to school. What can I do?

A: Grade seven can be a truly vile time for adolescent girls. Appearance is so closely tied to self-esteem at this age, yet grade seven bodies rarely measure up to Cindy Crawford's. Tie this in with the thinking and attitudes of pubescent males, with *their* increasing awareness of sex and *their* own anxiety about what's happening, and you have a situation that can be vicious if adults are not able to support and counsel both sides.

So listen to your child and don't negate the importance of the comments coming at her and how she feels in response. Advising her to ignore suggestive comments is often a reasonable start, but rarely a full solution. Sometimes lack of response or making an equally nasty comment back simply says "I'm in this game—and it makes me feel part of the group." An assertive "I don't like you making those comments. Please stop" can tell the others that it's not a game to her. A strong refusal to tolerate harassment will warn the bullies about follow-up if adults get involved.

A visit with the homeroom teacher or guidance counsellor by your daughter or both of you (if she's nervous about such a discussion) is also in order. Good schools don't take lightly abusive behaviour of any kind. If you allow your daughter to hide at home and not confront the situation, you'll create a vulnerability and helplessness that can be very harmful as she's growing up.

A School Alphabet

A Advocate for your child to get the best for him at school.

B Base your actions and discussions with school personnel on facts, not personalities or rumours.

C Calm yourself before reacting to an upsetting situation. *Then* call the teacher or principal.

D Develop a positive connection with the school principal. Don't let your first visit wait until your child gets in trouble.

E Evaluate the school and program yourself rather than make judgements based on hearsay.

F Find opportunities to help with or participate in your child's schooling. Read the class newsletter or talk to the teacher to find out how.

G Gather and give enough information on your child through regular notes, calls, reports and interviews.

Q: My child has been suspended from school for what they call "unruly" behaviour. How should I handle it with the school, my child, as well as with her younger brothers?

A: Chances are this isn't the first time you've been in contact with the school about your daughter's behaviour. Your other children will also be aware that there have been some problems, even if you didn't tell them. Of course, your daughter probably did, and perhaps even bragged about some of her activities. That's another reason that you have to act to make sure *everyone* knows something serious has happened. If you laugh it off, minimize the importance or blame the school, you'll doom both your daughter and the other children to continuing problems.

So let the other children know that what your daughter did is just not the way to act. Explain that you and the school will be working together to make sure that your daughter learns from this mistake. And then do just that. If you really think the school is being unfair to your daughter, start shopping for a new one.

Q: I'm uncomfortable with the friendship that has developed between my grade ten daughter and her male music teacher. How can I address it without taking her out of the music program or implying a problem that may not be there?

A: Start by making an appointment to talk with the teacher. It would probably be less embarrassing for your daughter if you left her out of this first meeting. Explain very clearly your concerns and the signals that have alerted you to the situation. It's not unusual for girls to develop crushes on adult males who are important in their lives. What is unusual—and illegal—is for a teacher to respond sexually to the attention.

It may well be that the teacher just enjoys your daughter's enthusiasm and interest in music.

H Help your child to establish good homework practices. But don't do the homework for him.

I Investigate complaints from your child about bullying by other kids or adults. No child can learn when he's fearful or intimidated.

J Join the parent organization and promote the activities that interest you (e.g., parenting seminars, curriculum issues, policy development, information nights, etc.).

K Keep the school informed of things on the home front that could affect your child's interest, attention, attitude, health, friendships and progress in school.

L Let your child develop the skills to handle small-scale problems on his own.

M Model the behaviours of a learner or reader by letting your child see you engaged in these activities.

N Notify the school when your child is going to be absent for a period of time and work out what you can do at home to help her keep up with her studies.

O Observe your child for signs of boredom, confusion or frustration and be prepared to work with the school to overcome them.

P Prepare for interviews and conferences with the teacher by talking with your child. Have her tell you what she has done well, what she finds difficult or is having problems with and what the teacher will say about how she works in class.

Q Question teachers and administrators in an honest, forthright, but not confrontational manner. In this way you'll get useful answers and have a good chance of working out a satisfactory solution.

R Read to, with, in front of or alongside your child every day.

Possibly he doesn't recognize the signals he's giving to the student through this "friendship." Once the matter is brought to his attention, he'll probably cool the relationship without another word being said. On the other hand, there is always some danger that your daughter's crush on this teacher is being encouraged in order to feed the man's ego. If your discussion with the teacher produces an embarrassed, surprised and shocked apology, then the teacher probably has been somewhat oblivious to what you've seen—and likely quite innocent of what you might be imagining. However, if the teacher becomes defensive, evasive or dismisses your concerns lightly, then the next step will be to let the school administration in on what you suspect and the steps that you have already taken.

Q: I've heard from neighbours that some of my daughter's grade eight friends are into drug use. How can I tell if my child is involved ? And should I tell the principal?

A: Call your local community police or family service bureau to find out what information, meetings or courses are available in your area dealing with teenage drug use. These will provide you with the necessary information to recognize signs of drug use, as well as indicators of the situations that lead kids to get involved. In these meetings the police are usually able to give you a realistic set of strategies for talking to your child about drugs in a way that will work for both of you.

Going to the school with your suspicions about the other grade eights may be quite helpful to the school principal, but don't exaggerate what you suspect or demand instant action on his part. Often a principal needs information from two or three different sources before he confronts the students or calls in the local police.

Q: I have real concerns about the violence that seems to be moving into the schools. Last week my son said he saw a child in his class pull out a knife in the playground. How can I get the school to listen and not think that I'm simply an alarmist?

A: First you'll want to make sure that you've got solid information to go on. Too often, parents and kids exaggerate stories based on rumour. Talk to your child about the schoolyard and some of the incidents that he may have seen. If your child is young you may find that he will respond to your concern with stories that he's just heard about but not experienced. Rumours can spread very quickly among this set.

On the other hand, there is more violence among children now than ever before. Talk to your child and his teacher to find out about the school rules and code of behaviour. Ask how these are communicated to the children and what the consequences are for students who are aggressive, hurtful, abusive or violent. If there is no behaviour code, offer to work with the school and the parents' group to come up with one.

Q: We've planned a family vacation in Florida for a week in February when the travel agent got the best deal. The teachers at our son's elementary school have no problem with that, but the teachers at our sixteen-year-old daughter's school are giving her a tough time. What should we do?

A: Short of moving the vacation, the only real solution is to come up with a deal for your daughter's teachers. Schools have varying policies about family vacations, often depending on how your children are doing at the school. Most can accommodate a week without much trouble, ten days with greater difficulty. Two weeks is really the outside limit. After all, if you take two weeks

S Select your child's preschool as carefully as you and she will choose her college or university.

T Teach your child good home study habits by helping him organize his time, space and materials.

U Understand that your child's performance in class as well as on tests or examinations may be affected by situations that have occurred outside of school.

V Volunteer to help your child's teacher in the class, on trips or at home.

W Wean your child of being too dependent on you. Teach him strategies for working alone or resolving conflict situations with peers.

Z Zip into action quickly when the school warns you of a problem with your child's behaviour or progress. Ignoring signals or delaying dealing with situations only makes things worse in the long run.

Behaviour/Discipline Codes

Good schools always have one. This statement should include:

- rationale for behaviour/discipline code;

- shared beliefs about the learning environment;

- positive statements describing acceptable behaviour;

- expectations, rights and responsibilities
of students;

- expectations, rights and responsibilities
of teachers;

- expectations, rights and responsibilities
of parents;

- consequences and follow-up for unacceptable behaviour.

Some boards have begun to require automatic expulsion for any student who
engages in violent behaviour involving a
weapon. This kind of knee-jerk policy
makes it difficult for a good school principal to use all the disciplinary resources at
her disposal: detentions, counselling, peer
resolution, alternative school service, stopping out, suspension, class withdrawal,
removal of privileges, "breakfast clubs,"
involvement of the resource teacher, even
cleaning chalkboards. Let's hope most of
Canada keeps some faith in the wisdom of
the people appointed as school principals.

in the middle of the school year, aren't you really
telling your kids that education isn't important?

But you only want a week, so the solution is to
have your daughter bring some work with her.
She can read a novel for English, do some math
questions and study two chapters in science, all
while sitting on the beach. Teachers respond far
better to students who explain their absence in
advance and ask how to make up the work than
they do to parents who simply announce, "We're
going on vacation, so there." A little work on
vacation will help your daughter keep her marks
up and her work up-to-date. We're just surprised
your son's school didn't ask for the same deal.

**Q: I can't get my grade school child to sit and
do homework. It's a constant battle and we
both end up angry and upset. What can I do?**

A: First you need to check and make sure that
the homework is appropriate both in kind and
amount for your child. There is probably a school
homework policy that has been reviewed by parents and teachers that outlines reasonable expectations for homework assignments. If everything
checks out and you feel that your child really
should be able to do the work, you may have to
look at the setting that you're providing. Asking
your child to sit and do homework when everyone else is at a fun activity will make her resentful, angry and frustrated.

So try to set a comfortable place, close to
where others are reading or working quietly: the
kitchen table is often best. Make sure that everything she needs is at hand and include a clock to
help you chop the tasks and time into manageable
bites. If you have other young scholars, try to have
them work at their homework at the same time.

Go over the tasks with her and decide with her
how long it should take to write out the spelling
words, or complete the paragraph, or answer the
ten math questions. Then stick around. Your

presence makes the homework important and gives you the chance to answer the occasional question or deliver the soothing "You can do it" when she gets frustrated.

Q: The teacher has said that my grade seven daughter is "lazy" and doesn't apply herself in school. I don't find her that way around the house. What's happening?

A: Many so-called lazy students have difficulty picking up a concept on the first round of instruction. If there isn't a second or alternate presentation to ensure everyone's on track, these students simply don't know where to start a follow-up assignment or practice. Because they are quite aware that they are not keeping up with the rest of the class, they are the last ones to ask for help or another explanation. Instead, they chat or stare or doodle or use whatever avoidance technique they can to avoid being found out.

A discussion between you and the teacher will help pinpoint the reasons for your child's apparent laziness in school. A good teacher should be able to come up with some strategies that will help her to find the work more understandable and relevant. If the teacher is entirely without ideas, then you'd better start putting in time at night to help your daughter understand the material that wasn't effectively taught during the day. Sorry, but it's the only quick solution.

Q: Yard supervision at my child's school is very lax. There is a lot of roughness, swearing and bullying taking place. The principal won't admit that there is a problem. She says that there is adequate staff on duty for the number of students. What can I do?

A: In any surveys of parent satisfaction with school, the issue of yard supervision is always right near the top of the list. There is never enough supervision and it's never strict enough,

Could My Child be on Drugs?

According to the Addiction Research Foundation, these are five signs that *may* indicate that your child is abusing drugs:

- your child shows a sudden change in behaviour, appearance or attitude;

- your child becomes more secretive;

- your child's school grades suddenly drop;

- money around the house goes missing;

- your child has a new group of friends—and he doesn't bring this group home anymore.

Solutions are not easy. The ARF warns against angry scenes and confrontations with your child. The best approach, they say, is to calm down first and then raise the issue. A parent should have specific events in mind, rather than vague accusations. The discussion should focus on the effect of drugs on your child and on the family. Emphasis should be placed on support, not blame. After that, you should all decide to change family routines, or seek help through your family doctor.

More information:
Addiction Research Foundation
33 Russell Street
Toronto, Ontario M5S 2S1

Employability Skills:

According to the Corporate Council on Education, this is what Canadian employers want from employees.

A person who can...

- listen, understand and learn;

- read and use written materials, including graphs, charts and displays;

- write effectively in the languages in which business is conducted;

- understand and solve problems involving math;

- think critically and act logically;

- use technology, instruments, tools and information systems;

- access and apply specialized knowledge;

- show self-esteem and confidence;

- be persistent in getting the job done;

- be accountable for actions taken;

- plan and manage time and money;

- suggest new ideas;

- work with others;

- understand the company's goals and work within the culture of the group;

- continue to learn for life.

at least according to the parents who respond to surveys. Even in schools where there is a clear policy and firm enforcement there are always situations that come up when the supervisor or teacher in charge is turned in the other direction. Schools often have a process for students to report problems and teachers are expected to take appropriate action. Since the teachers who are out on "guard duty," as the primary children call it, are the same ones who have to doff their coats and get the next class of twenty or thirty students under way, it's not unusual for less serious incidents to be dealt with abruptly. Teachers aren't always available right after the event to help the principal or vice-principal get to the true story. However, if you see staff simply chatting together instead of walking and watching the children, you should bring this to the attention of the principal again. And then call your school superintendent if the situation doesn't improve.

Q: There seems to be a constant stream of requests for money from my child's school—for activities, special supplies, special lunches, fundraising. I pay high taxes and a large portion of that goes to education. How much extra should I be expected to pay?

A: One of the realities of cutbacks to government services, and schools in particular, is that users will be subsidizing the activities and programs through a variety of fundraising activities. Call it another form of taxation, if you will, but in order to do the job that parents have come to expect of a good school, additional money must be found. One approach to deal with the constant "Gimme, gimme" is to ask for an estimate, by month, of the expenditures expected of you. These should include fundraising lunches, trips to the orchard, musical or theatrical performances, special activity fees, book-club purchases and ski trips. When schools are asked to list these expenses up front administrators may look over the whole picture and make choices to ensure that the demands on parents' wallets are within reason.

Q: I am concerned about the topics that may be raised in my child's family life or sex education classes. How can I ensure that the teaching is consistent with our own family values?

A: You can't—the course and the textbook are ordinarily laid down by provincial and board or district committees. But you can call the teacher of the course and ask to review the topics and materials that will be used in your child's class. Most teachers will be ready to go over the program with you. Then you can request to have your child excluded from those parts that you feel are inconsistent with your family values. Of course, children will get their sex education somewhere. Home is the first choice. School provides an unbiased, factually accurate second choice. Then there are always whispered street-corner conversations, X-rated movies and direct experience. We think options one and two look a lot better.

Q: How are books selected for use in classrooms and libraries? Teachers use a certain reading series in my school that my neighbour said has Satanic messages.

A: We think your neighbour spends too much time reading newspaper tabloids. School textbooks are usually vetted by both provincial ministries of education and teacher committees at the local board or district. School library selections often must pass by a committee of teachers, librarians and parents. The likelihood of a truly offensive or Satanic book making its way into a school is remarkably low. The real danger is that textbooks and libraries will end up devoid of anything the least bit controversial, and then a TV-jaded generation won't find anything worth reading.

A Few Acronyms

A great deal of school talk is done in acronyms these days. Here's a sampling of quasi-words to help you understand what the teachers are talking about in the staff room.

ABC: Association for Bright Children, for parents of gifted kids

ABE: adult basic education, for adults who return to school to get a grade twelve diploma

ATF: Alberta Teachers' Federation, the teachers' union; viz: BCTF, NTF, STF, MTF, OTF, et cetera

BD: behaviourally disordered, a special-needs child, usually in a contained classroom

BO: board office (or DO, district office); it usually smells just fine

CEC: Council for Exceptional Children, for teachers and parents of kids with special needs

CPF: Canadian Parents for French, supporting French immersion programs

CUPE: Canadian Union of Public Employees; their locals represent many secretaries, caretakers and supply teachers

DD: developmentally delayed

DDM: decentralized decision making; where the principal—not the board or district—calls the shots

DND: Department of National Defence, which runs its own schools overseas

ESL: English as a second language

FI: French immersion

GLD: general learning disability

IEP: individualized education program (British Columbia)

IPRC: Individual Placement and Review Committee, for special ed. designation in Ontario

IRA: International Reading Association

LA: language arts (trendier than plain old English)

LAC: learning assistance centre, with a resource teacher to help out designated special needs students

LDAC: Learning Disabilities Association of Canada

LRC: learning rescource centre, same as above

Some groups of parents have gone on the warpath to ban everything from *Duddy Kravitz* to *The Diviners*. A good school usually manages to deflect pressure from overly outraged citizens by vetting teacher choices through committees of parents. A weak school just caves in and pulls the book off the library or classroom shelves.

A related question—and a better one—has to do with "age appropriate" materials in the school. This is really a question of judgement rather than censorship. A grade three student probably wouldn't be interested in a novel about teenage pregnancy, so there's little point in making such a novel the class read-aloud. Teachers have little difficulty pegging the appropriate age for materials used by the whole class. The problems arise when kids begin reading for themselves at the school library. Parents whose concept of "appropriate material" lies way outside the mainstream shouldn't expect school to police their children's reading. Nor should schools eliminate books to satisfy the demands of a vocal fringe element in their community.

Q: My school district has a policy that does not allow students to be bused if they live within 1.6 kilometres of the school. We live 1.4 km from the school and my child has to walk past a park area that is well-known for drug deals and nightly violence. How can I get the district policy changed to have my child picked up and delivered by school bus?

A: School policies on transportation are governed almost entirely by budgetary considerations. Policies are based on what is reasonable in terms of the child's needs (many exceptional or special education students are transported for reasons of distance or safety) and geographic or safety situations. You may have a case for your community if the park area is a known haunt of dangerous persons. Of course, one additional bus route costs about $30,000, so don't expect school officials to welcome your suggestion with open arms.

You might also talk to your school principal to see if there are any other parents who have had the same concerns and have come up with solutions. Likely some of your neighbours have made arrangements to have their children walk in groups along a route that passes several of their "safe" homes. This might easily resolve your problem without requiring any change of district policy.

Q: Every year there are more students in each class in my child's school. It looks as if these numbers are going to continue to increase as our subdivision grows. I'm very concerned about the amount of attention and help my child will be getting. How can I get a cap on class sizes?

A: The simple answer is money—taxpayer money. Increases in class size will continue as long as schools are experiencing funding cutbacks. Since actual costs of operating school buildings are increasing with inflation and maintenance of aging facilities, the major way to cut costs is to reduce the number of teachers and increase class size. If it's any consolation, class size is not the be-all and end-all of effective education. It is true, statistically, that measured learning improves in classes under twenty pupils and that learning declines in classes over thirty. The reasons are obvious: there really *is* more individual attention in smaller classes and a much wider range of lesson styles can be used; there really *can't be* much individualization in a very large class and more lessons will end up lecture-style. If classes at your school are often larger than thirty students, it's time for political action.

Q: My child has a very severe allergy that could be life-threatening. He is just starting in kindergarten. How can I ensure that he will be

OBE: outcomes-based education

PA Day: professional activity day; kids stay home so teachers can fill out reports or conduct parent interviews

PE: phys. ed. by acronym

PH: physically handicapped

PO: purchase order; how teachers and principals get supplies

PD (or Pro-D): professional development; workshops, conferences and seminars for teachers

SLD: specific learning disability

SO: supervisory officer, usually a board official

TA: teacher assistant, to aid special students

TMH: trainable mentally handicapped

VP: vice-principal; doing hard time waiting to be principal

Parents as Partners

The parents at Ramer Wood Public School north of Toronto were quite clear about what they wanted from their school and what they were willing to do. Here are their responses to a questionnaire.

What the parents wanted:

94 percent: newsletters, classroom notices

88 percent: the chance to respond to surveys on issues like curriculum, discipline and evaluation

50 percent: the opportunity to attend presentations, by grade level, on math, languages, science and the arts

48 percent: information on board meetings and decisions made there

What the parents would do:

37 percent: volunteer time to work in their child's classroom

35 percent: supervise field trips

29 percent: help with fundraising

15 percent: help in the library

10 percent: be a reading booster

7 percent: assist with house league sports

5 percent: serve on a committee

monitored and looked after while he is at school?

A: Schools are quite used to maintaining a variety of personal health kits, including inhalers and injectible allergy kits for individual students. Some students are on regular insulin injections or may be on medication to control other types of physical or emotional disorders.

When you register your child, be sure to bring in the necessary medication and instructions so that you can explain to the principal, teacher and the office staff the precautions that must be taken, the symptoms the child exhibits and the exact treatment and follow-up that are necessary. After informing the staff, you will probably be asked to sign a form to allow them to administer immediate first aid. Then make sure that your child also knows the importance of reporting any symptoms immediately to the teacher or office.

Q: My fifteen-year-old son has been struggling with his courses over the past few years. He will soon be sixteen and wants to quit because he says that school is boring and he's not learning anything useful. What can I do?

A: We suspect that your son has been on this road since he was a little guy, which only makes changing direction now that much more difficult. If the urge to quit school is more recent, chances are you're looking at the influence of friends, or increasing frustration at school, or some sense that his current "career path" doesn't require graduation. (How many rock bands require a lead guitarist with a high school diploma?) Either way, it won't be easy to turn this around. Here are three approaches:

Change is sometimes a good enticement to stay in school. If your son feels his current school career is at a dead end, why not suggest a transfer to a different school or, better yet, an alternative school in your area. These schools often permit students to stay in school part-time so they can earn some ready cash while still making progress toward a diploma.

Talk also can work wonders, but probably not more talk from you. See if there's a teacher at school or a coach your son respects who might talk to him. Sometimes older brothers or friends can lay down some wisdom in a way that's more believable than when you try to do it. Maybe there's someone in the family who's given your son's dream a try and can explain that getting on the road to rock stardom isn't as easy as driving onto the Trans-Canada Highway.

Finally, bribery sometimes works where reason fails. You can talk till you're blue in the face about long-term goals and real life at age forty, but your son might respond more to the promise of a car when or if he graduates.

Teenagers have all sorts of reasons they can verbalize about dropping out, mostly based on whatever fund of wisdom they've attained at age fifteen or sixteen, but the *real* reasons for dropping out are often quite hidden. Kids stay in school because they're involved—in class, in extracurriculars, in sports, in the social life—and they quit when they feel left out. Sometimes it's better for teenagers to stop out for a semester, just to see how boring "real life" is, than to cajole them to stay in school.

Q: My family thinks that my son has severe behaviour problems. (My brother-in-law is a teacher!) The school hasn't said there is a problem, although Jonathan is squirmy like most six-year-olds. He is a boy, after all. Should I just ignore my family and quit worrying?

A: Probably. Kids don't always behave in the same way at school, in playground, at home and when visiting relatives. If that teacher in the family works with older children or maintains a very

There's Always Switzerland...

If you're convinced that Canada's schools are going to hell in a handbasket, you can always move to another country...like Switzerland. There kindergarten students are expected to shake hands with their teachers at the end of the day and half-hour-a-day homework begins in grade one.

Students in Swiss schools are rigorously evaluated at age eleven through standardized tests and teacher observations, then streamed for further education. Students in the "classical section" of *secondaire II* become proficient in at least four languages—and only 7 percent of these students will make it into university. Other students in the top half go off to a *gymnase cantonal, école supérieure de commerce* or *école technique.* Students in the bottom half (there's little mobility between streams) go off to trade schools.

Canadian teachers in Switzerland report that Swiss children are at levels about two grades ahead of Canadian students. Classrooms are teacher centred and traditional (tests are handed back from highest mark to lowest), extracurricular activities are few and children can be expelled for writing graffiti on a bathroom wall.

Could Canadian society support a system like this? We doubt it. Could be that each country gets the school system it deserves.

The Future Is Mostly Blurry

Ontario high school students who agreed with these statement about their futures:

"I have a good idea what I will do after I finish high school": 62 percent

"I find it difficult to imagine what I will be doing in ten years' time": 57 percent

"I expect to be unemployed when I leave school": 17 percent

"I intend to marry someday": 81 percent

"I will probably be married within five years of leaving high school": 29 percent

"I have a good chance of getting an interesting job after I finish my education": 71 percent (82 percent of A students agreed; only 60 percent of C or D students)

traditional classroom, he may have no idea what would be appropriate for a six-year-old in school—or at your home.

The real question is whether your son is learning the things he needs to in grade one and managing to stay on task well enough to get the work done. You might want to review Chapter 7 and then ask the teacher directly whether she thinks your son is working well in class.

Of course, there's always a chance that your child really does have a problem staying on task, and maybe your "boys will be boys" attitude is making that worse. Keep your ears open to what the teacher has to say and try to be honest with yourself. Attitudes and behaviours are pretty much set at an early age, so if change is needed, then this is the time to start. If Jonathan is just fine, then the next time your brother-in-law begins blabbing on, stifle a yawn and ask him to pass the mashed potatoes.

Q: The textbook that my grade five son brings home is very old and in poor condition. The teacher says that these are only being used as an extra resource, and that the main textbook is much better, but they only use it in school. Shouldn't all students have good-quality textbooks for home and school?

A: Unfortunately, the first place school trustees tend to slice budgets is in book buying. In the past, schools tried to replace texts about every six years, but these days school texts are used until they are literally falling apart at the seams. Another concern is an older book's appropriateness in terms of content. Some older texts won't meet the standards we expect of new books in presentation, readability and attitudes toward women and minorities. While we don't think books should ever be burned, there's something to be said for burying some until some archeologist wants to dig them up.

Q: My daughter has had several detentions lately for not completing homework and also not getting her work done in class. It's a real problem for me to pick her up after all her friends have already walked home together. Is this a reasonable practice for grade four?

A: Yes, it is. But your getting involved can be a good thing for both you and your daughter, providing you do it in the right way.

Detentions are rarely the first-choice response for a good teacher, but that doesn't mean they aren't an effective last resort. The detention tells your child that school work is important, that dawdling is not an effective life skill and that the teacher cares enough about the problem to give up some of her time at the end of the day. Sometimes detentions provide one-to-one time with the teacher that can help explain difficult areas or even lead to conversations on personal problems.

But if detentions are happening all the time, for many children in the class, you should reread Chapter 3 and speak directly to the teacher and principal. A teacher is unlikely to change her disciplinary techniques because *one* parent complains, but nothing ever changes until someone begins the process by speaking up. Perhaps that should be you.

However—and this is a big however—if your daughter thinks you're going to bat for her only because the detentions interfere with *your* routine, we guarantee that she'll continue to avoid her work both in class and at home. Why? Because she wants more of your time and attention. If the only way she can see evidence of your concern is to get in trouble at school, that trouble will certainly continue. The school principal can help you find a strategy that will help both you and your daughter break out of this destructive pattern.

Parents Want to Know...

A sampling of parents from twenty-five elementary and secondary schools in 1992 indicated that parents' concerns are varied and extensive. Here are the top eighteen:

- Standards
- Automatic promotion
- Safety
- Safety on the streets
- Basics
- Methods of instruction
- Homework
- Special education
- Integration of special students
- Equal opportunity for students
- Equal access for parents
- Racism
- Evaluation
- Report cards
- Yard supervision
- Spelling
- Canadian levels of achievement
- Learning outcomes

And here are the next twenty:

- Field trips
- Hidden costs
- Involvement in decisions
- Lack of communication
- Lack of consistency
- Curriculum content
- French program
- Lunch arrangements
- Daycare
- Baby-sitting (for meetings)
- Split grades
- Student placement
- Teacher selection
- Budget
- Portables
- Washroom facilities
- Class size
- Teacher personalities
- Teacher competence
- Teacher experience

Q: My grade two child's report card has great quantities of jargon-filled comments and no marks or grades. I find that I don't know whether or not she is able to do grade two work. How can I get a clearer picture of how she's doing?

A: The simple answer: talk to the teacher.

Report cards have become such political documents over the past few years, and so incomprehensible with their lengthy descriptions of outcomes and goals, that it's really hard to get straight answers in print on questions like "Does my child know how to read" or "Can she do grade two math?" So try talking instead. You should ask the teacher for general expectations for achievement in her classroom. Ask to see some samples of your child's work, which you can compare with examples in this book or the other work posted on bulletin boards in the classroom. This should give you some idea of how she's doing at her grade level. But remember that the most important question isn't how your daughter compares with other children; it's how she performs in relationship to what her ability appears to be. Improvement there may require real encouragement at home and at school.

Q: Our school has a parent-teacher organization that works with the school on some projects. These tend to be primarily fundraising and don't deal with any of the educational issues that some of the parents would like to change. How can we have more influence on what's really important?

A: A couple of members of your executive should make an appointment to meet with the principal to discuss some of the issues that you'd like to tackle. These may include student behaviour, standards across grades, homework policy, means of reporting, book selection, race relations or dozens of others. Some of these areas are probably already being handled by committees of teachers, so the most that you can expect is to add a parent voice to them. Some are probably being debated by committees at the provincial and school-board level, so you might have to delegate someone to serve there. And some of these areas will involve regular meetings between the executive and the principal, so you've got to be prepared to invest both people and time to your involvement. The profits from this investment, though, can be substantial.

Other topics—say, safe schools or evaluation—can perhaps be handled by a joint staff-parent presentation for the entire HSA or parent group. This would show other parents that your group is not simply about fundraising and help expand your membership to those who would rather not spend their time marketing chocolate bars or recipe books.

Q: My child doesn't appear to be doing as well as the other kids I see in grade three. I would like him to repeat the year, but the teacher feels that he should move ahead with his friends. I'm very concerned that he's going to end up even further behind. What should I do?

A: The issue of retention (what was once called repeating or flunking a grade) is still as difficult as ever. When Canada was still a dominion, there was a certain body of knowledge to be learned between September and June, and if a student hadn't learned enough of it, then he spent whittlin' time worrying about being left behind with the younger kids while his friends moved up to the next row. This created schools with fifteen-year-old grade eight students just dying to drop out when they hit their sixteenth birthday.

The futility of this approach gave rise to the more informed approach of today, where individual needs are identified and programs adjusted

Board or District Committees that May Include Parents

- school buildings and utilization
- community school planning
- extended school year
- curriculum advisory
- assessment and evaluation
- staffing and promotions
- board homework policy
- safe schools
- cooperative education
- early school leaving procedures
- alternative schools
- reporting to parents
- board communications
- race relations
- strategic planning
- French-language programs
- special education advisory
- response to ministry initiatives
- business partnerships

To apply for membership, contact your local trustee and write a letter to the director indicating your interest and the expertise that you can contribute to such a position. Provide your principal with a copy of the letter and discuss your interest with her. In many cases principals are asked to recommend parents who have shown a particular interest at the school level.

to allow students to learn at their own rate. But trying to avoid the stigma of repeating has left many schools with automatic promotions and too many teachers who don't really have time to individualize their programs. Some children are getting short-changed in the shuffle, graduating without many of the requisite skills in literacy and mathematics.

So there is no simple answer. Your school should be able to provide you with an outline of the expectations for children in grade three and a plan of how they are going to get him to that level. Ask about tutoring, small group support, extra help, homework programs, special education, resource teachers—anything that might help him learn what's essential for the grade four program. Then consider all the options, including placement in a combined or split grade three-four class. Generally, research comes down quite solidly against retention in grade school—but certainly there have to be some good safety nets in place for those students who are simply pushed on to the next year.

CHAPTER 16

The Real Issues Our Schools Face

W hile there is a lot of thunder and lightning about schools in our media, there is not much light being shed on the real issues in education. Our larger Canadian papers regularly bemoan declining standards, violent kids, taxpayer expense and virtually any kind of innovation. Our smaller papers are often boosters of educational trivia, saluting local school teams and the new computer lab, while they fill empty column space with horror stories from American inner-city schools. The average taxpayer, who does not have children in school, gets his images from these conflicting print sources and what he sees on mostly American television, and concludes that our schools are god-awful and certainly not worth any more of *his* money. The average parent, who knows a bit more about what is really happening, tends to be happier with the school *her* kids go to, but wonders about all those others she reads about and sees on television. The result, understandably, is confusion.

This is not a book about educational reform, but about making use of the schools that already

What Schools Should Be About

You'd think a list like this would be obvious, but it will make more sense when you check the opposite page...

- learning essential skills: reading, mathematics, geography, reasoning, scientific methods;

- mastering a certain body of knowledge: various literatures, history, scientific knowledge;

- learning about Canada and how it works;

- learning what business will demand: computer facility, business math, spreadsheets, languages;

- learning about the self: competencies, psychology, awareness;

- learning useful skills for later life: sports, music, carpentry, auto repair;

- practising and learning about real-life situations: shops, family studies;

- experiencing the arts, both for personal enrichment and skills development;

- working together and communicating with others.

exist in Canada. Nonetheless, if you've borne with us for the advice of the past fifteen chapters, perhaps you'll allow us a few pages of quick diagnosis for some of the real issues we see in Canadian education over the next twenty years.

The kid gap. Our kids come to school with a wide range of abilities and attitudes—the proverbial sailboats, tugboats and rowboats of primary class groupings. Gliding across the waters, we have the sailboat children from advantaged households—read to every night, competent on the family computer since age four, carrying the hopes and dreams of successful parents and supportive, on-looking families. Then there are the tugboat kids, who have to work their way through subject after subject, but get reasonable support both at home and at school. And finally we have the rowboat kids, the many, many children who don't have advantages at home, who may be raised by only one overstressed parent cut off from larger family, who not only don't get read to but sometimes don't get fed or bathed. It is the job of our schools to do their best for all these students, but doing so means putting extra effort—and resources—into the rowboat kids. If we fail to do so, the advantaged kids will literally sail away with all the goodies schools have to offer while the less-advantaged kids will be left at the dock.

Sadly, our schools are no longer working as well to narrow the gap between the sailboats and the rowboats. Some of this failure has to do with the disintegration of young families, some has to do with increasing poverty among children and some has to do with budget cutbacks. No wonder teachers feel overwhelmed. The growing *social* problems of their students almost outweigh their educational needs. Nonetheless, we feel it is time for Canada's schools to remember that education is the single most powerful tool for social equality. Through the 1980s and 1990s, too much of the emphasis in school has been on the gifted, the identified special student and the child whose parent is watching school closely. For the year 2000, we would like to see a renewed commitment to the *other* disadvantaged students, those kids without parental or system advocates. Such a commitment would affect everything from lunch programs, to length of the school day, to board or district budgeting, but it's essential to restore some kind of equality of opportunity for *all* the children coming to our schools.

The time/curriculum crunch. We can't keep on demanding more and more from schools that are limited, as they were at the turn of the century, to a five-and-a-half-hour instructional day and a 185-day agricultural year. We can't keep on expecting our kids to learn more, master more skills and deal with issues ranging from multiculturalism to ecology, when many of our less advantaged younger children don't spend time at home reading or studying and more than half our teenagers are working at part-time jobs. Not only have demands risen, but the total number of hours available for schooling and larger education after school have contracted.

We feel it's time to expand the school day. Everyone knows the curriculum is bigger, that more skills are required, that extracurricular activities are important. Let's act on what we know by adding an hour to the school day—some of it in class, some of it as an extended lunch hour for extracurricular activities, sports, bands, clubs and extra help for kids who need it. This is exactly the kind of compensatory education that will help to lessen the gap between the sailboat kids and the rowboat kids. At the same time, a lengthened day will provide the time required for all the new program requirements, teaching techniques and teacher collaboration that modern education demands.

What Schools Are Not Necessarily About

Our schools have been laden with all sorts of jobs that aren't really theirs. Our first list is plenty for schools to try to do. Here's where they're much less effective:

- fixing families that are in trouble;

- building self-esteem to the extent of turning kids into praise junkies;

- doing social work or psychology;

- providing test results that politicians can use for re-election;

- carrying the moral freight of society: drunk driving, AIDS, sexual responsibility (though talking about these issues isn't a bad idea);

- teaching driving, knitting or basket weaving—unless there's time and money left over after the essentials.

Ironically, good schools tend to do many of these things in an offhand way, but the vast majority of schools had better stick to the real goals.

Six Overinflated Issues in Education

These issues are real enough, but just don't rate all the attention they get in the press and on television:

- year-round school: a fine idea in Florida, but few Canadians want to give up the two or three nice months we have north of the forty-eighth parallel;

- provincial testing: it's expensive and time-consuming and rarely leads to real changes—not a bad idea, just an idea that hasn't been made to work;

- national curriculum: a big issue in England, but not that many Canadian kids move province to province; let's work on province-wide curriculums first;

- whole language: sorry, there are no hidden devils in the pictures, and phonics by itself never worked all that well either; we need a balance;

- declining standards: probably true, but complaints about falling standards go back to Aristotle, so by now we should all be morons; it's not all that bad;

- school violence: it's not nearly as bad as in the U.S. (though we may be heading that way); the vast majority of our kids will never see or experience anything more lethal than a bloody nose.

We recognize that even a modest extension of the school day represents an overwhelming change for most provincial school systems. Legislation must be rewritten; unions will complain, if not threaten strike action; thousands of bus schedules will change; and any number of parents—all those advantaged families—will say this interferes with ballet lessons and hockey practice. But the vast majority of our kids today are not spending their time immediately after school in any kind of productive way. Today's workday—unlike the farm day of 1880—goes to five or six or seven o'clock and most moms are simply not home to greet the kids, offer cookies and suggest that homework be attended to. The reality is that most of our kids spend the time leading up to supper simply propped in front of the TV. We feel that an extra hour in school, and an hour less staring at the tube, would acknowledge the family realities of this century and pay enormous dividends for our students in the next.

If we can find the will to make such a revolutionary change, we should then organize the extra school hour in the right way. Let's ask the teachers and parents in each school community how *they* want to use the extra time, what would work best for *their* students. For too many years we've been mandating change from the top, only to see it die in the corridors of the school. The way for change to succeed is to give it a nudge from above and then let the stakeholders in each school decide how to make it work at their level.

Failure to innovate. With only a few exceptions, Canada's schools are so similar to one another that they might have been stamped out with a cookie cutter. This doesn't mean that educational innovations aren't attempted—they are—but they are performed on all the schools at once. The grief we've seen in British Columbia's revised curriculum, in destreaming grade nine in Ontario, in whole language as it was brought to Alberta all speak of what happens when innovation is done on too large a scale.

The solution to "cookie cutter" schools will not be found in a voucher system, charter schools or massive funding for private schools. Such schemes haven't worked in the United States and they will simply debilitate the public and separate schools here. What we need is more variety and innovation in *public* education. Even today, most of our schools and boards are run on a nineteenth-century industrial model—a top-down hierarchy—that business has been abandoning for twenty years. Business has been busy encouraging employee commitment, team building and site-based management, yet many schools still limit staff involvement to a monthly staff meeting where the principal tells the teachers what the latest Ministry or Department of Education thrust happens to be. Should we be surprised that our schools and classrooms change at a snail's pace?

We could do much to improve Canada's schooling by giving teachers and parents more say in what happens in the neighbourhood school. We could do much to create more variety and real choice among schools by encouraging—and funding—public schools that have defined their own special vision or programs. We could offer some encouragement to schools that want to approach the curriculum in their own special way, or with their own time structure, or with different kinds of teacher or subject organization. Who says, for instance, that every student in grade three needs exactly ten months of that year to complete the grade three math program? Some kids may need six months, some kids two years, but our schools don't have the flexibility to accommodate these differences. Why not? Boy Scout and Girl Guide merit badges have no time limitations. A child wins the badge when he or she completes the task. While it's complex to set

Six Real Issues in Education

These are the issues that we and other insiders would like to see addressed:

- the growing gap between advantaged kids and disadvantaged kids;

- report cards: they're not reporting honestly and effectively;

- lack of flexibility: our schools aren't encouraged to innovate and too many are cookie-cutter imprints of every other school;

- lack of time: there's not enough time to master an expanded curriculum and make up for declining after-school learning in many households;

- teachers as professionals: this means real professional development, real professional tools and real licensing demands;

- accessing the family: more than ever, schools and teachers need to reach out to the family at home to provide effective education for kids in school.

schools up so kids proceed from subject to subject, year to year in discrete units, it's not impossible. As our public schools are currently funded and governed, few can even experiment with such alternative structures.

Regional Curriculum—It's Coming.

Since the average child will move four times in his school career, the issue of curriculum coordination is one parents must face again and again. In Manitoba, percentages are taught in grade five, in Alberta in grade six and in B.C. not until grade eight. The kids are pretty much the same, but provincial curriculum committees have set up different timetables for learning various subjects.

Fortunately, this situation is changing. In the West, four provinces and two territories are collaborating on common standards for curriculum development, starting with mathematics. In the Maritimes, the three provinces are working on a common core curriculum and a single statement of "expectations" for high school graduates. In Ontario, the common curriculum may actually bring some order to the fiefdoms of individual school boards.

Curriculum coordination is not the be-all and end-all of education. It tends to stifle some experimentation and often produces more documents on the teacher's bookshelf than change in classroom practice, but it's increasingly necessary in a mobile society. Perhaps by the year 2000 we'll be halfway there.

Professionalism and accountability for* every *teacher. Teachers are the only professionals who don't get a telephone. By and large, they get no secretarial help. Except for monthly staff meetings, they have virtually no time set aside to work together in teams, exchange ideas or engage in ongoing professional development.

It's time to change this. We'd never tolerate a doctor doing thirty-year-old medicine or an engineer building a 1950s bridge, but we can't seem to find the time or the funds to bring all of our teachers up-to-date or to let them organize in the most effective way. Teachers need time to think about teaching—company time—the way hospital doctors take once a month for grand rounds. The average board or district of education spends less than 1 percent of its budget on professional development; the average large company spends close to 10 percent of its revenue in training and retraining its employees. The bottom line for education is this: what happens in the classroom will improve only when the teacher in that classroom is capable and involved. Part of this can be dealt with by allowing more time for teachers to work together and learn from one another, as the Japanese do in their schools. Part of this requires ongoing teacher education as a requisite for keeping a teaching certificate, as most jurisdictions already do in the United States. And part of this requires a school management team that expects and demands the best of teachers.

Our impression is that 10 percent of the current teaching force should be in another line of work (and most teachers we checked with think our figure is conservative). A competent school management team would help less able teachers figure a way out of the profession, or push them out if a push is required, or help them access the joy and excitement in teaching that could be theirs if they knew how to find it. Sadly, our schools have not had enough of that kind of management. It is not a matter of teacher unions being too strong; it is a matter of management feeling itself too weak to make the tough personnel decisions that are essential for excellent schools. We think school systems could learn much about "total quality management" by looking to business models, by doing brief exchanges of senior executives with corporate Canada and by shifting supervisory courses from studies of school law and student behaviour to studies of effective personnel management.

Involving parents. Despite years of rhetoric about parents as partners, schools rarely treat parents as even junior associates, or clients, or customers. Too often they ignore the rest of the family altogether, focussing all their efforts on one child for six hours a day, 185 days a year, as if the other ten waking hours and 180 days didn't exist. Despite everything we know about the importance of home involvement and support for education, few schools make more than a token nod in that direction. Why are parent meetings called interviews rather than conferences? Why must parents always come to the school and not teachers to the home? Why can't public schools expect—as some private and alternative schools do—that parents will be involved in committees, activities, even maintenance? In Canada, we mandate by law that a child attend school 185 days a year, but we have no legal requirement that a parent show up even once. Nor have we trained our teachers to do the outreach necessary that would connect our schools to parents, businesses and the larger community.

Parent Council Roles

Parent councils are appearing in more provinces in response to the call of parents like you for a say in the decisions that affect your child's education. Parent councils generally operate at the school level and reflect the specific needs of each school community; others represents parents for the whole province. Some issues parent councils *may* address are:

- curriculum requirements
- reporting to parents
- hiring, staffing and promotion
- equity and opportunity for all students
- school goals
- behaviour or discipline codes
- homework policy
- standardized evaluation
- accountability
- budget
- fundraising

If you are interested in participating in your school's parent council you will probably have to be nominated by a number of parents in your community and meet some criteria relating to time, availability and interest. The best school councils are not simply parent groups, but a joint council comprised of parents, administrators, teachers and students. That gives the council some clout with the principal and other administrators.

On the Virtues of Music Education

Since the time of the ancient Greeks, educators have known that studying music improves students' capacity in mathematical theory and practice. Now we have research to indicate that it helps in reading, spelling and general study skills as well.

- In the United States, students taking music courses score an average of twenty to forty points higher on both math and verbal sections of the SAT (a university-entrance test).

- Students who took four years of music scored thirty-four points higher on their verbal SAT than those who took music for less than a year.

- Students who participate in their school band or orchestra are 52 percent more likely to go on to university and graduate than students who do not.

- Music majors have the highest rate of admission to medical school of any group of university students.

The question *Why?* looms large in all these figures. Is music the domain of advantaged kids or supportive parents? Are we looking here at association or cause and effect? We don't have answers to this yet, but urge you to remember all this the next time your board or district decides to cut back on arts programs.

Of course, the parents of advantaged children *are* involved already, and making sure the schools do the best by their kids. It is the parents of the less advantaged children we worry about—those who might well benefit from the skills and experience that can be found in schools. We do not think that schools should be doing social work—that's not their job—but we do think education should involve many aspects of a child's life. Some of the most effective literacy programs in New Zealand and the United States have nothing to do with school instruction; they direct their efforts at offering models of effective home teaching. The spinoff benefit for involved families is that the adults, too, often decide to further their education or improve their family circumstances.

Our schools and teachers are wonderful public resources not often used by disadvantaged portions of the population, whose past experience in school may not have been a good one. This situation will not be improved with cosmetic solutions—opening the school up for tennis lessons in the gym on Wednesday night—but it can change with a concerted effort to reach out to groups of parents who would not otherwise be involved. Then, and only then, will we see a real narrowing in the gap between the haves and have-nots.

The need for bigger basics. We said at the outset that education is more than just schooling, but that certainly doesn't mean that schooling needs to be as narrow as it is. The real thrust of the 1980s "back to basics" movement was a return to the narrow 1950s curriculum. What we needed—and still need—is some serious thinking about the demands on our kids in the year 2000 or 2020, a sense of the bigger basics that our kids will need in the future. It may be wonderful that a child understands the difference between a metaphor and a simile, but we think the capacity to handle a spreadsheet or visualize three-dimensional graphs will be far more important in the real world of the next century. Judgement calls have to be made in curriculum, especially when budgets are tight. Such calls can't be made on the basis of nostalgia for penmanship or spelling lists or the ability to do square roots by hand. The calls have to be made on the basis of future business and personal needs. In the next century, computer and media literacy will be part of the bigger basics; so will handling spreadsheets, doing flowcharts and conceptualizing problems; so will collaborative document revision, business planning, mastery of multiple languages. And all this will be in *addition* to the three Rs, which we nostalgically call the basics today.

Interestingly, some of the most traditional subjects appear to be the best preparation for what business and higher education are demanding. Music education, for instance, develops such important skills as memorization, concentration, physical coordination and a capacity to rise to the demands of performance. Similar virtues could be cited for art and dramatics—both for their intrinsic worth and for the skills they develop that will be useful to our kids later on. Yet these arts are often the first places where boards or districts begin cutting budgets unless parents speak up.

What we need in our schools is not more old-fashioned basics, but bigger basics for an increasingly complex world. A longer school day would certainly help in this undertaking. With a longer day, it should be possible to break out of some of the narrow "subject ghettos" and offer real interdisciplinary teaching: science and family studies, English and geography, history with music and art. With a longer day, it would be possible to integrate participation in lunchtime band with general music courses; to offer drama as a regular (not once a year) part of the program; to allow teachers to explore with students their own special areas of expertise—gourmet cooking, or astronomy, or short wave, or navigating the Internet. Our advantaged students are already getting all this—at home and in lessons after school. It's up to our legislators and trustees to extend such advantages to the children who can't access them from their parents.

We would hope that our schools in the near future would become more innovative and more responsive than they are now so that we might see some real experimentation with different kinds of organization and teaching techniques. We would hope for an end to simplistic solutions like "back to the basics" or "charter schools," which do not in themselves address the bigger problems our schools face. We would hope to see more parents involved in school, not just as volunteers, but in a decision-making or powerful advisory role. And we would hope to see schools welcome that involvement, with teachers and principals reaching out to tap the time and skills and expertise of the adults in their communities.

A collective will is required to renew our schools so they can provide a first-rate education for *all* our children. For their sake—and for our children's children still to come—we must find the strength and resources to do better.

Acknowledgements

The authors would like to thank the people whose knowledge, research and close reading made it possible for us to write this book: Sarah Davies at Random House, Chris Ball at the OSSTF library, Lillian Lahe & Ted Tipping in Newmarket; Barbara Parsons and Paul Brandon in Toronto; Joyce McCorquodale and Sandra and Ray Varey in Hamilton, Ontario; Christine Rhodes and Jennifer Holder in Winnipeg; Floyd and Betty Spracklin in Newfoundland; Diana Cruchley in British Columbia, Hervé and Ione Langlois in Saskatoon, Emma Adam in Minneapolis, Dr. John Flynn of the Canadian Catholic School Trustees Association, the parents, staff and students at Westdale Secondary School in Hamilton, Ramer Wood Public School in Markham and Oak Ridges School in Richmond Hill (especially Lori Baskin, Christine Alderman, Carol Huycke and Rochelle Sufrin) and the hundreds of other parents, teachers and students who contributed ideas or material.

Paul Kropp's personal thanks go to Gale Bildfell, who encouraged him daily on the writing, and to his five children, who never realized they might end up as exemplary material in a book like this. Lynda Hodson would like to thank her mother, Mable Gravelle, her sister Arlene Petrie as well as Cheryl, Sara and Stacey Golden and the Stea Family—Nick, Julie, Michael and Adria. She offers a special thanks to her daughter Laura Davis, and two friends, Mike Jarvis and Melissa Guthrie, who have never let her forget the difference that the *right* teacher can make.

Notes on Sources

Chapter 1. School finance is well covered in *Scrimping or Squandering? Financing Canadian Schools*, edited by Stephen Lawton and Rouleen Wignall (OISE, 1989); updated figures from Statistics Canada. Mark decline estimates are based upon anecdotal reports to authors. "CTBS norms" sidebar as reported in the *Globe and Mail* and in follow-up phone discussions with the publisher. Public attitudes were reported in *Canada's Schools: Report Card for the 90's* (Canadian Education Association, 1990). Comparisons done by the International Association for the Evaluation of Education Achievement are reported in *A World of Differences* (ETS, 1989) and Warwick Elley's *How in the World Do Students Read?* (IRA, 1992).

Chapter 2. On the influence of elite private schools, see Peter C. Newman's *The Canadian Establishment* (M&S, 1975). Jonathan Kozol's book on home schooling is entitled *Teach Your Own* (Dell, 1981). For a critical view of French immersion, see "False Immersion" by Carol Milstone in *Saturday Night*, September, 1994.

Chapter 3. The composite teacher portraits are drawn from statistics in *Teachers in Canada* (Canadian Teachers' Federation, 1992) as are many of the sidebars here and in Chapter 4. Further information from Alan King's *The Teaching Experience* (OSSTF, 1988).

Chapter 5. Statistics on families from the Vanier Institute's *Profiling Canada's Families* (1994) and Statistics Canada. A popular book on birth order is Ari Kiev's *Breaking Free of Birth Order* (Ballantine, 1993).

Chapter 6. There are many studies on the importance of early childhood stimulation and the value of preschool for low-income families, see especially Edward Ziegler's *Head Start and Beyond* (Yale, 1993). Daycare and early-childhood statistics from Statistics Canada and as cited in the *Toronto Star* (August 28, 1994) and the *Financial Post*.

Chapter 9. Kim Zarzour's *Battling the School-yard Bully* (HarperCollins, 1994) talks about the bullying issue at length.

Chapter 10 and 11. Disquieting statistics on teenage sexuality come from many sources: see especially Reginald Bibby and Donald Posterski, *Teen Trends: A Nation in Motion* (Stoddart, 1992). A wide range of information on teenagers and high schools can be found in Alan King's *The Adolescent Experience* (OSSTF, 1986) and his follow-up study, *The Good School* (OSSTF, 1990).

Chapter 15. The "Initials" sidebar is largely from *Talkin' Langley Talk* by Diana Cruchley of Langley, B.C. Information on Swiss schools came from James McMurtry's article, "Swiss school days full of work and rigour" in the *Toronto Star*, May 6, 1994.

Index